Praise for THE JEWISH AMERICAN PARADOX

"In a remarkable book at once deeply personal and deeply learned, one of America's leading intellectuals invites us to a fascinating conversation about what it means to be Jewish in contemporary America and the challenges facing the American Jewish community. This book deals with issues that have preoccupied me personally for many years, and after almost every chapter I wanted to pick up the phone and continue the conversation Mnookin started. It will make a wonderful gift to our kids and grandchildren, who are living the paradoxes he outlines."

—Robert D. Putnam, professor of public policy, Harvard, and author of *American Grace: How Religion Divides and Unites Us*

"An accomplished facilitator of negotiation, Robert Mnookin offers a master course in negotiating the most important questions a person—or a people—can confront. His focus on the contemporary challenges of Jewish identity—whether religious, social, familial, or ethnic—illuminates the larger issue of what it is to be self-critically human in a world for which few feel sufficiently prepared, much less at home. *The Jewish American Paradox* is an important book for Jews, Americans, and everyone who hopes for a better future."

—James Carroll, author of *Constantine's Sword* and *The Cloister*

"Mnookin presents a terrific case that Judaism should be a welcoming umbrella. My whole Jewish education was based on what you cannot do, what you cannot eat, when you cannot drive, play ball, etc. This book focuses on what you can do—embrace an ancient tradition and identify with a group. It is a call to stop feeling oppressed—an optimistic, almost non-doctrinal, evangelism."

—Harold Holzer, director of Roosevelt House Public Policy Center at Hunter College and Historian

"*The Jewish American Paradox* is a powerful combination of meditation on faith and rigorous legal analysis of the dilemmas facing American Jews in the twenty-first century. The author's late-in-life journey invites the reader to join his journey, and to learn surprising insights along the way."

—Steve Weisman, author of *The Chosen Wars: How Judaism Became an American Religion*

"Robert Mnookin's important new book is a brilliant analysis with positive prescriptions at a critical time for the American Jewish community. The rampant intermarriage by non-Orthodox American Jews and the policies of today's Israeli government, the most conservative in its 70 year history, require candid dialogue and bold solutions. Robert Mnookin provides just that....It is a book that must be widely read and its message absorbed into an action agenda."

—Ambassador Stuart E. Eizenstat, author of *President Carter: The White House Years*

THE JEWISH
AMERICAN
PARADOX

Also by Robert H. Mnookin

Kissinger the Negotiator:
Lessons from Dealmaking at the Highest Order
(with James K. Sebenius and R. Nicholas Burns)

Bargaining with the Devil: When to Negotiate, When to Fight

Beyond Winning: Negotiating to Create Value in Deals and Disputes
(with Scott R. Peppet and Andrew S. Tulumello)

Dividing the Child: Social and Legal Dilemmas of Custody
(with Eleanor Maccoby)

Barriers to Conflict Resolution
(with Kenneth Arrow, Lee Ross, Amos Tversky, and Robert Wilson)

THE JEWISH AMERICAN PARADOX

EMBRACING CHOICE
IN A CHANGING WORLD

ROBERT H. MNOOKIN

PUBLICAFFAIRS

NEW YORK

PublicAffairs
Hachette Book Group
1290 Avenue of the Americas, New York, NY 10104
www.publicaffairsbooks.com
@Public_Affairs

Printed in the United States of America

First Edition: November 2018

Published by PublicAffairs, an imprint of Perseus Books, LLC, a subsidiary of Hachette Book Group, Inc. The PublicAffairs name and logo is a trademark of the Hachette Book Group.

The Hachette Speakers Bureau provides a wide range of authors for speaking events. To find out more, go to www.hachettespeakersbureau.com or call (866) 376-6591.

The publisher is not responsible for websites (or their content) that are not owned by the publisher.

Library of Congress Control Number: 2018959205

ISBNs: 978-1-61039-751-3 (hardcover), 978-1-61039-752-0 (ebook)

LSC-C

10   9   8   7   6   5   4   3   2   1

In memory of my grandfathers—
Jacob Mnookin and George M. Sittenfeld—
whose love, generosity, and pride in being Jewish Americans
inspires me today

Contents

INTRODUCTION

WHEN I WAS thirty-six I was forced to confront my own ambivalence about being Jewish.

Recently tenured as a professor at Berkeley Law School, I was spending a sabbatical semester in Oxford, England, with my family. My wife, Dale, and I had enrolled our two daughters—Jennifer, then eleven, and Allison, eight—in English schools.

Over dinner one night at the start of the school year, Jennifer told us about her new class, Religious Education, taught by Miss Kay, the formidable headmistress at Oxford High School for Girls.

"Miss Kay asked, 'Who here is Anglican?'" Jennifer reported. "Almost everyone raised her hand. Then Miss Kay asked, 'Do we have any Presbyterians?' A few more kids raised their hands. 'Catholics?' A couple of kids raised their hands." Miss Kay had even asked about Mormons, as Jennifer recalled, but there were none. "Then she asked, 'Is there anyone here not of the Christian faith?'"

I asked Jennifer what happened next.

"Well, I raised my hand. And Miss Kay gave me a funny look and asked, 'And what are you, my dear?' I told her, 'I'm Jewish.' Miss Kay paused for a second and said, 'Oh, how *interesting*.' Then she asked whether my parents would object if, as part of this course, we read parts of the New Testament as well as the Old Testament. I told her you would not object."

Dale and I told Jennifer that she had responded quite appropriately. "How did all of this make you feel?" I asked.

She looked at us and asked, "When are we actually going to become Jewish?"

Dale and I were a little stunned. I responded, slightly defensively, "Your mother and I have always thought of ourselves as Jewish. We are not really religious, but we *are Jewish*." Left unsaid, but implicit, was the idea I had grown up with: being Jewish was not something you needed to *become*; you just *were*, whether you liked it or not. By birth Dale and I were Jews. Therefore, so was Jennifer. Descent alone was enough.

One thesis of this book is that for my grandchildren this will no longer be true.

JENNIFER WAS NOT SATISFIED when I told her that Dale and I had always thought of ourselves as Jewish. She shot back, "You know what I mean!"

"I'm not sure I do," I responded.

"I want to have a bat mitzvah," she said.

Dale and I looked at each other, baffled. Where had this idea come from? Not from us. Neither Dale nor I had ever been bar or bat mitzvahed. We had grown up in the Midwest in the 1950s in highly assimilated families. Our parents and grandparents were longtime members of Reform Jewish congregations, which at the time did not even celebrate bar or bat mitzvahs. No Hebrew school for us. Instead, like our Protestant friends, we had been sent to Sunday school at our "temple"[1] until tenth grade, when we were confirmed. Twice a year our parents took us to services on the High Holy Days of Rosh Hashanah and Yom Kippur. We received presents for both Hanukah and Christmas, the latter celebrated as a secular holiday with gifts under a Christmas tree.

In the Midwest of the 1950s every Protestant, Catholic, or Jewish family—whether religiously inclined or not—had been expected, as a matter of social convention, to belong to some church or synagogue.[2] But unlike our parents, Dale and I had never bothered to join a temple, even after our children were born. As a young couple living in Cambridge, Washington, DC, and Berkeley in the late sixties and seventies, we had never felt any social pressure to do so. Nor to this point had we provided our children with any religious education or even taken them to temple on High Holy Days. But now our daughter was telling us that our passive form of being Jewish wasn't good enough. (As we learned later, Jennifer's interest in Judaism had been sparked by the fact that some of her friends back home had started studying for their bat mitzvahs.)

After a few moments of silence Dale and I recovered enough to make a few comments. Initially we tested her resolve. She'd have to learn to read Hebrew, we warned her, and it would be a lot of work. By the time we got home to California she would be behind her friends in bat mitzvah study. Dale asked whether Jennifer was really willing to give up some of her favorite after-school activities—music, art, dance—to fit it all in. Jennifer was determined to do it.

Meanwhile eight-year-old Allison sat quietly eating her dinner.

"I'm the only American kid in my class," she commented finally. "And I'm probably the only Jewish kid. But no one has asked, and I haven't said anything. I don't see any reason to bring it up."

Boy, could I relate to the approaches of both daughters! As an assimilated Jewish kid growing up in Kansas City, I had learned to be very quiet about my Jewish identity. If someone inquired if anyone was Jewish, I would raise my hand. But if no one asked, I wouldn't bring it up. It wasn't that I was afraid of anti-Semitism; I had never personally encountered a single anti-Semitic remark. But I was aware that being Jewish was somehow different and that I wasn't supposed to make an issue out of it. The idea wasn't to deny being Jewish but rather to fit in.

I certainly never had any sense that being Jewish was somehow an advantage. In fact, it was clear to me that it was a *disadvantage*. I was fully aware that Jews were a minority and that social discrimination still existed. The all-male prep school I attended had an unacknowledged Jewish quota of around 10 percent or so—I was one of five Jewish kids in my class. Absorbing all this as a teenager, I gathered that I was supposed to be proud of being Jewish, on the one hand, but to downplay it, on the other—and not to let it get in the way of my brilliant career. I handled these mixed messages by accepting my Jewish heritage, if not exactly embracing it, and then thinking about it as little as possible. Because I wasn't religiously inclined, this approach worked for me well into adulthood.

But now Jennifer was challenging Dale and me to rouse ourselves from our apathy and to step up and affiliate for her sake. So we told her that when we returned to Berkeley we would join a temple and enroll her in its religious school so she could begin cramming for her bat mitzvah. When we got home we enrolled Allison as well.

Allison initially objected to going to religious school, which she correctly saw as "Jennifer's thing." I insisted she go. Paying hefty temple dues for the first time in my life, I was determined to reap some economies of scale. For the money we were spending, why shouldn't Allison also learn something about her religious heritage? But because I was a little reluctant to force her to go, I bribed her. At the time she was obsessed with horseback riding, so I told her that if she went to Hebrew school and had a bat mitzvah, she could get a horse of her own for at least a year. That did the trick. So off both girls went to religious school, where they learned to read Hebrew, if not understand it. Blessedly, by the time Allison celebrated her bat mitzvah at thirteen, she had lost all interest in horses.

My response to Jennifer's challenge turned out to be only a tiny step on the journey that led to this book. I call it a "tiny step" because initially I didn't do much more than write a check. My own connection to Judaism remained slight while the kids were growing up, and so did Dale's. We took the children to temple on High Holy Days. Most years we held a Passover Seder in our home, celebrating with both Jewish and non-Jewish friends its message of freedom. With regret, we stopped having a Christmas tree, which the Reform movement now strongly discouraged. That was more than enough religion for us.

FIFTEEN YEARS AFTER THAT dinner table conversation, Dale and I moved back to Cambridge, Massachusetts, where I had been recruited to lead the Program on Negotiation at Harvard Law School, my alma mater. The Program deals with conflicts of all sorts: family disputes arising from divorce, complex commercial disputes, and international disputes, especially ethnic conflicts. As part of my work as a negotiation expert, in an attempt to contribute to the resolution of the Israeli-Palestinian conflict, I started facilitating confidential dialogues among clashing factions in Israel.

During the entire two-year period of those talks, I didn't see my interest in Israel as having anything to do with me being Jewish; I thought of the work as being motivated by my professional interest in dispute resolution.

I did much of this work with a gifted young Israeli graduate student named Udi Eiran. Udi's view was that even the most assimilated Jew harbored a "Jewish spark,"[3] a tiny pinprick of light that might someday be fanned into a blaze that fully illuminated one's life. Whenever I would claim that the work was just part of my professional life, Udi would tease me. "No," he would say, wagging his finger, "I can see the Jewish spark inside you!" At the time I laughed about it. But in retrospect Udi was probably right. It would take me another fifteen years to find that spark, but as you'll see in this book, I ultimately found a way to connect powerfully with my heritage.

What fanned that spark was the birth of my four grandchildren. In my late sixties I began to realize that I fervently hoped they and their children would take pride in a Jewish identity. Continuity suddenly mattered to me. The irony of this development wasn't lost on me: I had never given the slightest thought to "Jewish continuity" when raising my daughters. Jennifer and Allison had found their own Jewish identities, no thanks to me. As they entered their teens, Dale and I had never suggested that they should find Jewish mates. Religious tests of this sort would have been inconsistent with our values. When Jennifer married a Jew and Allison married a lapsed Episcopalian, Dale and I were delighted with the men they chose. When each couple eventually had two children, Dale and I never asked how they planned to raise the children religiously. In retrospect I was spectacularly lucky that both couples decided to raise the children as Jews.

But why did I care that my *grandchildren* would think of themselves as Jewish? That's what puzzled me. And what did this sudden interest in continuity say about how my own Jewish identity had changed? These questions led me deep into an inquiry into Jewish identity, the nature of identity itself, and the challenges facing the American Jewish community.

WHO COUNTS AS JEWISH? The first part of this book is dedicated to this complicated question. What has being Jewish meant historically, and how well do the answers of the past serve American Jews today? The traditional "answers" essentially rely on descent—an ascribed status that is inherited. For my grandchildren's generation, these traditional answers are no longer adequate.

I have also concluded that the American Jewish community faces four critical challenges, each of which creates conflict within the community, our families, and sometimes ourselves. These challenges anchor the second half of the book. Can the American Jewish community survive, given that:

- *Most American Jews don't practice the religion?* A commitment to Judaism provides a solid foundation to Jewish identity and a natural way to transmit that identity to the next generation. But today many Jews are, like me, uninterested in affiliating with a synagogue or observing much more ritual than a yearly Seder. Nearly half of American Jews say they are agnostic or do not believe in God, and only three in ten Jewish adults belong to a synagogue or temple. The challenge for Jews like me—and it's no small challenge—is to clearly articulate to our children and grandchildren what our Jewish identity consists of and which values we hope to pass on.
- *American Jews are no longer persecuted for being Jewish?* For centuries Jewish identity was reinforced by the need to band together for survival. In America, especially between about 1900 and 1950, Jews were barred from schools, professions, and neighborhoods. I was lucky to be born in 1942; by the time I applied to college, such educational quotas were largely gone, and today institutionalized discrimination has essentially disappeared. There are obviously still anti-Semites in America, but their hostility is no longer expressed through American institutions that hold the keys to power, prestige, and inclusion. My grandchildren will never experience the fear and discrimination that gave earlier generations such a strong bond. This freedom is a blessing for them, but it removes a potent reminder that they are Jewish. It is also the primary reason they will find it so easy to reject a Jewish identity if it doesn't appeal to them.

- *Israeli policies cause bitter conflict among us instead of unity?* Support for Israel and a commitment to its survival has long contributed to American Jewish identity. But today many of us find certain policies of the Israeli government increasingly offensive. Some of these policies relate to Israel's continued military occupation of the West Bank; others concern the monopoly given to the Orthodox rabbinate to define authentic Judaism.
- *Most American Jews now marry outside the faith?* For eighteen hundred years the vast majority of Jews married other Jews. Endogamy was required by traditional Jewish law and reinforced by social custom. In America this practice helped sustain Jewish identity for centuries. In 1900 the intermarriage rate was only about 5 percent. But for today's young couples, intermarriage is the norm. Among Jews who married after 2000, some 58 percent chose a non-Jewish spouse. Will they and their children think of themselves as Jews?

The situation of American Jews today is deeply paradoxical. On the one hand, some 94 percent of us express pride in being Jewish, as well we should.[4] The evidence of Jewish success in America is stunning. Although we constitute only 2 percent of the nation's population, as a group we enjoy outsized influence and esteem in virtually every facet of American life, including higher education, science, the law, the arts, entertainment, politics, business, and philanthropy. The percentage of American Jews who hold college degrees is twice the American average (59 percent to 27 percent)[5] and nearly triple for postgraduate degrees (28 percent to 10 percent).[6] Further, 44 percent of Jews have a household income over $100,000, compared to 19 percent of the general population.[7] Three of the nine Supreme Court justices are Jewish, as are one-third of American Nobel laureates.[8]

But in the face of the four challenges—weak religious observance, waning anti-Semitism, conflict over Israel, and rampant intermarriage—it's not clear how long we can collectively sustain a strong sense of Jewish identity.

Fears about Jewish continuity are hardly new, especially in America. In 1964 *Look* magazine ran a cover story entitled "The Vanishing American

Jew."[9] In 1997 my Harvard Law School colleague Alan Dershowitz wrote a best-seller with the same title.[10] More recently a 2013 study of Jewish Americans "unleashed a tsunami of doom and gloom punditry," in Professor Leonard Saxe's words, about the American Jewish future, largely because of its sobering statistics on intermarriage.[11] Some panicked souls even claim that we're about to disappear as a group entirely, that success and acceptance will accomplish what even the most vicious anti-Semitism never could.

I believe this emphasis on "vanishing" is nonsense. The American Jewish community will not vanish over the next fifty years. At least two of its subgroups will survive: the Orthodox Jews and the ardent Zionists. My fear is more specific: if these are the *only* two groups who survive, the community will lose its diversity and much of its vibrancy. Those who don't fit in—probably including my descendants—will be marginalized. Over time those who feel alienated or excluded from these "ways of being Jewish" will likely stop identifying themselves as Jewish at all.

THE TRADITIONAL APPROACH TO ensuring continuity, which many of today's Jewish leaders favor, is to set strict criteria for "membership in the tribe." I am extremely critical of this approach, which Dale and I first encountered personally about nineteen years ago when planning Allison's wedding. Allison had fallen in love with a wonderful man whose full name is Cornelius Olcott V. Needless to say, Cory was not raised in the Jewish faith. Religion was not a big deal to either family, and both the Mnookins and the Olcotts were delighted with the match. But Allison and Cory, like all intermarried couples, had some negotiations ahead: first with each other, then with the temple.

The negotiations with each other were easy. Allison told Cory that she wanted a Jewish wedding and hoped to raise their children as Jews. Cory had no objection. Nor did his family. Cory was not especially religious, but he had no interest in converting to Judaism. In this regard, he was typical of non-Jews who intermarry.

The negotiations with the temple were more complex. In 1999 most Reform rabbis refused to perform a Jewish wedding unless the non-Jewish

spouse first converted. (This is still the policy for Conservative and Orthodox rabbis.) Alli and Cory decided to get married in the Bay Area, where
they had both grown up. At our former congregation in California the
senior rabbi didn't officiate at interfaith weddings as a matter of "principle." But he referred Allison and Cory to the new junior rabbi who, he
said, had a more flexible attitude and would sometimes officiate, pending
an interview with the couple.

At the interview the junior rabbi asked Allison and Cory about their
plans. They explained that they intended to raise their future children as
Jews. They would join a temple and send the kids to religious school. The
kids would celebrate bar or bat mitzvahs. Allison intended to celebrate
Passover and Hanukah and take the kids to High Holy Days services. So
far, so good. But then the younger rabbi asked, "What about Christmas?"
Allison responded that they would not celebrate Christmas as a religious
holiday, but they *might* have a Christmas tree in the house. It meant something to Cory, and besides, her family had had a tree when she was young.

The rabbi immediately cut them off and said he would not officiate.
The interview was over.

Allison was devastated and humiliated. They had flunked the "Christmas tree test." I was furious at the rabbi's behavior. At the very least, I
thought, he should have used Allison's response as an opportunity for further conversation—perhaps to explain why he thought a Christmas tree
might send a confusing mixed signal to the children. But to slam the door
in their faces was hardly the way to welcome Cory to the Jewish world.
Indeed, it rudely reminded him, "You are not one of us." We ended up
hiring a rabbi who was unaffiliated with a temple.

If this incident was a step in my journey, it was probably a step back-
ward. Since then the Reform movement has increasingly welcomed interfaith couples, but I believe the community as a whole is still far too fond of
setting exclusionary rules for membership. To my mind, the issue is: *What
are we doing about the next generation?* Not, *How can we stop intermarriage?*

THIS BOOK, GROUNDED IN my struggle to come to terms with my
own Jewish identity, proposes a new way of thinking about who counts

as Jewish. It emphasizes choice in two directions. It accepts as part of the American Jewish community anyone who wishes to identify, no matter how many Jewish parents they have. It also allows people to leave the tribe without being condemned by other Jews for "denying their heritage." This approach violates centuries of Jewish tradition, but it meets critical contemporary needs and offers a sound basis for Jewish identity in America. It's a Big-Tent approach.

Inside the Tent the table is set with a smorgasbord of Jewish values, music, food, traditions, rituals, spirituality, language, philanthropic causes, and connections with Israel. At this table some will nibble; others will feast. But all will have options, and none will be turned away.

Once under the Tent, of course, Jews must be encouraged to stay: to affirm our Jewish identity rather than lapsing into apathy. Each of us needs to answer the question: Why do we care about being Jewish? Each of us must take responsibility for educating ourselves about our heritage and then *choosing* what's meaningful to us—and how we want to express it. In a very real sense the "chosen people" must become the "choosing people."

Let me say right here that I do not intend to tell anyone whether or how to be Jewish. There is no one right way. Nor do I presume to tell anyone *why* they should be Jewish. Each of us must figure that out for ourselves. But the importance of making these individual choices and their significance for the community as a whole is at the heart of this book. In these pages I invite the reader to accompany me on my own intellectual journey.

1

The Puzzling Nature of Jewish Identity

TO BEGIN INVESTIGATING the question of modern American Jewish identity, I start with the paradoxical life story of one of the world's most influential theorists on the subject of identity, Erik Erikson. I first met Erikson in 1975. At the time he had recently retired as a Harvard professor and, with his wife, Joan, had moved to Tiburon, California. Erikson's dear friends Bob and Judy Wallerstein had organized an informal faculty seminar of sorts to give him a friendly forum for trying out new ideas. I was fortunate to be invited to join the small interdisciplinary group of about twelve professionals who met with Erikson about half a dozen times.

Most of the other members of the seminar were prominent Bay Area mental health professionals—psychoanalysts, psychiatrists, and psychologists—who were considerably older than me. I was in my early thirties, a law professor at Berkeley with interdisciplinary interests, focusing primarily on child custody and children and the law. I leapt at the opportunity to join this distinguished group and to learn more about identity and human development from Erikson.

When I had been a student at Harvard in the 1960s Erikson had been a faculty celebrity. I didn't meet him in Cambridge, nor did I take any courses from him, but many of my friends did. Trained in Vienna as a child psychoanalyst by the Freuds themselves—primarily Anna, but also her father, Sigmund—Erikson was a professor of human development and a lecturer in psychiatry. His perpetually oversubscribed undergraduate course at Harvard, Social Sciences 139, "The Human Life Cycle," was popular, known for being very interesting and not terribly demanding.

My friends who took the class reported that a high point came when Erikson screened and discussed Ingmar Bergman's movie *Wild Strawberries*, about an old man looking back on how he had negotiated various stages of his life.

Erikson's worldwide influence sprang from his developmental model of identity, which posited that we work through particular challenges over eight life stages. (Freud's original theory of development had not extended past the years of early childhood.) He coined the concept of an "identity crisis," which related to an adolescent's struggle to develop a strong and cohesive sense of self. Erikson also championed the idea that a person's cultural context influenced identity development. He wrote best-selling biographies of Martin Luther and Gandhi, establishing the genre of psychobiography. In *Young Man Luther* he suggested that a series of identity crises for Luther, including a rebellion against his domineering father, had made it possible for Luther to rebel against the Catholic Church and launch the Reformation. *Gandhi's Truth* won the Pulitzer Prize and the National Book Award, rare feats for a book by a mental health professional.

Although I cannot claim to have gotten to know Erikson at all well over the course of the faculty seminars in Marin, I immediately took a liking to him. At seventy-two, he was a handsome man with blue eyes; a light, ruddyish complexion; and a striking mane of beautiful white hair. Although courtly, he dressed informally; like my grandfather George, he wore a western string tie with a striking piece of jewelry as a clasp. He was soft-spoken, with an accent that sounded German to me. From his name and appearance, however, I assumed he was Scandinavian.

Of our six or so sessions, I recall only one in which Erikson touched upon Jewish identity. He was talking about the challenges that a successful revolutionary regime faces in creating a new identity for its youth, and he used Israel and China as examples. In Israel, he said, Zionists had faced the challenge of creating a new kind of Jew—a native-born Israeli Jew (*sabra*) with a character different from that of the Diaspora Jew from Europe. The new Israeli Jew would devote his or her physical labor to cultivating the land; speak Hebrew, not Yiddish; and be a brave warrior, prepared to fight to protect the new Jewish homeland. This heroic image sharply contrasted with that of the stereotypical ghetto Jew, perhaps a peddler and a weakling, who was unwilling to fight even in his own self-defense. In China after the Revolution of 1949, Erikson said, the Communist regime had faced a similar challenge as it strived to create a new identity distinct from the old kowtowing "Chinaman" dominated by European colonialists.

I recall one other time when Erikson discussed Jewish identity in my presence. Dale and I had been invited to a dinner party at the Wallersteins' that the Eriksons attended. Dale was seated next to Erikson, and early in the evening he asked her what kind of name *Mnookin* was. When she told him that the name came from a Hebrew word meaning "at rest" or "peaceful," he asked Dale whether she was Jewish. When she replied that she was, he said, "You don't look Jewish." Then, as if to explain his questions, he said, with apparent modesty, "I write about identity, you know."

What neither of us knew at the time was the importance Erikson himself attached to *not* "looking Jewish" and *not* having a Jewish name. We found that out by chance, shortly after this dinner party, when Erikson suffered a crisis relating to his own complicated and confused identity.

The crisis was triggered by a book review in the *New York Times* with the provocative title "Erik Erikson, the Man Who Invented Himself."[1] The review, written by Marshall Berman, a City College professor and Harvard PhD who had studied with Erikson, appeared on the front page of the March 30, 1975, Sunday Book Review section and included a beautiful photograph of Erikson with his magnificent head of white hair. It addressed Erikson's most recent book, *Life History and the Historical Moment*, a collection of essays, most of which had been published before.

The first paragraph of the review gave no hint of what was to come. It could not have been more complimentary:

> Erik Erikson is probably the closest thing to an intellectual hero in American culture today. He has added striking new phrases to our language— "life cycle," "identity crisis," "inner space," "psychohistory"—words that signify new ways to interpret and confront our lives. As a psychoanalyst he has played with children and unraveled marvelous hidden depths and

resonances in their play. He has evoked the joy and dread of adolescence with a rare vividness and sympathy, and disclosed new dimensions of meaning in experiences we thought we knew all too well. In his many case histories he has shown us people in their full actuality, neither horribly grotesque nor transcendently holy, with needs and fears and longings in which we could recognize as our own.

Several paragraphs later Berman revealed what, for me, was a complete surprise: "Like many of the outstanding intellectuals of our time, Erikson grew up as a Jew in Imperial and Weimar Germany, and crossed the water [to America] during the Hitler years... [to fulfill] a vital inner need." Berman argued that Erikson's "inner need" was to abandon his Jewish and German refugee status and reinvent himself as a man of Danish gentile ancestry.

Berman's harshest criticisms focused on what Erikson had omitted from an autobiographical essay, included in the book, titled, " 'Identity Crisis' in Autobiographic Perspective." The "immediately troubling thing" about this essay, Berman wrote, was that the "crises are wholly left out." Reading "between the lines" of Erikson's essay, Berman detected an unwillingness "to be found out." According to Berman, "once we start to look, Erikson's bad faith is not hard to find."

As evidence of Erikson's "bad faith," Berman mentioned four things: First, that Erikson "cannot bear to say: that he is a Jew." In the essay Erikson had acknowledged that his stepfather, Dr. Theodor Homburger, was Jewish and that Erikson had been raised as a Jew. But Erikson had failed to state that his mother, née Karla Abrahamsen, was Jewish too.

Second, that Erikson had changed his surname as an adult after having grown up with Homburger's name and having been raised in his household. This name change, according to Berman, represented Erikson's "repudiation of his stepfather, whose Jewish name he should normally bear (though he has kept his stepfather in the background, as a vestigial 'H.')."

Third, that the new surname Erikson had chosen was not his birth father's name but rather a name he'd made up, drawing on his own first name. Berman noted "the cosmic *chutzpah* of his claim to be 'Erik Erikson,' his own father, in the most literal sense a self-made man."

Fourth, that Erikson didn't admit he'd been a refugee. "By refusing to confront himself as a Jew, Erikson represses at least one experience of dreadful suffering that we know he went through: He was a victim of Nazism." In the essay Erikson had asserted that he came to America voluntarily, not because "as a Jew, he *had* to go," wrote Berman.

The review did more than accuse Erikson of dishonesty about his Jewish heritage; it suggested that, in evading or denying his Jewishness, Erikson was inauthentic and had lived his life inconsistently with his own developmental theories, which emphasized "wholeness," a concept that, according to Berman, "means we should strive to accept our pasts, our parents, our diverse and disparate impulses and needs and yearnings" instead of "rejecting and repressing the parts of ourselves we fear."

Shortly after the review appeared, the seminar met for what I think was the last time. Erikson himself was not present. I suspected he was embarrassed and shaken by the review. (His biographer suggests that the review delivered a very upsetting blow.)[2] The rest of us, many of whom were Jewish, were stunned by the intensity of Berman's attack. We discussed what, if anything, members of the group might do individually or collectively to show support for Erikson. The consensus was that, whatever the underlying facts, Berman had unfairly attacked Erikson's character. Should a letter be sent to the *Times* in defense? If so, what might it say?

To my knowledge, no one in the group ultimately wrote a letter attempting to rebut Berman. None of us was confident we had all the facts about Erikson's background, although several members said they'd known that his stepfather was Jewish and that Erikson had been raised in a Jewish home. Someone pointed out that in his professional writings Erikson had not avoided the use of the Homburger name entirely; he had published some very early papers in the 1930s under the name of Erik Homburger. He had also kept the name *Homburger* as his middle name after changing his last name. Some of his better-known later works had been published under the name "Erik H. Erikson"—hardly a complete repudiation of his stepfather. Indeed, in a 1970 book on Erikson's work by Robert Coles, when asked about the Jewish part of his background, Erikson was quoted as saying, "I have kept my stepfather's name as my middle name out of gratitude (there is a pediatrician in me, too) but also to avoid the semblance of evasion."[3] This remark, made at least five years before the Berman review was published, suggests that Erikson was fully aware that his name change might be viewed as an attempt to conceal his Jewish heritage.

What we in the seminar group did not discuss were the issues relating to Jewish identity that arose, at least for me, from Berman's review. Berman seemed to assume that the way to determine whether someone was Jewish was to apply the matrilineal principle of Jewish law: Erikson's mother was Jewish; therefore, Erikson was Jewish. But did that mean he had to be forever Jewish? Was his biological father's background of no relevance? Was Erikson not allowed to forge his own identity? Moreover, I wondered, had Erikson converted to Christianity, and if so, shouldn't that be relevant to his identity as a Jew?

Like the others in our group, I was unwilling to criticize Erikson. I wished I had more facts. My guess was that Erikson no longer thought of himself as Jewish and, because of anti-Semitism, was reluctant to be identified publicly as a Jew. But no one in our group posed the most troubling question raised by the Berman review: Was this man we liked and admired, this man dedicated to identity and wholeness, a self-hating Jew?

I was raised to believe it was wrong to try to "pass" as a gentile. But when I think about Erikson, I wonder: Is it always wrong? What if a person feels no connection to Judaism as a religion or to the Jewish community? What if the burdens of anti-Semitism become unbearable, as they may have for Erikson growing up in Europe? Why should it be wrong to stop identifying yourself to others as Jewish under such circumstances? In other words: Why shouldn't you be allowed to opt out?

Questions like these lead me now—some forty years after my encounters with Erikson—to study in more detail his story and the various strands of his identity as an entry point into my own grappling with what it means to be Jewish. I believe many Americans of Jewish heritage will be able to relate to Erikson's complicated relationship to Judaism, whether they identify as Jewish or not. By untangling Erikson's story, I hope to reveal the complex questions of identity that arise when we consider the many different ways in which someone might be said to be Jewish—or not. And in doing so, I wish to expose the unsatisfying way in which American Jews today often categorize and pigeonhole each other as either "Jewish" or "not."

ERIKSON AND IDENTITY

What was Erik Erikson's identity? Over Erikson's lifetime, how did he shape his identity, and in writing about himself, what did he reveal and what did he attempt to hide? In evaluating the autobiographies of others, Erikson had written, "Nobody likes to be found out, not even one who has made ruthless confession a part of his profession. Any autobiographer, therefore, at least between the lines, spars with his reader and potential judge."[4] Thanks to Lawrence J. Friedman's terrific 1999 biography of Erikson, we now know more about Erikson's life—his family, how he was raised, and his life's trajectory—than we did when Berman raised questions about Erikson's Jewish identity in 1975.[5]

Berman's inference about Erikson's mother was correct: she was Jewish. Her maiden name was Karla Abrahamsen, and she came from a prominent, liberal Jewish family in Copenhagen. She was said to be "brilliant, and deeply intellectual. Indeed, she was one of the few women in the community to attend gymnasium."[6] She had a deep intellectual interest in the Danish philosopher Søren Kierkegaard and Christian spirituality; at the same time, she never questioned or in any way abandoned her own Jewish identity. She married twice—each time to a Jewish man. She kept a Jewish home, celebrated the Jewish holidays, and attended the synagogue. In fact, because of Nazi oppression, in 1935 she and her husband left Germany and emigrated to Palestine. She lived in Haifa, Israel, for twenty-five years, until her death in 1960.

In short, Erikson's mother was a Danish Jew. From adolescence on, Erikson emphasized the Danish part of his mother's heritage but was less explicit about the Jewish part. He was so evasive on this point that even his 1994 obituary in the *New York Times* got it wrong, stating that Erikson's "adopted father was Jewish and his mother's heritage was Lutheran."[7]

What about Erikson's biological father? The story is a murky one.

Theodor Homburger, Erik's stepfather, was Karla's second husband. In 1898, about four years before Erik's birth, Karla married Valdemar Isidor Salomonsen, a Jewish stockbroker. To say that the marriage was short-lived is an understatement. On her honeymoon in Rome Karla wired her brother in Copenhagen and asked him to bring her home. By the time her brother reached Rome, Salomonsen had disappeared. Erikson's biographer suggests that the marriage "did not last a night and was probably unconsummated."[8] In any event, Karla never saw Salomonsen again after her wedding night. After returning to Denmark, she kept the Abrahamsen surname but remained legally married to Salomonsen.[9]

About three years later, while living in Copenhagen, Karla became pregnant. To avoid scandal, Karla's family in Denmark insisted she go to Germany in the care of three aging spinster aunts for the later part of her pregnancy and have the baby there.[10] For this reason, Erik was born not in Denmark but in Frankfurt, Germany, on June 15, 1902. His birth certificate listed Valdemar and Karla Salomonsen as his parents. Valdemar could not have been Erik's biological father, but under Danish law a child born to a married woman is presumed to be the child of the wife's husband; therefore, Valdemar was Erik's legal father, and Erik was a legitimate child.

After Erik's birth, Karla remained in Germany with her aunts and began to study to be a nurse. When Erik was about two, Karla took him to a Jewish pediatrician named Theodor Homburger. Theodor's background was in many ways similar to Karla's: he came from a prominent, middle-class Jewish family that had lived in the Karlsruhe region since the early eighteenth century. An observant Jew, he was a leader of the more liberal synagogue in Karlsruhe. Karla became quite taken with Theodor. When Erik was not quite two and a half, Karla and Theodor became engaged. They were married on June 15, 1905—Erik's third birthday. He went on their honeymoon with them.

As a condition of their marriage, Theodor insisted Erik be told that Theodor was his biological father. This meant that from age three on, Erik bore his stepfather's last name and was raised as a Homburger.[11] Theodor and Karla subsequently had children of their own, two of whom, Ruth and Ellen, survived childhood.

At some point, likely between the ages of eight and fourteen, Erik confronted his mother and asked if Theodor was really his father.[12] Erik's suspicions were probably aroused by the fact that he looked nothing like Theodor. Tall, blond, and blue-eyed, Erik had a light complexion; Theodor was short and dark. Nor did Erik much resemble his mother physically.

Karla responded by acknowledging that Theodor was Erik's stepfather. She also told Erik the name of her first husband, Valdemar Salomonsen, claiming that he was Erik's father and had abandoned her while she was pregnant. This was, of course, a lie. Only later in his adolescence did Erik learn, likely from one of his Danish relatives, that Salomonsen had abandoned his mother several years before she became pregnant with him.

Karla never disclosed to Erik the identity of his biological father, and Erik never learned his father's name from anyone else. Nor did Erik ever press his mother on the question. He had many opportunities to do so, for Karla lived until age eighty-four. Although she lived in Haifa for her last twenty-five years, she regularly visited Erik, his family, and his half-sister in America.[13] According to Erik's biographer, "her silence on the question over the decades increased the possibility that she had been seduced or raped by a stranger."[14]

What did Erikson himself have to say about the identity of his father?

After the 1975 publication of the Berman essay, Erikson felt the need to explain his family background to his friends. He prepared a memorandum that he sent to Anna Freud and other friends and family. In it he acknowledged that after living in America for six years, he had changed his name during the American naturalization process. He wrote that "my mother was a Danish Jewess" and "my original father was a non-Jewish Dane."[15] In other letters Erikson wrote that he was "the offspring of a love affair between my mother and a Danish man who (so my family told me) was not a Jew and whose name was kept secret from all but a few who have long since died." At other times Erikson suggested that he had deduced over the years that his father was a "gentile Dane from a 'good family' and 'artistically gifted.' "[16]

None of these statements is demonstrably true. As his biographer wrote, "Erikson was preparing a narrative for the public record that appeared to resolve a matter that had not been resolved in fact."[17] According to the biographer, one of Erik's half-sisters later speculated that Karla had gotten drunk at a party hosted by her brothers and might have been too drunk or incapacitated to know who had impregnated her during a one-night stand. Another Abrahamsen family rumor suggested that Karla had named Erik after his biological father, whose name was also Erik, and that this Erik was a "Copenhagen court photographer."[18] But these were only speculations. As his biographer put it, Erikson "did not know for sure whether his real father was 'a non-Jewish Dane' and whether he was the son of Erik or any other Scandinavian gentile."[19] Nor was there any evidence that Karla's pregnancy had been the result of a "love affair" or that his birth father came from a "good family" or was "artistically gifted."

Regardless of who his father was, however, Erikson was a Jew by the standards of Jewish law and social convention. That was part of his struggle. He was raised in a world where, even if his father had been descended from Danish kings, he was inescapably categorized as a Jew. That had to be torment for someone determined to define himself on his own terms.

As an adolescent, Erikson was already deeply ambivalent about being Jewish. In school his German classmates sometimes taunted him as a Jew, while in Hebrew school his Jewish classmates sometimes teased him by calling him a "goy" because of his blond hair, blue eyes, and fair complexion. Erikson later admitted that he became "intensely alienated from [the] German middle class, [from] reform Judaism, [from the] doctor role."[20] Erik wanted none of that: he wanted to be an artist. Erik remembered "as an adolescent writing a long letter of disengagement to the rabbi." He recalled that this was "part of a quiet alienation from my whole childhood setting, German *and* Jewish."[21]

In sum, Erikson wrote that as an adolescent, "I set out to be different." His biographer characterized his stance as "living on the line" under "a stepson's identity"—neither fully Jewish nor gentile.[22]

These elements—the search for a romanticized missing father, the rebellion against a stepfather who had falsely claimed to be his father, the alienation from country and religion—all combined to create an "identity crisis" of the type Erikson would later define for the world. Although he never fully resolved this crisis, it arguably fueled the work that made him famous.

As an adult, he took actions that moved him further and further away from his Jewish origins. In his choice of a wife, he came down unambiguously on the gentile side of the line. Sarah Serson, who went by the name Joan, was an observant Protestant, the daughter of a Canadian Episcopal minister and an American mother. In 1929, at age twenty-six, Joan moved to Vienna to study dancing. She soon met Erik Homburger, who, after spending a few years in his early twenties pursuing the somewhat vagabond life of a young artist, had ended up in Vienna and begun his training in psychoanalysis. Soon they were a couple.

In 1930 Joan discovered she was pregnant. It appears that Erik initially balked at marrying her because of both "apprehension over permanent commitments and his fear that his parents would disapprove of marriage to a non-Jew."[23] But friends persuaded him not to repeat his father's mistake: "His child should not be born out of wedlock as he had been, and Joan should not be left alone with a newborn as Karla had been."[24]

By the time they married in Vienna, Joan was six to eight months pregnant, according to varying accounts.[25] They told neither family about the decision, "apprehensive about the serious misgivings each might have about this Jewish-Christian mixed marriage."[26] During a three-month period in late 1930 the couple had three wedding ceremonies, none of which Erik's or Joan's family knew about in advance or were invited to attend. One was an Anglican ceremony. But because Austria did not recognize Anglicanism, that marriage had no legal standing. The couple therefore had a civil ceremony, at which Erik registered as a Jew and Joan registered as a Protestant. The third was a Jewish ceremony, held so that Erik could later tell his parents that they'd had a Jewish wedding, but for this the bride and groom did little more than go through the motions. For purposes of this ceremony, they lied to the officiating rabbi and claimed that Joan was a convert to Judaism.[27]

After they married, Erik made no pretense of being in any way an observant Jew. Joan was a committed Protestant, and their children were raised as Christians. In short, I have no doubt that Erik abandoned Judaism as a religion.

The question of Erikson's relationship to Christianity is more complicated. Like his mother, Erikson had a serious intellectual interest in Christianity, especially its existential dimensions, as espoused by Kierkegaard and by Erikson's Harvard colleague Paul Tillich. But during most of their marriage Erik did not attend church services with Joan.

While at Harvard Erikson displayed a large crucifix in his Widener Library office. His teaching assistants didn't know what to make of it because they knew Erikson was not a practicing Christian. Finally, a teaching assistant named Gordon Fellman, who is now a professor of sociology at Brandeis, asked Erikson if he considered himself to be Jewish or Christian. "If you are anti-Semitic, I'm a Jew," Erikson reportedly replied enigmatically.[28]

What did he mean by this? That an anti-Semite such as Hitler would consider him a Jew? Or that, if confronted by an anti-Semite, he would identify himself as a Jew to take a stand against prejudice? Probably the former. The second interpretation seems inconsistent with his attempts to avoid Jewish labels—his name change and his reluctance to acknowledge his mother's Jewish ancestry.

But the question was what Erikson *considered himself*, and his answer was opaque and not responsive.

When Erik and Joan returned to California after his retirement from Harvard, Erikson's behavior strongly suggests that he did not think of himself as Jewish and may have thought of himself as Christian. As his friend Bob Wallerstein later wrote of these years, Erikson occasionally referred to his half-sister Ellen, who lived in Israel, as "my Jewish sister," as if Erikson himself were not Jewish. Wallerstein also wrote,

Over the fifteen years [in California] that we saw each other so regularly and professionally, talk was rarely about religion. It was not often that Erik made references like the one to "my Jewish sister." On one occasion, however, he asked me directly, "How come you Jews yearn so longingly for the coming of the Messiah and don't realize that the Messiah has already come?"

In using the phrase "you Jews" Erikson plainly implies that he is not one of them. Moreover, it suggests that Erikson thought Jesus was the messiah. Wallerstein further noted that "there was nothing Jewish about the Eriksons' home or their life."[29]

In California Joan found great comfort in belonging to an Episcopalian parish. Erikson occasionally accompanied her to church on Sunday.[30] In a private letter written in 1976, Erikson explained, "I do feel on occasion the need to participate with my wife in a church service in order to affirm and receive affirmation from the ritual formulations of a devotional community. My wife's church is ministered by a clergyman singularly able to convey the basic terms of original Christianity; and he is hospitable toward my kind." By "my kind," did Erikson mean a Jew by birth who wished to explore Christianity but had not formally converted?

On one occasion the Wallersteins accompanied the Eriksons to a special ceremony at Grace Cathedral in San Francisco to honor a monk whom Joan admired. Wallerstein wrote, "When parishioners went up to take communion, Judy and I were startled to see Erik go up with Joan. We thought we knew that only those baptized in that faith were authorized to take communion, and we had never heard that Erik had been baptized." Wallerstein was later informed, however, that "all those present at Episcopal services are invited to participate in communion whether baptized or not, and Erik was indeed invited to participate by the friendly minister."[31] Erikson's biographer also suggested that Erikson had never been baptized.[32]

Perhaps the most revealing statement by Erikson himself about his religious identity is found in a private letter to Hope Curfman, a social worker who was co-leading a Denver church workshop on Erikson. Curfman had written to him first, saying that she was often asked about his religious faith and asking, "Do you consider yourself to be a Christian?" Erikson's essay-length response was written in 1976, the year after the

Berman attack, and its depth suggests that perhaps he was working out an answer to his critics as well:[33]

A statement of faith...cannot be simple....All right, then: some passages in the Gospels—the Word made Flesh and the Child and the Kingdom—have always touched me....To me, the shining newness, above all, of Jesus' parables attests to the genuine presence of a singular man. His teachings are, of course, unthinkable without the elemental steps of Judaism.

Several paragraphs later Erikson wrote,

You refer to my "mixed Jewish and Christian origins." Does your question imply another one, namely, whether or not I consider myself a Jew? Yes, I went along to synagogue as a child, and I underwent Bar Mitzvah, the Jewish confirmation, at the proper age. But while I was touched by the rituals at home (such as Passover), the synagogue services, at the time, impressed me as rather ritualistic performances, and this probably because of their "reformed" style....Also, my mother was a faithful reader of Kierkegaard, and I early received from her a quiet and uncombative conviction that to be raised a Jew did not preclude a reverence for the core values of Christianity. Later, personal fate removed me from my background, and world events destroyed it altogether....Now to the point: I know that nobody who has grown up in a Jewish environment can ever be not-a-Jew, whether the Jewishness he experienced was defined by his family's sense of history, by its religious observances, or, indeed, by the environment's attitude toward Jews.

This last sentence is a remarkable statement. It seems to imply that although Erikson "experienced" Jewishness growing up, he never felt like a Jew; that his Jewishness was imposed on him by both his family and the anti-Semitic culture in which he lived; and that he would have preferred to "be not-a-Jew" but the "environment" made that impossible. In the next sentence, however, he accepts Jewishness as part of his history:

For that very reason, however..., to profess one's Jewishness can, in our day, imply a diversity of "confessions": from a proud affirmation of a unique racial history to the confirmation of the Judaic faith or to the mere undeniability of a fact; and from the eager claim to the potential right to become an Israeli (on the basis of having had a Jewish mother) to the survivor's admission that he (on the same statistical grounds) would have been eligible for the holocaust. None of these aspects can ever be stricken from the Jewish part of one's historical identity which, in fact, is made up of their unique combination.

At the end of this long letter Erikson returned to the question of whether he was a Christian:

I want to quote to you a phrase which my wife used when I asked what she (who happens to be an Episcopal minister's daughter) would say in response to your question. She said, "I would tell her that I am a Christian apprentice." I like this, because (as your own remarks indicate) it seems so much more important to recognize the frontier on which one is struggling for insight and commonality than to let oneself be totally committed to categories which—important as they are for the factual definition of one's daily duties—foreclose one's infinite search....All these words—do they tell whether I "consider myself a Christian"? I would say "yes" in the sense that in order to perceive and to study the living implications of Christ's message I am not only willing but determined to live on the shadowy borderline of the denominational ambiguities (whether national or religious, political or professional) into which I seem to have been born.

Upon Erikson's death Joan honored his wish to be cremated, which is not permitted in traditional Jewish practice. Joan arranged for his remains to be buried in the cemetery of the First Congregational Church in Harwich, Massachusetts, where the Eriksons lived during his final years; Joan's Episcopal minister from California presided over the service. According to Robert Wallerstein, Joan "had completed the Christianization of Erik H. Erikson, always her desire."[34]

So what do I make of Erikson's subjective religious identity? It defies easy categorization. He thought of himself as having both Jewish and Christian ancestry. He abandoned Judaism as a religion and had no connection to the American Jewish community. It appears he never embraced Christian orthodoxy enough to convert but instead saw himself as "an apprentice Christian." He admired Jesus and his teachings. In his letter to Curfman he described his faith as based on the "original Christian vision—rather than its institutional fate." Subjectively he lived on the "shadowy borderline of denominational ambiguities" and never fully resolved his religious identity.

At the core of Erikson's theories was the notion that human beings go through various developmental stages, each of which involves a particular challenge in which a person has to learn to live with the dynamic tension between competing needs. For example, during the early adulthood stage the tension is between intimacy and isolation. In the final stage it's between integrity and despair. According to Erikson, wisdom and maturity involve reaching a positive way to live with these tensions. I regret that Erikson never shared more explicitly how he came to resolve the tension between his Jewish heritage and the new self he wanted to create.

ERIKSON'S OTHER AMBIGUOUS IDENTITIES

Just as Erikson's religious identity was far from clear, he also lived on the "shadowy borderline" in terms of both his nationality—as a Dane, a German, and an American—and his profession, as an artist, a psychoanalyst, and an academic.

Erikson had a complicated national identity. He became a naturalized American in 1939 and took pride in that identity. Before that, was he Danish or German? He was born and raised in Germany, but his birth certificate identified both parents as Danish, and he no doubt would have qualified for Danish citizenship; however, when he was seven, in 1909,[35] Karla arranged that he become a naturalized German citizen, thus extinguishing any claim to Danish citizenship.

Growing up, Erik was very aware of his Danish heritage and often visited his Danish relatives in Copenhagen. However, he never learned to speak Danish, for his mother insisted German be spoken in the Homburger home. Indeed, Karla appears to have been "intent on maintaining a German household, not a Danish one, all the more because German was the 'official' language of continental Europe."[36]

As noted earlier, the adolescent Erik rebelled against German middle-class culture and wanted to think of himself as completely Danish. Alas, his love for Denmark would be unrequited.

Erikson and his wife were living in Vienna when Hitler rose to power in Germany. Both decided they had to leave Austria, Erik because he felt Nazism would soon arrive and Joan because she didn't like living in Vienna. At Erik's insistence they chose to go to Denmark, where he hoped to begin a psychoanalytic practice and eventually acquire Danish citizenship. "I was born a Dane so I went back to Denmark," Erikson once said in a somewhat misleading statement.[37]

Erik and Joan had to enter Denmark on visitor's permits, which did not allow either of them to work. With the help of his mother's relatives, Erikson petitioned the Ministry of Justice for the long-term residency papers he needed to set up a practice and eventually acquire Danish citizenship. On his application he claimed that his father was Salomonsen (his mother's first husband), that both of his parents were Danish, and that he faced difficult conditions in Germany as a Jew. But to his shock and distress, his petition was denied, meaning he could not work or teach in Denmark, become a Danish citizen, or even remain in Denmark for more than a few months.[38] At Joan's urging, they decided to emigrate to America and arrived in New York in the fall of 1933.

Was Erikson Danish? He certainly thought so, and perhaps in some ancestral sense he was, as both of his parents were from Denmark. But he wasn't a citizen, he didn't speak the language, and he'd never been immersed in the culture, so his Danish "national" identity was partly his own creation.

Erikson's professional identity was also complicated. In his youth he considered himself an artist, and an early woodcut reproduced in

Friedman's book suggests he had considerable talent. Because of his work in Vienna with Anna Freud, he ultimately became a member in full standing of the Vienna Psychoanalytic Society, which gave him automatic membership in the International Psychoanalytic Association.

But in America he never found a stable professional home. In the 1930s American psychoanalytic institutes generally required a medical degree in addition to psychoanalytic training to qualify for regular membership. The Boston Psychoanalytic Society and Institute made an exception for Erikson, but as a therapist without medical training, he never felt he had full standing with the American psychiatric community.

Nor was he ever securely situated as an academic. Departments of psychiatry were housed in medical schools, and Erikson was a psychoanalyst without a medical degree. Nor did he have formal training in psychology or the social sciences. He took courses in psychology in the 1930s and began a PhD program, but he never earned the doctorate normally required for a professorial appointment in a psychology, anthropology, or sociology department. Moreover, his work did not neatly fit into any standard academic department. He taught at both at Yale and Berkeley but never got a professorial appointment with tenure until 1949 at Berkeley, and that lasted only one year.[39] His next tenured appointment came from Harvard in 1960, and it was over the objections of some faculty who believed his written work was insufficiently rigorous. It was an "independent, nondepartmental appointment" as a "Professor of Human Development," not attached to a particular academic department.[40] The fact that Erikson never achieved a clear departmental identity as an American academic, despite his fame, mirrored the other ambiguities that marked his life's journey.

THE SLIPPERY NATURE OF IDENTITY

The subject of identity has fascinated social scientists for as long as the field has existed. Theories of identity have spread across all manner of academic disciplines, including psychiatry, sociology, social psychology, social anthropology, and cultural studies. And yet, according to the back cover of *The Handbook of Identity Theory and Research*:

Despite the wealth of findings across many disciplines, identity researchers remain divided over such enduring fundamental questions as: What
exactly is identity, and how do identity processes function? Do people
have a single identity or multiple identities? Is identity individually or
collectively oriented? Personally or socially constructed? Stable or constantly in flux?[41]

My own ideas of identity, especially Jewish identity, address all these
questions, and Erikson offers a way to illustrate them. The first idea is
that each of us has many strands to our identity. None of us is simply one
thing. For Erikson those strands included religion (Jewish and Christian);
ethnicity (Jewish and Danish); citizenship (German and American); profession (psychoanalyst and academic); and family (son, stepson, husband,
and father). As we've seen, some of these strands were a source of pride and
others a source of inner conflict.

The second idea is that the salience of any particular strand varies from
person to person and involves choice. This is certainly true of the Jewish
strand, the salience of which varies enormously among American Jews.
(Moreover, the Jewish strand may be composed of substrands: religious
and ethnic.) For the ultra-Orthodox, being Jewish is a dominant strand
that permeates every aspect of daily life. For others of Jewish heritage it
may be only the thinnest of strands: they may be nonobservant and unin-
volved with any communal aspects of Jewish life. Most American Jews
fall somewhere between the two extremes, and some, like Erikson, are
ambivalent about this strand. If the adult Erikson thought of himself as
ethnically Jewish at all, the strand was paper thin. By choice, his dominant ethnic strand was Danish.

The third idea is that the salience of each strand may fluctuate throughout one's lifetime, a process that also involves choice. For some Jews,
the Jewish strand may assume greater importance at certain times—for
example, when studying for a bar/bat mitzvah; planning their marriage
ceremony; deciding what sort of religious education, if any, to provide
their children; or coping with a serious illness or the death of a relative—
and ebb at other times. For others, like me, the Jewish strand may grow

more salient as they get older. By early adulthood Erikson chose to reject the religious strand of Judaism and to shrink the ethnic strand down to a wisp. By the end of his life he might not have considered himself ethnically Jewish at all, although critics like Marshall Berman did.

This suggests a fourth idea: that Jewish identity has a collective dimension based on membership in a group. This is true of other dimensions of identity, too. Belonging to a group—whether a family, a social class, or an ethnic or religious group—can be a source of pride and self-esteem, providing us with a sense of connection to others. But if we feel alienated from a group to which we are said to belong, membership may be a source of confusion and pain.

This highlights the fact that our identity isn't completely up to us to create. Other people have opinions about our identity as well, and these opinions can have enormous impact on us. As Erikson implied in his comment to his teaching assistant, any anti-Semite would consider him Jewish because of his background. Some Jews—Berman is an example—would consider him Jewish for the same reason. The flip side of this phenomenon is that groups can *deny* membership to individuals who want to belong. Erikson desperately wanted Danish citizenship and was rejected. There is an analogy within the American Jewish world: many people self-identify as Jews but are not universally accepted because their mothers are not Jewish and they have not formally converted. For some Jews, as we'll see, this sense of rejection can spark an identity crisis and can influence the development of their personal Jewish identity.

What standard of membership should apply to the American Jewish community today? Who should count as a Jew? In addition to matrilineal descent, there are several traditional ways of thinking about Jewish identity: as a religion, a race, and an ethnicity. Do any of these ideas offer a standard that makes sense in today's America? If not, how might we usefully define the boundaries of being Jewish? Or do we need to define them at all? Can we leave it up to each individual to choose whether or not to identify as Jewish?

2

THE MATRILINEAL PRINCIPLE

THE TRADITIONAL JEWISH law standard defining who is a Jew—what I will call the *matrilineal principle*—is easy to state: at birth you are automatically a Jew if your mother was Jewish. Without a Jewish mother, you are not Jewish unless you go through a formal and generally quite onerous religious conversion to Judaism. By religious law, being Jewish is an all-or-nothing proposition. There is no such thing as a "half-Jew." Having a Jewish father counts for nothing; if your mother isn't Jewish, you're a gentile.

The matrilineal principle creates an ascribed status that has nothing to do with personal choice. If your mother was Jewish, you *are* forever Jewish, whether you like it or not. Even if you convert to another religion, under traditional Jewish law (*halacha*) you remain a Jew[1]—that status is as permanent as your blood type.

I am not a fan of the matrilineal principle. In contemporary America—where children of mixed heritage are no longer an exception—I believe it produces results that are dysfunctional, arbitrary, and unfair. Intermarriage now produces hundreds of thousands of Americans with only one Jewish parent, and the matrilineal rule rejects about half of them.

But there are many adherents to this principle today who justify their allegiance to it on the basis of tradition and precedent. Tradition and precedent aren't necessarily bad reasons to continue doing something, but let's examine the origins of the matrilineal formula to see whether it makes sense on its own terms today.

THE ROOTS OF THE MATRILINEAL RULE

For about eighteen hundred years the matrilineal principle has been the dominant religious standard for determining whether a person is Jewish.

The rule has been a part of Jewish law for so long that some Jews view it as sacred, somehow sanctioned by God. But its religious pedigree is not nearly as solid as its rabbinical proponents today would claim.

The matrilineal rule did not exist in biblical times and can't be found in the Torah or the rest of the Hebrew Bible. In biblical times children inherited their Jewish status through the *paternal* line. Many Israelite men took foreign women as wives, and "there was never any doubt that the children were Israelite," according to Harvard history professor Shaye Cohen, who has studied the pedigree of the matrilineal rule in detail.[2] The Old Testament is filled with tales in which "Israelite heroes and kings married foreign women."[3] Cohen points out that "Judah married a Canaanite, Joseph an Egyptian, Moses a Midianite and an Ethiopian, David a Philistine, and Solomon women of every description."[4] There is no claim that the children of these patriarchs were not members of the tribe because their mothers were not. Nor is there any hint that the children suffered "any legal or social disabilities."[5] Indeed, simply by virtue of marriage, these women "joined the clan, people, and religion of [their] husband[s]."[6] The Bible contains no suggestion that these gentile wives had to convert to Judaism; the idea of conversion to Judaism did not yet exist.[7]

The matrilineal principle first appeared centuries later, Cohen argues, in the context of new rules about marriage. The oldest textual basis for the principle is found in four paragraphs of the *Mishnah*,[8] the first major work of rabbinic literature. Written in Hebrew about 200 CE, the Mishnah is an anthology of various legal rulings and debates, many of which were ascribed to various sages. The Mishnah came to be seen as a compendium of earlier oral laws put in writing to make sure they weren't forgotten.[9] However, Cohen concludes that the matrilineal rule cannot be dated "before the period of the Mishnah itself," at the end of the second century CE.[10]

By this time Judaism had adopted two important practices unknown to the Israelites: it prohibited marriage with all non-Jews[11] and permitted gentiles to convert to Judaism.[12] These innovations reflected new social realities. Cohen explains,

Since biblical Israel was a nation living on its own land, it had no need for a prohibition of intermarriage with all outsiders. Attitudes changed when conditions changed. In the wake of the destruction of the [first] temple in 587 BCE, Judea lost any semblance of political independence, the tribal structure of society was shattered, and the Israelites were scattered among the nations.[13]

Cohen explains further,

During the period of the second temple, with the loss of national sovereignty and the increased interaction with gentiles, the Jews sensed that their survival depended upon their ideological (or "religious") and social separation from the outside world. Since the Mosaic legislation was inadequate for their needs, they erected new barriers between themselves and the gentiles.[14]

By the time the Mishnah was published, Cohen says, the shift to endogamy was largely complete: most Jews married other Jews. But that didn't stop Jews and gentiles from having sexual relations, producing children outside of marriage, or sealing a union with a gentile marriage ceremony. The matrilineal rule needs to be understood in this context.

Cohen translates the key passage in the Mishnah as follows:

[A] Wherever there is potential for a valid marriage and the marriage would not be sinful, the offspring follows the male. And what [woman] is this? This is the daughter of a priest, Levite, or Israelite who was married to a priest, Levite, or Israelite.

[B] Wherever there is potential for a valid marriage but the marriage would be sinful, the offspring follows the parent of lower status. And what [woman] is this? This is a widow with a high priest, a divorcee or a "released woman" [*haluzah*, Deut. 25:5–10] with a regular priest, a *mamzeret* or a *netinah* [Ezra 2:43–58, etc.] with an Israelite, an Israelite woman with a *mamzer* or a *natin*.

[C] And any woman who does not have the potential for a valid marriage with this man but has the potential for a valid marriage with other men, the offspring is a *mamzer*. And what [man] is this? This is he who has intercourse with any of the relations prohibited by the Torah.

[D] And any woman who does not have the potential for a valid marriage either with this man or with other men, the offspring is like her. And what [man] is this? This is the offspring of a slave woman or a gentile woman.[15]

The first thing you notice about this passage is that the matrilineal principle isn't spelled out in a straightforward way. It has to be deduced from a series of convoluted statements relating to the validity of various types of marriage. The passage assumes that, under Jewish law, some couples have the "potential" for a valid Jewish marriage (see paragraphs A and B) and others do not (see C and D). The child's status as a Jew depends not on whether the parents are actually married but whether they *could* legally marry under Jewish law. As long as both parents are Jewish—and no sin is involved, such as adultery or incest—the Mishnah states that "the offspring follows the male."[16] In other words, the child inherits his or her religious status as a Jew from the father, as in biblical practice.

The second thing you notice is that the matrilineal principle applies only in cases of mixed parentage. If one parent is a gentile, the lineage is determined by the mother. When the mother is Jewish and the father is not (paragraph C), then the child is a *mamzer*, a Jewish child of impaired status.[17] If the mother is not Jewish (paragraph D), the child's status is "like her"—that is, not Jewish.

The big question with regard to mixed parentage, says Cohen, is: "What compelled [the rabbis] to depart from the biblical tradition and from the practice of the Second Temple period"—both of which were patrilineal?[18] We don't know. The rabbis left no explanation.

Cohen considers a number of popular theories and rejects them all.[19] He concludes that, in all probability, "the matrilineal principle is a legal innovation of the first or second century of our era...as a consequence of the influx of new ideas into rabbinic Judaism" related either to (1) Roman law or, (2) thought concerning the interbreeding of animals ("the mixture of diverse kinds").[20]

He makes a good case for the influence of Roman law, noting that the parallels are "striking."[21] The idea that a marriage could be legally valid or not—unknown in biblical times—closely mirrored Roman law, which governed marriage between Roman citizens and noncitizens.[22] The treatment of the offspring is also similar.

Cohen is less certain about the influence of the rabbinic laws regarding forbidden unions between animals, but he finds strong parallels there, too. He notes, perhaps with deliberate humor, "The union of a Jew with a gentile is akin to the forbidden union of a horse with a donkey."[23] In both cases the offspring follow the mother.

Although scholars don't know why the rabbis adopted this rule, it's tempting to speculate. We know that the narrow purpose of the rule was to determine the status of children who had only one Jewish parent. Why was a child's Jewish status important? Because a Jew could only marry another Jew. The community had to know who was allowed to marry whom.

What was the purpose of banning intermarriage? The Jews were now in exile, a minority governed by others. If assimilation and intermarriage took their natural course, the Jewish people might disappear. As Cohen suggests, endogamy might have been seen as necessary for survival.

If the overriding purpose of the rule was to discourage sexual relationships outside the tribe, why not limit Jewish status to children who had *two* Jewish parents? Cohen says there would have been little need for such a rule because intermarriage was already uncommon in first-century Judea and remained so for many centuries thereafter.[24] I see another possibility: fornication outside the tribe happened often enough, but a two-parent rule was too draconian; it wouldn't meet other social goals, such as providing community support for a Jewish single mother who had been abandoned by the gentile father. I must acknowledge, however, that the Mishnah itself did not require such community support and stigmatized the child as a *mamzer*, a Jew of impaired status.[25] The next question, then, is: Why didn't the rabbis accept *all* children of mixed parentage as Jewish? Why favor only the mother? This is the crux of the matter.

The most obvious justification is that the mother's identity is always known, but not the father's—the Roman principle of "mater certa, pater incertus."[26] Cohen rejects this justification mainly because the rabbis applied the rule only to cases of mixed parentage, even though paternity can also be uncertain for a child born of two Jews.[27] I disagree with his logic; indeed, if I had to speculate, the key reason for differentiating between fathers and mothers is that you *would* always know the identity of the mother.

Let's take married couples first.[28] If a married Jewish couple had a child, Jewish law—like that of most contemporary legal systems—presumed that the woman's husband was the child's father. Thus, the child inherited its status from the father.[29] For a variety of reasons it would be socially disruptive to question paternity in the context of marriage, especially before the era of genetic testing.

Now let's consider unmarried couples, to which the rule clearly applies. If a Jew and a non-Jew produced a child, what happened to mother and child? A child with a Jewish mother had verifiable Jewish ancestry, and the mother would likely remain in the Jewish community and raise the child as a Jew. But when the mother was *not* Jewish, how could one be sure that the father was? Especially if the Jewish man denied paternity? In that case the gentile woman would probably remain with her own tribe, where there was no chance the child would be raised as a Jew. So I suspect that the rabbis' decision was pragmatic, related to the likelihood that the child (1) had verifiable Jewish ancestry and (2) would be raised in the Jewish community.[30]

Whatever the original reason for the rule, its lack of biblical pedigree has been something of an embarrassment for rabbis who believe that Jewish law is God given. Rabbinic authorities have combed the Torah for "hooks" that might supply such a pedigree and have tended to rely on three passages in the Torah, none of which Cohen finds persuasive.[31]

The obvious disconnect between biblical practice and the matrilineal rule plagues religious authorities to this day. Recently someone sent the following pointed question to the website Chabad.org (an Orthodox Hasidic site): "Was Jewishness always matrilineal?" The questioner noted that Moses married the daughter of a non-Jewish priest and that Moses's children were clearly Jewish.[32]

When forced to confront the contradiction, Rabbi Tzvi Freeman acknowledged that biblical stories featured Jewish men marrying non-Jewish women with no mention of conversion, but he claimed that conversion was implied. "When a man marries a woman from outside the tribe, all understand that he is bringing her in to join the tribe, and so she must go through whatever rites are required to make that entry."[33] In other words, please assume the gentile wife underwent a conversion, even though the Bible never mentions such rites.

In all events, the matrilineal rule survived unopposed for centuries, largely because it wasn't invoked very often. For most of Jewish history—from the first century until well into the modern era—unions between Jews and gentiles were comparatively rare. Jews lived in segregated communities and faced almost insuperable social barriers to marrying out.

These tight boundaries began to break down in the nineteenth century as many Jews in America and Western Europe were granted citizenship and became integrated into the gentile world. As I will discuss later in the book, by the last quarter of the twentieth century intermarriage in America had become very common and the arbitrariness of the matrilineal rule had become conspicuous. Why treat children with a Jewish father differently from children with a Jewish mother if the intermarried couple wants to raise the child as a Jew?

In 1983 the Reform movement broke ranks and set a new standard: any person with one Jewish parent is Jewish as long as they are raised in a Jewish home or make some affirmative declaration of commitment.[34] The result is that American Judaism now has two competing religious standards. Both the Orthodox and Conservative denominations reject this innovation and adhere to the principle that only those with a Jewish mother are Jews by birth.

These two standards don't coexist easily. The traditional matrilineal rule retains a powerful grip on the Jewish psyche, even on many who prefer the Reform standard. The rule continues to wield pervasive cultural influence. If you asked any random person on the street who counts as Jewish, my hunch is that most gentile Americans would reply, "Your mother has to be Jewish."

So we must ask: How well does the matrilineal rule serve the Jewish community today, given current social realities? In my view it has significant defects.

THE MATRILINEAL PRINCIPLE IS UNDERINCLUSIVE: IT EXCLUDES PEOPLE WHO ARE LIVING THOROUGHLY JEWISH LIVES

If the original purpose of the rule was to embrace only those children who unquestionably had Jewish "blood" (relying on the "mater certa" principle), that rationale doesn't hold up today. It's quite a simple matter to determine paternity through genetic testing.

If the original purpose of the rule was to embrace only those children of mixed parentage who were likely to be raised as Jews, it fails to achieve that purpose. Today many such children with Jewish mothers are not being raised in Jewish communities or being taught much about Judaism. Conversely, many individuals with Jewish *fathers* have been raised as Jews since birth, have been bar or bat mitzvahed, celebrate Jewish holidays, and identify themselves as part of the Jewish community.

The irrationality of the rule is demonstrated by the life of Angela Warnick Buchdahl, the child of a Jewish father and a Korean Buddhist mother. She is now the senior rabbi of Central Synagogue in New York City, one of the leading Reform congregations in the country. Under her leadership Central Synagogue serves almost twenty-four hundred member families, and its reach extends far beyond Manhattan: hundreds of people view its live-streamed Shabbat services on Friday nights, and at least twenty-five thousand people in forty-nine different countries watched its services on recent High Holy Days.[35] In terms of leading a Jewish life, how could you find someone more dedicated? And yet under the terms of the matrilineal rule she is not Jewish.

Buchdahl's case illustrates the psychological costs of the matrilineal rule.

Admittedly, her situation was more complicated than most. Her mother was not only a gentile but also of a different race. Although Buchdahl was raised Jewish and recalls the family being welcomed by their Reform synagogue and community, she was intensely aware of her outsider status in the wider Jewish world. "My greatest fear," she told *Hadassah Magazine* in 2013, "was that I was a fraud, that I wore the cloak of a Jew but somehow deep down inside I wasn't authentic."[36]

These feelings came to a head during a college summer in Israel, where she felt "marginalized and invisible." She wrote an article about her experience for the Jewish online journal *Sh'ma*, describing that time as a "period of crisis":

> After a painful summer...I called my mother to declare that I no longer wanted to be a Jew. I did not look Jewish, I did not carry a Jewish name, and I no longer wanted the heavy burden of having to explain and prove myself every time I entered a new Jewish community. She simply responded by saying, "Is that possible?" It was only at that moment that I realized I could no sooner stop being a Jew than I could stop being Korean, or female, or me.[37]

Buchdahl ultimately resolved this identity crisis, as Erikson would surely have called it. She majored in religious studies at Yale, attended the Hebrew Union College–Jewish Institute of Religion in New York, and became a Reform rabbi. Today her congregation welcomes all comers, including interfaith and interracial Jewish families, and she makes a point of celebrating this diversity.

THE RULE IS OVERINCLUSIVE: IT LEAVES NO ROOM FOR CHOICE

The matrilineal rule claims as Jewish those people who have no Jewish identity and who may even follow another religion. Consider, for example, the case of Madeleine Albright, the former US secretary of state.

Albright was born Marie Jana Korbelova in 1937 in Prague, Czechoslovakia. All four of her grandparents were Jewish. Her parents were highly assimilated and not observant. Her father, Josef Korbel, was a diplomat.[38]

When Albright was almost two years old, Nazi Germany occupied parts of Czechoslovakia. Ten days after the invasion the Korbels fled to London, where they spent the war years as part of the Czech government in exile. In London both of her parents converted to Catholicism. Albright was raised as a Catholic, and her parents never told her about her Jewish ancestry. They said only that her grandparents had died during the war.[39]

After the war the family returned to Prague, where Albright's father served as the Czech ambassador to Yugoslavia. But when the Communists took over Czechoslovakia in 1948, her family fled again, this time to the United States. The Korbels settled in Denver, where Josef became a professor and eventually a dean at the University of Denver. Albright attended Wellesley College on a scholarship and graduated in 1959. Soon thereafter she married Joseph Albright and adopted his religion, becoming an Episcopalian.[40]

The fact of her Jewish roots didn't emerge publicly until she became secretary of state. When President Clinton nominated her in 1996 the *Washington Post* began to research her family history as part of a profile. The *Post* learned that more than a dozen of her relatives, including three of her grandparents, had died as Jews in the concentration camps. Some were killed in the gas chambers of Auschwitz; others died of typhoid and malnutrition at the Terezin holding camp in Nazi-occupied Czechoslovakia.[41] The *Post* also learned, from interviews conducted in the family's home village, that Albright came from a family of Czech Jews who had owned a building-materials business before the war.[42]

In early 1997, just a week after Albright was sworn in as the first female secretary of state, *Post* reporter Michael Dobbs met with her to present the results of his research and seek a response. "It was a very emotional moment for her and a slightly difficult interview," Dobbs recalled later. "She sort of thanked me for the information, but she was shocked by the revelations."[43]

The story broke a week later. "This was obviously a major surprise to me," Albright told the Associated Press. "I had never been told this."[44] The

Post quoted her as saying, "I have always thought of myself as a Czechoslovak Catholic."[45]

But how surprised was she? Albright told the *Post* that she had been receiving letters about her family background for years, especially after she became US ambassador to the United Nations in 1993, and that some of these letters had referred to her family's Jewish origins. The *Post* further noted that some of Albright's relatives and family friends in the Czech Republic were well aware of the family history.[46]

The story sparked a minor furor over whether Albright had been intentionally hiding her Jewish origins before the *Post* confronted her with solid proof. A spate of articles—many by writers who identified themselves as Jewish—appeared with headlines such as "Did She Know?"[47] Frank Rich of the *New York Times*, referring to Albright's claim that the discovery had been a "major surprise," wrote that she seemed to be "shading the truth." What was "troubling to many Jews, myself among them, is her lack of curiosity about her roots," he wrote, noting that she had received letters about her Jewish heritage from the mayor of her father's hometown and from a Jewish first cousin. "What smart, serious, sensitive student of history, let alone Nazi refugee, makes no effort to find out how her grandparents died?"[48]

Albright offered a number of explanations. The early letters sent to her had been full of inaccuracies, so she didn't take them seriously. After she was nominated for secretary of state the letters became more specific and credible, but she was "working 20 hours a day" and didn't have time to do the follow-up research she wanted to do on her own.[49] "I was not surprised about my Jewish origin," she clarified in one interview. "What I was surprised about was that my grandparents died in concentration camps."[50]

Dobbs, the *Post* reporter, didn't buy it. Two years later he published a book on Albright in which he wrote,

> As I completed the research for this book, I came to the conclusion that Madeleine learned the essential details of her family's past long before February 1997. It is quite probable that her parents kept her and her siblings in the dark about their origins for many years. But too many

people, both in America and in Europe, knew what had happened for the secret to be kept forever from such an intelligent, inquiring woman. As I explain in the course of this book, there are simply too many contradictions and inconsistencies in her story for it to be believable.[51]

But even if she willfully ignored the signs, so what? Why did this attract so much attention from American Jews? There were at least two reasons.

The first reason stems from the matrilineal rule and its emphasis on ascribed status. According to this rule, Albright is a Jew. Ancestry is irrevocable.[52] It doesn't matter how she was raised or how she thinks of herself or even what she knew. Significantly, Albright didn't go along with this view; after the *Post* article ran, she said she still considered herself an Episcopalian.[53] Perhaps this response struck the wrong note with some Jews who were eager to claim her as a member of the tribe and may have hoped she would embrace her Jewish identity.

The second reason the story hit a nerve was the sensitivity of American Jews to the issue of hiding one's origins. As Frank Rich noted in his *Times* piece, many Jews had tried to shed their Jewishness in America, especially in the postwar period. "Even the Holocaust was not talked about too loudly among American Jews in the 1950's," Rich wrote. "However unintentionally, Madeleine Albright actually lived the darkest fantasy of the most assimilationist American Jews of that time. Her family's obliteration of its Jewish past—extreme case though it may be—wouldn't resonate so loudly if it didn't awaken guilty memories in so many other American homes."[54]

My own view: it is true that as an adult she didn't pursue hints about her family background. It is remarkable that a person with her experience, professional insight, and integrity remained unaware of her heritage for so long. But family secrets, particularly relating to identity, have their own dynamic.

Insisting that someone is Jewish, regardless of self-identity or how they are living their life, is wrong. In my view Albright should not be considered a Jew, because she does not think of herself as a Jew. She was fifty-nine when the *Washington Post* story ran. As she said years later, "At 59—and now, I'm 75—it's a little hard to change every way that one thinks" of oneself.[55]

After leaving office in 2001 she spent years researching her family's heritage through classified documents and interviews in Czechoslovakia. The result was a book, *Prague Winter: A Personal Story of Remembrance and War, 1937–1948*, published in 2012, in which she reported that at least twenty-five members of her family had been killed in the camps.[56] When asked why she was writing the book now, her answer suggested that she was still stung by the attacks on her integrity made fifteen years earlier:

> I did not have time [before]. The way I describe this, it is like being asked to represent your country in a marathon and just as you are to start running, somebody gives you a heavy package and says 'unwrap it while you run.' Here I was trying to become the first woman secretary of state and all of a sudden all this devastating kind of information came.[57]

By the time her book was published, Albright had unwrapped the package. Her family, too, had evolved: her youngest daughter, Katherine, had married a Jewish man; the couple was raising their children Jewish, and Albright's youngest grandson was preparing for his bar mitzvah. Later that year Albright celebrated both Hanukah and Christmas with her family.[58] At seventy-five, she had this to say about her identity:

> I'm very proud of my Czechoslovak background, but my identity the way I describe it now: I am an American, I am a mother, I am a grandmother, I am a Democrat, I came from Jewish heritage, I was a Roman Catholic, I am a practicing Episcopalian, I am somebody who is devoted to human rights, I am somebody who believes in an international community and I can't separate those things. . . . I can trace these various parts as having a profound influence on me in one form or another.[59]

In one sense, the story of her "outing" is somewhat reminiscent of Erikson's: both were publicly attacked for denying their heritage. But there is an important difference between the two. Erikson was raised as a Jew. His mother was openly Jewish. He had a bar mitzvah. He knew the truth about his maternal heritage and obscured it. Albright, however, was never told that her parents had converted to Catholicism. She was raised as a Catholic. After she discovered her Jewish roots, she chose *not* to change her religious identity: she remained a Christian.

THE RULE IS ARBITRARY

The matrilineal principle is a test based on ancestry and descent. In an age when intermarriage is common, it produces arbitrary and irrational results.

For example, each of us has eight great-grandparents. If your mother's maternal grandmother was Jewish, you are 100 percent Jewish under the matrilineal rule, even if the other seven great-grandparents were not. However, if seven of your great-grandparents were Jewish but your mother's maternal grandmother was not, you are not considered seven-eighths Jewish; instead, you fail the test.

THE MATRILINEAL RULE HAS at least one major benefit: it's a clear, bright-line rule that is generally easy to apply. It depends on an objective fact that is typically easy to ascertain: whether your mother was Jewish. But for me, that benefit isn't nearly enough to overcome its drawbacks.

3

MUST A JEW PRACTICE JUDAISM?

WHAT IF BEING a Jew required a commitment to Judaism as a religion?

Demanding religious beliefs and observance in order to be a member of a religious community is hardly a radical idea.[1] A priest would scoff at the notion that an atheist who never set foot in church qualified as a Catholic simply because his mother was Catholic. The same would be true among Muslims. Yet in the Jewish world a totally nonobservant atheist would be considered a Jew by all Orthodox rabbis simply because his mother was Jewish. This has often baffled gentile friends of mine. One friend said to me, "I thought Judaism was a religion. How can a religion require so little?"

Judaism *is* a religion, but not in the same sense as the other two monotheistic religions. First, it has no catechism of agreed-upon tenets of faith. Second, the major Jewish denominations don't agree on the standards for observance. Finally, the matrilineal rule requires neither faith *nor* observance. On average, we American Jews are not very observant and include a surprisingly large number of agnostics and atheists. Most of us, myself included, would flunk any religious standard that was at all demanding.

THE ROLE OF FAITH IN JUDAISM

When interviewed on NPR about his religious background, David Javerbaum, the writer of the hit Broadway show *An Act of God*, briefly stunned the host. "Judaism is a thoroughly, totally ironic religion," he said. "It is the first religion that no longer believes in God."[2]

That was an overstatement, but the role of faith in Judaism is hardly straightforward. Unlike Christianity and Islam, Judaism is not a confessional

45

religion where members must formally assent to certain shared doctrines. Catholics, Anglicans, and Lutherans all have a catechism.[3] To be a Muslim, one must affirm a belief in God and a belief that Mohammed was his prophet.[4] In Judaism there are no required beliefs.

Jewish scholars in the Middle Ages tried and failed to develop such a creed.[5] The most famous and influential of these efforts was the "Thirteen Principles of the Jewish Faith" by Moses Maimonides, the great thirteenth-century Jewish philosopher, who expressed them as follows:

1. Belief in the existence of the Creator, who is perfect in every manner of existence and is the Primary Cause of all that exists.
2. The belief in God's absolute and unparalleled unity.
3. The belief in God's non-corporeality, nor that He will be affected by any physical occurrences, such as movement, or rest, or dwelling.
4. The belief in God's eternity.
5. The imperative to worship God exclusively and no foreign false gods.
6. The belief that God communicates with man through prophecy.
7. The belief in the primacy of the prophecy of Moses our teacher.
8. The belief in the divine origin of the Torah.
9. The belief in the immutability of the Torah.
10. The belief in God's omniscience and providence.
11. The belief in divine reward and retribution.
12. The belief in the arrival of the Messiah and the messianic era.
13. The belief in the resurrection of the dead.[6]

It's not a bad list. To this day, in morning prayers, some Orthodox congregations recite a more poetic version of his thirteen principles, beginning with the words *Ani Maamin*—I believe.[7] But today many religious Jews, especially the non-Orthodox, would have a difficult time accepting some of Maimonides's principles, particularly those relating to an afterlife, divine reward and retribution, and the eventual arrival of a Messiah.

If I were to distill my own list of the fundamental tenets of Judaism, it would include belief in four elements, only two of which were recognized by Maimonides: one God, the divine origin of the Torah, the covenant between God and the Jewish people, and the special bond between the people and the land of Israel.[8]

The point is that Maimonides failed in his theological project, which was to make acceptance of all thirteen principles a condition of being Jewish. He argued that his principles were the "fundamental truths of our religion and the very foundations" of Judaism and that one had to accept these principles to be a member of the "community of Israel."[9] He failed because other medieval Jewish scholars disagreed with him on one or more of these tenets.[10] Given the Jewish propensity for argument, this is hardly surprising. Indeed, some modern Jewish theologians and scholars go so far as to claim, "Religious dogma is anathema to Judaism."[11] That may be an overstatement, but Judaism has no pope or any other centralized institution for enforcing consensus, and none has ever developed around Maimonides's principles or those of anyone else.

But what about this belief in God? Judaism was the first monotheistic religion, so a belief in God would seem to be a required minimum. The biblical stories suggest that each Jew is expected to work out his own relationship to God, which is not one of simple obedience. Instead, a religious Jew is free—and even encouraged—to argue, negotiate, and struggle with God. Abraham bargained with—or, according to some interpretations, challenged—God on behalf of the righteous people of Sodom and Gomorrah. Jacob, after wrestling with an angel, was renamed "Israel," which literally means "to struggle with God."[12]

Through the ages Jewish scholars have struggled not only with God but also with the meaning of God. *Must a Jew Believe Anything?* is the provocative title of a superb book by Menachem Kellner, retired professor of Jewish thought at the University of Haifa and an observant Orthodox Jew. Kellner claims that the Old Testament does not require Jews to "believe in" God, in the sense of having a conviction that God exists, but rather demands "primarily trust in God expressed in concrete behaviour"—namely, obedience to God's commandments found in the Torah and Jewish law.[13] "Loyal behaviour, not systematic theology, is what is expected and demanded."[14]

Liberal rabbis and Jewish thinkers go further than Kellner. Rabbi Harold Schulweis has suggested that the theological emphasis of Judaism should be shifted from God to godliness.[15] Once again, the emphasis is on behavior, not beliefs. Reform Rabbi Eugene Borowitz insists that a belief in God is "fundamental to being a good Jew," but he is completely open-minded about what "God" means.[16] In his book *Liberal Judaism* he writes, "'My' good Jew believes in God but not necessarily in my view of God. We have numerous differing interpretations of what God might mean to a contemporary Jew." In other words, Borowitz says, Judaism remains a theistic religion but is "not...very dogmatic about it."[17] Rabbi Mordecai Kaplan, founder of the Reconstructionist movement, rejected the notion of a personal God who intervenes in human affairs in favor of a definition of God as a force within nature.[18]

Furthest out on the progressive end of the spectrum is a small movement known as Humanistic Judaism, a completely nontheistic form of Judaism that fits Javerbaum's hyperbolic claim. There is no mention of God in its liturgy, even when observing Jewish holidays or life-cycle events such as bar and bat mitzvahs, weddings, and funerals.[19] Instead, the movement celebrates Jewish history and culture, the Jewish people, and humanistic values that are seen as consistent with liberal Jewish ideals.[20]

This nontheistic approach intrigues me because I'm an agnostic, and I like the fact that it sparked lively debate within the Reform movement. In 1994 a Humanistic congregation (Beth Adam of Cincinnati) applied to join the national organization for Reform congregations, thereby forcing the Reform movement to grapple with the issue of theism. Beth Adam's rabbi, who had been ordained by the Reform movement, argued quite correctly that Judaism does not *require* a belief in God and that many Reform congregants are either agnostic or atheist. His logic posed a serious dilemma for the Reform movement— and, indeed, his application was *welcomed* by the Reform association's president, who knew it would generate debate and test the theological limits of the Reform movement.[21] It was true that many Reform Jews were not believers. But embracing a congregation that eliminated the idea of God was beyond the pale. After extensive debate the Reform association ruled that it would not accept congregations that denied God's existence altogether.[22]

So the debate continues. I love this open, elastic quality of Judaism, which encourages every Jew to define his or her spiritual beliefs for him- or herself. I love the fact that the religious tradition encourages Jews to grapple intellectually and spiritually with God and with each other.

WHAT DO AMERICAN JEWS ACTUALLY BELIEVE ABOUT GOD?

Perhaps not surprisingly, a large proportion of American Jews don't believe in God—at least, not in a traditional God who intervenes in human affairs in response to prayer. A 2011 study found that half of all American Jews have doubts about the existence of God, compared to 10 to 15 percent of other American religious groups.[23]

In 2013 the Pew Report found that only about one-third of American Jews are "absolutely certain" about their belief in "God or a universal spirit."[24] Nearly a quarter of the Jewish respondents do not believe in God.[25] Another 38 percent fall in the middle, saying they "believe but [are] less certain."[26] Perhaps most relevant to Jewish identity, about two-thirds of all Jews "see no conflict between being Jewish and not believing in God."[27]

BELIEF IN GOD (*percentage*)

Absolutely certain	34
Believe but less certain	38
Do not believe	23
Other	5

Source: Pew Research Center, "A Portrait of Jewish Americans," 2013 Pew Report, 74.

DEED, NOT CREED: THE ROLE OF TRADITIONAL JEWISH LAW

Judaism has always emphasized behavior over belief. As one rabbi told a congregant, "God doesn't care whether you believe in him or not. All that he cares is that you do the right thing."[28]

What is the right thing? With respect to broad ethical obligations, various American Jewish denominations are in essential agreement. Hillel, the great sage of the first century BCE, characterized the essence of Judaism by saying, "That which is hateful to you do not do to another."[29] A century or so later Rabbi Akiva located the essence of the entire Torah in Leviticus 19:18: "Love your neighbor as yourself."[30] Acts of loving kindness, compassion, and the pursuit of justice are all emphasized.

Where the major denominations differ is in their attitude toward Jewish law (halacha). Halacha is a comprehensive legal system derived from the Torah (the five Books of Moses) and the Oral Law (a set of oral traditions said to be codified in the Mishnah, the Talmud, and other postbiblical texts). The denominations differ in three respects: (1) whether halacha has divine origins, (2) whether it should control the details of religious observance, and (3) the degree to which it can be flexibly interpreted to accommodate social change.

For the Orthodox—about 10 percent of American Jews—halacha is sacred and cannot be changed, only interpreted. Observing the law consumes nearly every waking moment, much as it did centuries ago. The Ten Commandments are just the tip of the iceberg. The Torah is said to contain 613 commandments, or *mitzvot*,[31] and the Oral Law adds many more. This elaborate legal regime covers not only ethical behavior but also food, Sabbath observance, prayer, marital sex, and a vast number of other subjects.

Although the Orthodox community is quite diverse[32] and its subgroups observe halacha in different ways, all forms of Orthodoxy require tremendous discipline. Orthodox life is hard. It's inconvenient. And it's meant to be. For readers who are unfamiliar with this way of life, I offer a few examples.

The dietary laws (*kashrut*) dictate not only what you eat but also how you prepare food and how animals are killed. Pork and shellfish are forbidden. You may eat any animal that has cloven hooves and chews its cud, but it must be slaughtered under rabbinic supervision, according to rules designed to minimize pain to the animal. Foods containing milk and meat cannot be eaten at the same meal or even off the same plates; a kosher household typically has at least two sets of pots, pans, dishes, and utensils—one for meat and one for dairy. The two sets are not supposed to touch. For people who don't own a double set of ovens, microwaves, and dishwashers, rabbis offer work-arounds to avoid contamination. Although many non-Orthodox assume that the dietary laws were created for health reasons, there is no evidence for this, and the Torah itself doesn't provide a reason.[33] Some scholars believe that the primary purpose of kashrut was to minimize social contact between the Jews and their Persian and Roman conquerors.[34]

The Sabbath, the day of rest, is meant to be a joyous release from work of all kinds. The Friday night meal is a special family occasion that includes ritual blessings over bread and wine. From sundown Friday to sundown Saturday, one is forbidden to do "work" of any sort, including writing, handling money, or carrying objects. One can't engage with machinery or electronics. That means no driving or riding in cars or other vehicles, using the phone, watching TV, or turning lights on or off. Food must be prepared in advance; you can't light a fire or push a button on the oven. But again, there are work-arounds. Automatic timers for lights and appliances are permitted if set in advance;[35] many modern ovens have a "Sabbath mode" for this purpose. Another taboo, pushing the button of an elevator, creates a major headache for those who live in high-rise buildings. To ease the burden of climbing the stairs, a few apartment buildings and hospitals have installed elevators that, from Friday to Saturday evenings, are programmed to stop automatically at every floor.[36]

The food and Sabbath rules, among others, are strong anchors that keep the Orthodox tied to their communities. You can't observe the Sabbath unless you live within walking distance of a synagogue. Without access to a kosher butcher, finding meat that has been appropriately slaughtered is difficult. Although not all Orthodox observe every rule, it's very hard to be observant at this level without community support.

Consistent with halacha, Orthodox men and women have sharply differentiated gender roles. Only men can be rabbis or read the Torah to the congregation. Religious services are conducted almost entirely in Hebrew, and the seating of men and women in the synagogue is strictly segregated: the women are often seated in the synagogue's upper level, the men downstairs. Jewish law imposes both affirmative and negative obligations on men, only prohibitions for women. For example, only men are affirmatively obligated to pray every day. Women are not. Both sexes are prohibited from engaging in adultery or lies. Endogamy is strictly enforced, and no Orthodox rabbi will officiate at a wedding unless both members of the couple are Jewish by halachic standards.

A less well-known area of law governs sexual relations between men and women. Premarital sex is forbidden, as is homosexual conduct.[37] The sex drive is seen as natural but needing structure to channel it within marriage. Within marriage sex is seen as sacred, and sexual intimacy is considered a woman's right. The primary purpose of sex is not procreation but to "reinforce the loving marital bond between husband and wife."[38] Birth control is permitted. However, sex is forbidden for at least twelve days a month—during the wife's menstrual period and for seven days afterward. Before sexual relations are resumed, a woman should visit the *mikva* (ritual bath) and immerse herself. The Torah does not indicate the reason for this rule of separation, but its benefits have been widely noted: it gives the couple a rest from each other, heightens the pleasures of reunion, and is conducive to conception.[39]

Reform Judaism takes a radically different approach to halacha. Reform rabbis view Jewish law not as God given or sacred but as rabbinical adaptations to historical conditions and, therefore, open to change. To the extent that the law is inconsistent today with scientific knowledge or the needs of contemporary life, it can be ignored. Modern religious observance should honor the best of Jewish heritage but not be bound by outmoded rules.

The Reform movement first appeared in America in the mid-nineteenth century, only slightly later than its appearance in Germany. It flourished in America as a modern option for Jews who sought a way of remaining Jewish while becoming part of the social and economic fabric of American life. Indeed, the early Reform rabbis thought they were saving Judaism from oblivion, fearing that if they didn't modernize the religion, American Jews might abandon it altogether. The rabbis' chief goal was to make it possible for Jews to be both Jewish and American. By many measures they succeeded: Reform today is the largest denomination, constituting about 35 percent of American Jews.

The Reform have maintained what they see as the essential core of Judaism: the celebration of holidays and life-cycle events, the focus on the Torah, and an emphasis on ethical behavior, especially *tikkun olam*, the doctrine of "repairing the world."[40]

What they've eliminated are most of the traditional rules regulating the details of daily life. In the Reform synagogue men and women participate in religious services on an equal basis, and there are now many women rabbis. The services have been modernized to include more English and contemporary commentary that is seen as relevant or inspirational. In the home Reform Judaism imposes no dietary restrictions. I know of no Reform Jew who keeps kosher. A few may avoid pork; many more follow a gluten-free diet or are vegetarians. Most enjoy lobster, scallops, and bacon.

One ongoing challenge for Reform Judaism is to define the limits of adaptation. As we'll explore later in this book, the movement's attitude toward intermarriage has evolved in just the last thirty years. Not only has the movement abandoned the matrilineal principle, but about half of Reform rabbis are now willing to officiate at a wedding where the non-Jewish spouse has not converted. Homosexuality is fully accepted, and same-sex marriages are regularly performed.

The Conservative movement, founded around 1900, was created by American Jews who wanted to modernize the religion but thought the Reform movement had gone too far. In their eyes Reform synagogues looked and felt too much like Protestant churches, with their organs and choirs, prayers in English instead of Hebrew, and worshippers who didn't wear yarmulkes or prayer shawls. Orthodoxy, however, didn't seem flexible enough.

In an attempt to balance tradition with change, Conservatives took the somewhat paradoxical view that halacha is binding but can be adapted when necessary. Even today the liturgy in Conservative synagogues remains similar to that in Orthodox services. In other areas, however, the movement has made concessions to modern life. In 1950, as Jews moved to the suburbs, the movement allowed members to drive on the Sabbath. Few Conservative Jews feel compelled to observe the more Orthodox interpretations of the "no work on the Sabbath" rule; I suspect nearly all will handle money and turn on lights. The Conservative attitude toward gender roles is much more like Reform: synagogue seating is mixed, women fully participate in the services, and there are now female rabbis. Conservative rabbis even have the discretion to officiate at same-sex weddings—as long as both spouses are Jewish, of course—and many do.

But the movement draws the line in two areas: intermarriage and the matrilineal principle. A Conservative rabbi is not permitted to preside at an interfaith wedding and is not even allowed to attend the ceremony. (Somewhat paradoxically, however, the movement now welcomes intermarried couples *after* the wedding and even allows the non-Jewish spouse to join the congregation.) The matrilineal principle is still sacrosanct. A child with a Jewish father but not a Jewish mother is not Jewish without formal religious conversion.

RELIGIOUS DENOMINATION (*percentage*)

Orthodox	10
Conservative	18
Reform	35
Other denomination	6
No affiliation ("just Jewish")	30

Source: Pew Research Center, "A Portrait of Jewish Americans," 2013 Pew Report, 177.

How Observant Are American Jews?

Compared to their Christian neighbors, American Jews on the whole are not very devoted to religious observance. Only about one-fifth (19 percent) pray weekly, compared to about half (47 percent) of other Americans.[41] Only 31 percent of American Jewish families are dues-paying members of a synagogue or temple.[42] Synagogue attendance is spotty. Except for the Orthodox, Jews attend religious services far less often than other Americans. Whereas about half of Americans report attending religious services at least once or twice a month, only one in five Jews (23 percent) does the same.[43] Another one in five Jews (22 percent) report that they "never" attend services. The remaining half fall in between: 35 percent attend services on the High Holy Days—Rosh Hashanah (the Jewish New Year) and Yom Kippur (the Day of Atonement)—and 19 percent "seldom" go to synagogue.[44]

Most American Jews are similarly relaxed about observing religious rituals in the home, especially those that demand daily or weekly effort. The overwhelming majority— more than three out of four—do not observe kosher dietary laws. (Only 22 percent say they keep kosher in the home.) Sabbath observance has dropped to the same low: only about 23 percent of Jewish families always or usually light candles on Friday evening. Even fewer (13 percent) mostly the Orthodox—avoid handling money on the Sabbath.[45]

But the Yom Kippur fast and the Passover Seder, which take place only once a year, are still going strong; they've been so thoroughly absorbed into Jewish culture that even Jews with little religious commitment, myself included, often observe them. More than half (53 percent) of Jewish adults fast for all or part of Yom Kippur.[46] I observe the fast for two reasons, only one of which I can defend: I like the idea of doing penance for things I've done that I really regret, and I've been a little overweight for many years and think fasting isn't a bad idea.

Passover, which is celebrated in the home, is the most popular annual Jewish holiday in America. The Seder is an elaborate meal that celebrates the Jews' deliverance from slavery in ancient Egypt.[47] About 70 percent of all American Jews observe this ritual with family and friends, often adapting it to their own preferences.[48] For example, I am very uncomfortable with much of the tribalism expressed in the traditional service, which emphasizes the wickedness of the Egyptians who oppressed the Jews, so I either use a modern *Haggadah* (the book that guides participants through the Seder) or go online to create my own. To me the holiday is an affirmation of freedom and a condemnation of slavery and discrimination. I'm not alone in this regard. The internet abounds with guides to customizing Seders with references to discrimination and oppression around the world. There are also guides to feminist Seders, Buddhist Seders, LGBTQ Seders, and the like.

WHY A RELIGIOUS STANDARD WOULDN'T WORK

Initially it seems appealing to say that to be Jewish, one must practice Judaism as a religion. Many Orthodox Jews, both here and in Israel, believe this is necessary in order to be a "good" Jew. But as a principle for defining the entire American Jewish community, it won't work. As I've said, Judaism has no catechism of required beliefs, and the denominations don't agree on the standards of observance. Even if you wanted to impose a religious standard for belonging, who would set the standard? The rabbis would never agree on a standard, and there is no pope or College of Cardinals who can impose consensus.

Even if the rabbis miraculously managed to agree on a religious standard, they would never try to apply it as the *sole* criterion for membership. It would be a disaster. Nearly half of all American Jews are either agnostics or atheists, and about a quarter report they "never" attend services in a synagogue. Requiring a religious commitment would expel from the tribe too many of us who take pride in our Jewish identity.

This poses a serious challenge, however, for sustaining our identity as Jews. Religious commitment is a powerful identity anchor. It enables you to express your Jewishness through prayer and ritual, both at home and in synagogue with other Jews. It also provides a clear path by which you can pass Judaism on to your children. For those of us who are not committed to the religion, what is the source of our Jewish identity? What exactly are we passing on? Is it *just* descent—or something more?

4

THE PUZZLE OF "JEWISH BLOOD"

NOT LONG AGO Dale and I were invited by friends to attend an evening event at the Chilton Club, one of Boston's most exclusive social clubs. Originally a women's club, it was named after Mary Chilton, said to be the first woman to step ashore from the Mayflower. Like the Somerset Club and the Country Club, the Chilton has long been a bastion of Boston's WASP elite. I had visited the elegant clubhouse several times as both a dinner guest and featured speaker, but it's the kind of place that makes me wonder: *Does this club have any Jewish members?*

On this particular evening Susan Butler, a freelance journalist, gave a talk about her new book, *Roosevelt and Stalin: A Portrait in Partnership.* The talk focused primarily on the complex relationships among Stalin, Roosevelt, and Churchill and their meetings in Tehran and Yalta during World War II. I remember that Butler worshiped Roosevelt, admired Stalin, and loathed Winston Churchill, who is one of my heroes.

But what I remember most is that, during the course of her talk, she offhandedly used the phrase "Jewish race"—not once but several times. My reaction was visceral. Her use of this term, particularly at this club, hit me like a punch in the gut.

How is it possible, I asked myself, that in this day and age, an otherwise educated person would think there was a Jewish race? Didn't Butler know that this idea had been thoroughly discredited, especially after the Holocaust?

For the rest of the talk I mused about whether to say something to her. Her use of the phrase may well have been innocent. But I experienced it as what my students would call a *micro-aggression*—a casual remark that a member of a minority would experience as an indirect and perhaps unintentional insult. I thought she would want to know that she was causing offense. I certainly would if I were in her shoes as a speaker.

After the talk I approached Butler and said, in what I hope was not an accusatory tone, "I'm sure you meant no offense, but American Jews today associate the idea that Jews are a distinct race with the Nazis and the Ku Klux Klan. I'd urge you to avoid the phrase in your next presentation." Her response was noncommittal, neither defensive nor welcoming. When I saw that she was not inclined to engage, I yielded my spot to others waiting to talk to her. I had at least spoken up. But it wasn't a satisfying conversation.

Now that I have studied the matter, I wouldn't be quite so sanctimonious if I were to have a longer conversation with Susan Butler today. Indeed, this chapter represents what I would hope to say in any long discussion, with anyone, about the Jewish race. I would begin by acknowledging that the story is much more complex than I imagined just a few years ago.

First, I would admit that "race" is a fuzzy term: people define it in different ways. *My* definition refers to heritable physical differences between groups, and that's the focus of this chapter. To me the term *Jewish race* stands for the proposition that Jews inherit *distinctive physical or biological characteristics* that are fixed, like skin color or your genes. Butler may have had in mind a broader definition that includes group differences that are cultural or ethnic and relate to a sense of a shared history. These, too, may be passed down from generation to generation. I exclude them from my definition of race because they are not biological or physical—they must be taught. These "learned" elements of group identity, in my view, are better captured by the notion that Jews are a "people," a "nation," a "tribe," or an ethnic group, a cluster of ideas I explore in Chapters 5 and 6.

Second, I would acknowledge that the idea of Jews as a distinct race has deep roots and was never the exclusive province of anti-Semites. To the contrary, both Jews and gentiles often used to employ the term—in a biological as well as cultural sense—to describe Jewish group identity.

Third, although the idea of a Jewish race is no longer politically correct, biology is now being invoked to suggest that there are distinctive

Jewish bloodlines. Scientists have done pathbreaking work to identify and prevent diseases (such as Tay-Sachs, Gaucher, and Canavan) that are most prevalent among Jews. More importantly, the new field of "population genetics" and the use of modern DNA testing have led to a profusion of hyperbolic marketing claims by companies purporting to identify one's Jewish ancestry on the basis of genetic markers.

All of this is to say that the idea of Jewish blood deserves attention and is more interesting than I had originally thought. But don't get the wrong idea. As you will see, neither race nor genetics provides a useful basis for identifying who should count as Jewish.

THE "JEWISH RACE" AS A BADGE OF HONOR

It's not crazy to think of Jewishness in terms of bloodlines. The idea of race is closely connected with the notion of descent, which is central to Jewish identity. The Old Testament describes Israelites as being descended from Abraham, his son Isaac, and his grandson Jacob, whose descendants were the progenitors of the twelve tribes that developed into the Jewish people. The matrilineal principle is explicitly ancestral: it defines being Jewish as a birthright inherited by anyone with a Jewish mother.[1]

Throughout the ages both Jews and gentiles have used the term "Jewish race" in a benign or even positive way. In Roman times the Jewish historian Flavius Josephus, the author of the first-century *The Jewish War*, identified himself as "I—Josephus, Son of Matthias, a Hebrew by race."[2] In the nineteenth century British prime minister Benjamin Disraeli, a born Jew whose father baptized him as a Christian, repeatedly championed his "Hebrew race."[3] George Eliot's novel *Daniel Deronda*, published in 1876, took a sympathetic view of its Jewish characters and is laced with references to Jews as a race.[4]

What may be more surprising to some readers is that, in the late nineteenth century, many American Jews openly and proudly described themselves as a race. This trend began in the 1870s as acculturated Jews were becoming more socially integrated with non-Jews. As historian Eric Goldstein suggests, Jews viewed this increased social mixing with both enthusiasm and anxiety.[5] "Much of this anxiety stemmed from the tension between Jews' impulse for integration and their desire to maintain a distinctive Jewish identity," he writes.[6] The closer Jews came to acceptance by gentiles, the more pressure they felt to articulate their specialness as a group, and for a time they expressed this bond in racial terms. "Their conception of Jewish distinctiveness," Goldstein emphasizes, "was one rooted not only in cultural particularity but in biology, shared ancestry and blood."[7]

The language of race served at least two purposes. The most important was that it reinforced endogamy—the notion that Jews should only marry other Jews. Although marriage between Jews and gentiles was still rare in the late nineteenth century, it had increased enough to spark alarm,[8] and some Jewish leaders responded with rhetoric that may seem jarring to modern sensibilities. "No people on the face of the globe can lay claim with so much right to purity...and unity of blood," declared Leo Levi, a leader of B'nai B'rith, arguing that Jewish survival depended on preserving Jews as a race.[9] Some rabbis spoke of the importance of racial purity for Jews to carry out their mission,[10] and paeans to blood purity appeared in popular novels by Jewish authors and in editorials in Jewish newspapers.[11] As long as Jews protected their bloodlines through endogamy, the argument went, it was safe to mix socially with gentiles. Even hard-liners like Levi agreed, saying that Jews who were "proud of their lineage" and determined to "bequeath an unmixed strain of Jewish blood" to their children would come to no harm by socializing with gentiles.[12]

A second purpose of this rhetoric was to reinforce the notion that Jewish group identity was indelible. "The great appeal of racial language," Goldstein writes, "was its unique ability to capture the strong attachment of Jews to Jewish peoplehood, a feeling heightened during a time when many markers of Jewishness were receding."[13] It was an ingenious "rhetorical strategy"[14] that affirmed Jewish identity while not interfering with assimilation.[15] Indeed, many Jews of this period "found in race a comforting means of self-understanding, one that provided a sense of security as they continued toward their goal of greater social integration."[16]

Although anti-Semitism in America was on the rise from the 1880s until the end of World War II, some Jews continued to affirm their identity as a race well into the twentieth century, according to Goldstein. They didn't see this as inconsistent with being American—or with being "white." American society was organized on a framework in which the "crucial [racial] distinction was between whites and non-whites," and Jews were seen as securely lodged in the white category.[17] But after the turn of the century, as anti-Semitism took on an increasingly racial tone, most Jews found it problematic and even dangerous to describe themselves as a race and gradually abandoned the practice.[18]

THE ROOTS OF RACIAL ANTI-SEMITISM

Over the centuries anti-Semitism has taken many different forms, but the most pernicious of these is racial anti-Semitism. It rests on the premise that Jews are a distinctive and inferior race whose insidious traits are handed down from generation to generation.

The first clear-cut example of racial anti-Semitism arose in mid-fifteenth-century Spain with the doctrine of *limpieza de sangre*, or "blood purity." According to author and historian James Carroll, the Catholic Church played a critical role in developing this doctrine, which had far-reaching consequences.

From its very early days the Church held as an explicit goal—even an "obsession"—the conversion of the Jews.[19] Beginning in the Middle Ages a variety of coercive measures sought to force Jews to convert to Catholicism. In the late fourteenth century, violent attacks on Jews in parts of Spain led thousands of Spanish Jews to convert. Many more were pressured into conversion when, in 1492 and 1502, King Ferdinand and Queen Isabella issued decrees expelling all Jews and Muslims unless they converted. Jews who converted to avoid expulsion were called *conversos*, or "new Christians," and were not readily accepted. Because they had converted under duress—in some cases under threat of death—their sincerity was always questioned. The Spanish and Portuguese Inquisitions were set up to root out "false converts" among these Jews, who were suspected of secretly practicing some elements of Judaism.

At about the same time, some in Spain also became obsessed with the idea that Jews were an inferior race that threatened Christian society and that only "pure Christians" were qualified to hold public office or positions of authority in the church. According to Carroll, "This embrace of the blood-purity standard marked the epoch-shaping move from religious anti-Judaism to racial anti-Semitism."[20] Applicants for the priesthood, for example, had to prove that their family had no Jewish blood—*mala sangre*, or "bad blood"—dating back to their grandparents or even further.[21] As the ideology spread, statutes were passed barring conversos and their descendants from professions, universities, guilds, and the military.[22] (This practice was not outlawed in Spain until 1870.) The doctrine even spread beyond Spain: in the early seventeenth century the Jesuits enacted rules that went back five generations: "No one will hereafter be admitted to this Society who is descended of Hebrew or Saracen [Muslim] stock... to the fifth degree of family lineage."[23]

As we will see, the Nazis' Nuremburg Laws can be interpreted as descendants of limpieza de sangre.[24]

SCIENTIFIC RACISM

In the nineteenth century, first in Europe and later in America, anti-Semites began to buttress their racial attacks on Jews with appeals to modern science, a practice that became known as *scientific racism*. As nationalism rose in both Germany and France, various "scientific" theories were used to justify discrimination against Jews as members of an alien, inferior race.

Although the details of these "scientific" claims varied, the core ideas were that (1) human beings could be sorted into groups based on racial differences, (2) racial differences drove human behavior, and (3) the "races" could be ranked hierarchically. Scholars measured different physical characteristics, attached different labels to their groupings, and identified different numbers of races. But the results were similar: white Europeans always ranked higher than Asians or Africans, and among whites, the northern European "Nordic" or "Aryan" races were at the very top, while Jews were ranked near the bottom.

Georges Vacher de Lapouge (1854–1936), a French anthropologist, published a theory of races that illustrates these ideas. In his 1899 book, *The Aryan: His Social Role*, he offered a scheme of racial classifications based primarily on head measurements. At the top he put the "Aryan white race," which he claimed were "dolichocephalic" (long headed). At the bottom he put the "brachycephalic," or short-headed races, best represented by the Jew. Between these extremes he identified three other groups. In the same year an American academic, William Zebina Ripley (1867–1941), published a similar theory based on head measurements, stature, and eye and skin color. In his book *The Races of Europe: A Sociological Study*, Ripley classified Europeans into three races: Teutonic, Alpine, and Mediterranean.

In America the best-known, most influential, and today most infamous proponent of scientific racism was Madison Grant. In 1916 he published *The Passing of the Great Race*, which became a national bestseller. Grant initially divided human beings into three broad races based primarily on skin color: Caucasoids (based in Europe), Negroids (based in Africa), and Mongoloids (based in Asia). He then subdivided the European white races and ranked them much as Ripley had done. At the top was the "Nordic" race, based in Scandinavia. Below the Nordics were the Alpines, who lived near the Alps, and the Mediterraneans, who inhabited southern Europe, North Africa, and the Middle East. Jews were presumably in this third category.[25] Hitler would later refer to this book as his "bible."[26]

Closely related to scientific racism was the eugenics movement, which made similar claims to science and drew on notions of Darwinian evolution. The core ideas were that both positive and negative human traits were hereditary; that their prevalence could be influenced by breeding, just as with plants or livestock; and that humans should use this knowledge to improve the hardiness of their genetic stock. Proponents, including academics and scientists, urged that people with undesirable traits not be allowed to reproduce. The movement also provided fodder for

American "nativist" claims that racial mixing was harmful because it degraded "native stock."

In early twentieth-century America these two powerful movements fed a growing political backlash against immigrants. Between 1880 and the 1920s the United States experienced immigration on an unprecedented scale. Our country's population in 1880 was only fifty million; during the next fifty years over twenty-five million immigrants would pour into America.[27] Unlike their English, Scottish, German, and Scandinavian predecessors, the so-called New Immigrants came mostly from southern and Eastern Europe. "These newcomers were often described by what they were not: not Protestant, not English-speaking, not skilled, not educated, and not liked," in the words of author and PBS host Ben Wattenberg.[28] Indeed, as the American historian Frederick Jackson Turner lamented in 1901: "It is obvious that the replacement of the German and English immigration by southern Italians, Poles, Russians, Jews and Slovaks is a loss to the social organism of the United States. The congestion of foreigners and localities in our great cities, the increase of crime and pauperism are attributable to the poorer elements."[29] To members of the Protestant elite who were alarmed by this influx, scientific racism supported the view that these immigrants were inferior, and eugenics stoked fears that the newcomers would outbreed those of native stock or, perhaps worse, mate with them.[30]

In America a growing number of academics—many of them Jewish—mounted fierce opposition to scientific racism. A pioneer in this effort was Franz Boas (1858–1942), an assimilated German Jew, now credited as the founder of cultural anthropology, who carried out "a life-long assault... on race."[31] From his command post at Columbia University, he set about debunking the idea of race as a determinant of behavior or intelligence, instead emphasizing the importance of culture in explaining differences among groups.[32]

Although Boas's work would eventually influence the entire field of anthropology, it had no impact on American public policy in the early twentieth century. Scientific racism and the eugenics movement, however, had enormous impact, contributing to the passage of restrictive immigration policies. The Immigration Act of 1917 explicitly banned from entering the United States a long list of undesirables, including alcoholics, anarchists, feeble-minded persons, idiots, imbeciles, insane persons, and paupers.[33] The Immigration Act of 1924 imposed stringent country quotas aimed at substantially limiting immigration of southern and Eastern Europeans, especially Italians and Jews.[34] The most direct impact of the eugenics movement was the passage of state laws permitting compulsory sterilization of people seen as mentally disabled.[35]

In Europe the most profound impact of these movements was in Germany.

NAZISM AND THE HOLOCAUST

The Nazis' racial ideology was a kind of feverish amalgam of limpieza de sangre, scientific racism, and eugenics. Like the sixteenth-century Spaniards, the Nazis were consumed with blood purity and viewed Jews as a degenerate race. But the Nazis went much further, carrying scientific racism and eugenics to their ultimate conclusion: genocide.

The Nazi racial program was based on the belief that Germans belonged to the Aryan "master race," which was superior to all others. According to Hitler's ideology, the Jews were the Aryans' greatest enemy, threatening to weaken and perhaps destroy the Aryans through racial contamination.

The Nazis' initial goal was to maintain the purity of their racial stock by isolating the Jews and driving them out of Germany. To implement these policies, the Nazis had to decide who counted as a Jew. Like any legal system that differentiates on the basis of race, the Nazi regime faced the challenge of developing standards, a task that is most difficult when dealing with people of mixed blood.

In 1933 the Nazi government passed a law aiming to dismiss all "non-Aryans" from government positions, including educators and those practicing medicine in state hospitals. The definition of a non-Aryan was a simple ancestry test: anyone who could not prove they had four Aryan grandparents was a non-Aryan. This meant, of course, that a person who had at least one Jewish parent or grandparent was non-Aryan.

In 1935 the so-called Nuremberg Laws stripped Jews of German citizenship and prohibited them from marrying or having sexual relations with anyone of "German or related blood."[36] These laws required a more elaborate racial scheme, which was the result of considerable debate within the Nazi leadership as they struggled to align various policy goals. Within Germany the scheme included three racial categories: Jews, Germans, and those of "mixed race" (*Mischlinge*).

Most of the Mischlinge were Protestant or Catholic: the descendants of Jews who had converted to Christianity, intermarried with gentiles, and assimilated into Christian society.[37] For Nazis determined to prevent further racial contamination, this population had to be identified and regulated.

Under the Nuremberg Laws, a "Jew" was defined as a person with at least three Jewish grandparents. Where the scheme got complicated was in classifying people who had only *two* Jewish grandparents—and there were many who fit this description. The test for such people involved additional factors such as affiliation with a synagogue, whether the person's spouse was Jewish, and the like. If one of these "extra" Jewish factors applied, the person was categorized as a Jew. If not, he or she was a Mischling of the first degree, which was not much better. Those who had only one Jewish grandparent were Mischlinge of the second degree. (Those who were one-eighth Jewish or less were classified as belonging to the German race.)[38]

As a practical matter, first-degree Mischlinge suffered some of the same educational and marriage restrictions as Jews, but second-degree Mischlinge had more freedom. This led to a brisk business in reclassification, often accomplished by bribery, as Jews or first-degree Mischlinge sought documentation showing that they were second-degree Mischlinge or German.[39]

In 1941 the Nazis secretly decided to implement the Final Solution—the program of herding Jews into ghettos and camps and murdering them. Within Germany the Nazis applied the Nuremberg racial scheme: German Jews would be deported and killed; Mischlinge merely risked sterilization. Outside Germany, however, the Nazis offered no such leniency to those of mixed blood; they regularly sent to the death camps anyone who had one Jewish grandparent.

Is it any wonder that, like most American Jews today, I recoil at any mention of the Jewish race? Under the Nazis it led to the death of six million Jews.

JEWS AND RACE IN AMERICA TODAY

Even as late as World War II Ashley Montagu, a Jewish cultural anthropologist (whose birth name was Israel Ehrenberg), bemoaned the fact that "Jews are nearly always referred to in popular parlance as a 'race.' This is done not only by the so-called 'man in the street' but also by many scientists, medical men, philosophers, politicians, historians, and members of many other professions."[40]

This is no longer true. Virtually no one thinks of American Jews today as having a racial identity: race is associated primarily with skin color, and most Jews in America are considered white. More generally, race itself is no longer considered a meaningful scientific basis for categorization. How and why did this shift occur?

The critical turning point was the discovery of the Holocaust. The racial atrocities of World War II sparked such revulsion that the term *race* became almost taboo, especially as applied to Jews and sometimes more generally.[41]

In 1950, in recognition of the Nazi horrors, the UN Economic and Social Council (UNESCO) convened a distinguished group of social scientists, headed by Montagu, to summarize where modern scientists stood on race. The result was a ringing declaration, called "The Statement on Race," that came close to discounting the idea of race altogether. In the universalist spirit of the times, it began: "Scientists have reached general agreement in recognizing that mankind is one: that all men belong to the same species, Homo Sapiens."[42] It went on to outline scientific views on race that have endured to this day: that humans are more genetically alike than different, that biology is not a predictor of behavior, that pure races don't exist, that no race is biologically superior or inferior to another, that racial mixing does not produce biologically disadvantageous results, and that ethnic groups are not races.[43]

But in their zeal to combat race prejudice, the authors arguably went a bit too far, stating, "For all practical social purposes 'race' is not so much a biological phenomenon as a social myth."[44] They concluded, "Lastly, biological studies lend support to the ethic of universal brotherhood."[45]

This aspect of the 1950 statement was widely criticized as a political manifesto rather than an accurate summary of scientific consensus. Especially indignant were the physical anthropologists and geneticists whose disciplines had not been represented on the original panel.[46] UNESCO promptly convened a second group, composed largely of physical anthropologists and geneticists.

The result was a more nuanced statement in 1951 that affirmed most of the first group's scientific conclusions but conspicuously omitted any mention of "universal brotherhood"—and insisted that races did exist. As the authors of the 1951 statement observed rather tartly: "The physical anthropologists and the man in the street both know that races exist; ... the latter from the immediate evidence of his senses when he sees an African, a European, an Asiatic and an American Indian together."[47] The authors went on to suggest, "In its anthropological sense, the word 'race' should be reserved for groups of mankind possessing well-developed and primarily heritable physical differences from other groups."[48]

So the idea of race has not disappeared. Many application forms ask people to identify their race. Americans often speak of race in everyday conversation, especially in relationship to claims of discrimination. As of 2010 the US Census collected demographic data in five racial categories, all relating primarily to skin color: White, Black or African American, American Indian or Alaska Native, Asian, and Native Hawaiian or Other Pacific Islander. Separately, the 2010 survey included a box to check for "Hispanic origins," which the government characterized as an ethnicity.[49] The census survey has never included a question asking Jews to identify themselves in any way, either as a race or an ethnicity.

But as in earlier periods, there is still no consensus on how to define race. One researcher surveyed the field and found a broad range: "As few as three and as many as 37 races have been described."[50] This scholar concluded that "just what constitutes a race is a hard question to answer, because one's classification usually depends on the purpose of the classification, and various approaches to taxonomy often have a built-in bias."[51]

Nor has the idea of a "Jewish race" completely disappeared in America. The Ku Klux Klan still claims that Jews are not white but rather a separate race.[52] The Nationalist Socialist Party of America, a neo-Nazi group active in the 1970s, stated among its "fundamental principles" that "the Jew is the Ultimate Enemy." The party's newspaper read,

> The single serious enemy facing the White man is the Jew. The Jews are not a religion, they are [a] ... *race*, locked in mortal conflict with Aryan man which has lasted for millennia, and which will continue until one of the two combat peoples is extinct.[53]

In fact, it was neo-Nazi activity that led to an unusual US Supreme Court ruling in the 1980s, holding that Jews can state a claim of *racial* discrimination—even though virtually no one still thinks of them as a race. The case began in 1982 after eight young neo-Nazis painted anti-Semitic symbols and slogans on the walls of a synagogue in Silver Spring, Maryland. The congregation filed suit, claiming that the vandals had violated a civil rights statute prohibiting racial discrimination. The lower federal court threw the case out, ruling that "discrimination against Jews is not racial discrimination" because Jews today are not considered "a racially distinct group."[54]

A unanimous Supreme Court reversed the decision, reasoning that at the time the law was passed in 1866, race was defined differently from how it is today. "The question before us," the Court wrote, "is not whether Jews are considered to be a separate race by today's standards, but whether, at the time [the statute] was adopted, Jews constituted a group of people that Congress intended to protect."[55] The legislative history of the statute made clear that "Jews and Arabs were among the peoples then considered to be distinct races, and hence within the protection of the statute," the Court wrote.[56] The case marked a rare time in human history when the notion that Jews are a separate race was used not to justify discrimination but to shield them from it.

A Jewish Gene?

In recent times the idea of "Jewish blood" has resurfaced in the context of genetic testing, which suggests that people of Jewish heritage are biologically identifiable on the basis of their genes. There are more than half a dozen companies that claim to assess your "Jewish DNA," some for as little as $100.

"Are you Jewish?" asks the website iGENEA, then explains,

A DNA test from iGenea provides you with clear evidence of whether you have Jewish roots. Based on your specific genetic characteristics, we can identify whether you are of Jewish descent, which line the Jewish descent is from (paternal, maternal or both lines) and even what percentage you are Jewish.

As I'll later show, this is nonsense. There is no genetic test that can accurately identify whether a person is Jewish. There is no "Jewish gene." But the field of so-called Jewish genetics has given new life to the idea that Jews as a group are united by biological ties.

For my birthday about four years ago my daughters gave me a subscription to 23andMe, a direct-to-consumer genetic testing service. After receiving my "home-based saliva collection kit" in the mail, I took a swab of spit, put it in a test tube, and sent it off to the lab as instructed. About six weeks later I was notified that my report was ready: I could go online and find out my ancestry, any health risks and inherited conditions I might face, and who my DNA "relatives" are.

Companies like 23andMe compare sections of your DNA to that of various "populations" defined by ethnicity and geographic location. The basic notion is that if you look at various genetic markers, there are some that vary systematically between populations. These markers are used to create a reference set for each population. Your DNA is then compared to the various reference sets to analyze statistically the number of matches.

One key question is the one that biologists Richard Lewontin, Mary-Claire King, and Marcus Feldman posed in the scientific journal *Nature*:

"Is it possible to find DNA sequences that differ sufficiently between populations to allow correct assignment of major geographical origin with high probability?" Their answer to this question is yes.[57]

A second question is: How strong is the evidence that people who identify themselves as Jewish share genetic markers? Here, too, the answer is clear. Ashkenazi Jews share long stretches of DNA.

According to my DNA report from 23andMe, am I ever Jewish! My ancestry report indicates that I am 99.8 percent European and that 96.3 percent of my genes match a single subgroup, Ashkenazi.[58] (The remaining 3.5 percent was labeled "broadly European.")[59]

The website offered me a "Chromosome View" of the data where I could see, for each of my twenty-three chromosomes, the extent to which my DNA sample matched the reference set for "Ashkenazi Jewish." To illustrate how all this works, let me dig a little deeper into what I learned.

One set of tests relates to the Y chromosome, which is only found in men. The Y chromosome is passed down largely unchanged from father to son, making it relatively easy to study. The research often focuses on something called a haplogroup, a set of genes that share a common ancestor.

My paternal Y chromosome line is a haplogroup known as E1b1b1c1a. According to 23andMe, although this cluster is "common throughout the Near East, reaching levels of 5 percent among populations such as the Bedouin, Omanis and Druze, it appears particularly elevated in Jewish populations" now living around the globe. "Given the clearly elevated frequency in all Jewish populations, E1b1b1c1a was very likely present in the ancestral Jewish population from the Levant that dispersed throughout the Old World about two thousand years ago."

According to a major study published by the National Academy of Sciences in 2000, there is a strong scientific consensus to "support the hypothesis that the paternal gene pools of Jewish communities from Europe, North Africa, and the Middle East descended from a common Middle Eastern ancestral population, and suggest that most Jewish communities have remained relatively isolated from neighboring non-Jewish communities during and after the Diaspora."[60]

The evidence on maternal lineage is more complex and suggests a good deal of intermarriage between Jewish men and non-Jewish women. This is consistent with the biblical tradition in which Israelite men took foreign wives. It also suggests that after the Diaspora, some Jewish men may have traveled alone throughout Europe and taken gentile wives from local communities.[61] For example, a 2013 study estimates that 80 percent of Ashkenazi maternal ancestry comes from women indigenous to Europe.[62] The evidence also supports the hypothesis that these male pioneers did not simply blend into gentile society but instead established Jewish communities that, once settled, accepted few additional converts.[63]

The key to the genetic similarities among Jews is endogamy. Jews are not unique in this regard. Many other populations share genetic characteristics, including Finns, American Indians, Icelanders, and certain West African tribes.[64] To the extent that a population is isolated and does not intermarry with other groups, it tends to preserve the genetic makeup of its "founders." What's remarkable about Jews is that they retained these common genetic markers despite being scattered all over the world.

In sum, the genetic research implies that if I meet another Jew today—even one whose ancestors came to America from a very different place in the Diaspora—our common roots may go back centuries to the ancient Middle East. In fact, in his book *Legacy: A Genetic History of the Jewish People*, Dr. Harry Ostrer claims that the major Jewish groups do share a common Middle Eastern origin. For example, Ashkenazic and Sephardic Jews are somewhat similar genetically, even though they were geographically separated many centuries ago.[65] As Stanford geneticist Russ Altzman puts it, "The shared genetic elements suggest that members of any Jewish community are related to one another as closely as are fourth or fifth cousins in a large population, which is about 10 times higher than the relationship between two people chosen at random off the streets of New York City."[66] I must caution, though, that comments like these are easily misunderstood. Altzman is not saying that all Jews are fourth or fifth cousins, merely that the data *suggests* a distant family relationship *similar* to that of fourth or fifth cousins.

Geneticists are wary of taking these conclusions too far, even when the evidence is astounding. One of the most attention-grabbing studies of Jewish genetics focused on the Cohanim—those Jews named Cohen, Kahn, or some variant. By oral tradition the Cohanim are descendants of a priestly caste said to be linked by paternal descent from Aaron, the first biblical priest. In ancient times the Cohanim played an important and exclusive role in religious rituals. Membership in the priesthood was hereditary, and strict rules governed who the Cohanim could marry. Since the destruction of the Temple, these "priests" don't have much of a role to play and enjoy few special privileges, but many people of Cohen lineage are immensely proud of it. (Among Orthodox Jews, Cohanim are still the first called to the reading of the Torah.) There is no written proof of Cohen lineage; Cohen status is passed down orally through the family.

Because the Y chromosome is passed down only to males, the Cohanim seemed tailor-made for study. Could their lineage be traced all the way back to Aaron? Genetic researchers conducted their first study in 1995 with an ingenious strategy for collecting saliva samples: they went to Jerusalem during High Holy Days, set up a table at the Western Wall, waited for Jewish men to finish praying, and persuaded as many as possible to spit into test tubes. The scientists ended up with the DNA of about two hundred Jewish men: half Ashkenazim, half Sephardim, and about a third claiming to be Cohanim. When the researchers analyzed the data, they found to their astonishment that 98.5 percent of the self-described Cohanim had the same genetic marker, no matter where in the world they had come from. The same marker was found in only 3 percent of the Jews who did not identify themselves as Cohanim.[67]

These findings, which seemed to lend support to the biblical story of Aaron and the priesthood, were first published in *Nature* and drew wide—at times, hyperbolic—coverage in the mass media. The researchers were promptly inundated with requests from Jewish men who wanted to be tested for proof of priestly lineage.[68]

For a second study the researchers collected DNA samples from some three hundred Jewish men, about one-third of whom claimed to be Cohanim. Again, the results created quite a stir. The Jews who did not claim to be Cohanim turned out to be genetically diverse, but more than half of those who self-identified as Cohanim shared a cluster of six identical markers. The researchers named this cluster the "Cohen Modal Haplotype (CMH)."[69]

The chance of such a precise match occurring at random was estimated to be less than one in ten thousand.[70] Moreover, the researchers were able to estimate the existence of this cluster back to a time during the biblical period.[71] Later studies found the CMH marker in less than 10 percent of Jewish men generally. The CMH was also found in some non-Jewish populations, including Iraqi Kurds, Armenians, southern and central Italians, Hungarians, and Palestinian Arabs.[72]

It is easy to exaggerate what these DNA findings demonstrate. Jon Entine, a journalist whose enthusiasm for population genetics often seems to exceed that of the scientists whose findings he uses, acknowledges that the Cohen studies "cannot definitively prove the existence of a single founding father for the Jewish priesthood, let alone confirm that the marker originated with Aaron."[73] Genetic researchers Neil Bradman and Mark Thomas, who led the Cohanim studies, are even more emphatic about the broader issue: "There is no Jewish haplotype and genetics cannot 'prove' whether someone is a Jew.... Nor can genetics decide whether a particular community is or is not Jewish."[74]

Because of these discoveries, and the suggestion that many Jews share some genetic markers, is it now appropriate to characterize Jews as a race? I think not. What these discoveries show is that many Jews share a common ancestry or geographic origins.

Nicholas Wade, the *New York Times* science journalist, expressed his resentment over the use of the term *ancestry* rather than *race* to describe genetic findings, asserting that "race is a perfectly good English word."[75] Harvard professor of genetics David Reich strongly disagrees:

> But "ancestry" is not a euphemism, nor is it synonymous with "race." Instead the term is born of an urgent need to come up with a precise language to discuss genetic differences among people at a time when

scientific developments have finally provided the tools to detect them. It is now undeniable that there are nontrivial average genetic differences across populations in multiple traits, and the race vocabulary is too ill-defined and too loaded with historical baggage to be helpful. If we continue to use it we will not be able to escape the current debate, which is mired in an argument between two indefensible positions. On the one side there are beliefs about the nature of the differences that are grounded in bigotry and have little basis in reality. On the other side there is the idea that any biological differences among populations are so modest that as a matter of social policy they can be ignored and papered over. It is time to move on from this paralyzing false dichotomy and to figure out what the genome is actually telling us.[76]

JEWISH DISEASES

The most promising use of "Jewish genetics" lies in the prevention and treatment of so-called Jewish diseases. It is now scientifically accepted that the incidence of certain inherited genetic disorders is much higher among Jews.

The best-known Jewish disease is Tay-Sachs, a fatal neuro-degenerative disorder that typically strikes infants. The disease is caused by a defective gene and is inherited in an autosomal recessive pattern. This means that if both parents are carriers, a child has a one-in-four chance of inheriting the disease.

The defective gene is most commonly found among Ashkenazi Jews. According to the Center for Jewish Genetics, approximately one in thirty people in the American Ashkenazi Jewish population is a Tay-Sachs carrier.[77]

Effective screening for Tay-Sachs carriers was one of the first great successes of genetic testing. It began in 1983 within the Orthodox Jewish community, when a rabbi developed a program called Dor Yeshorim to encourage unmarried couples to engage in confidential genetic testing to determine whether they were "compatible"—that is, whether their offspring would be free of the disease. If the couple were both carriers of the disease, they were informed that they were not compatible and were offered genetic counseling. Today the organization Dor Yeshorim, based in Brooklyn, New York, screens twenty-five thousand young people a year around the world for a range of "Jewish genetic diseases."[78]

Thanks to this genetic screening, Tay-Sachs has been virtually eliminated among Jews in North America and Israel. As the *New York Times* reported in 2003, "The disease is now so rare that most doctors have never seen a case."[79]

Tay-Sachs is just one of many Jewish genetic disorders. In fact, the Center for Jewish Genetics claims that one in four Jews is a carrier for one of nineteen disorders.[80] None of these conditions appear only in Jews; rather, their incidence among Jews is much more common—from twenty to one hundred times more common—than in the general population.

Genetic defects have also led to greater susceptibility to common diseases such as cancer. Jewish women are twenty times more likely than other women to have the BRCA1 and BRCA2 genetic mutations, putting them at high risk of developing breast and ovarian cancer.[81]

Science owes these findings to a geneticist named Mary-Claire King, who, with others, carried out the seminal research on BRCA1 and BRCA2 in 1996. King is in a unique position to assess the intersection of genetics and identity. Until she was in college, she believed she was a WASP with Pilgrim roots extending back to the *Mayflower*. She also believed her mother's maiden name was Clarice Gates—that's what her mother had told her. But one Christmas, while home from college, Mary-Claire found on a bookshelf an old dictionary with the name "Clarice Cohen" written on the inside cover, unmistakably in her mother's handwriting, Mary-Claire carried the book into the kitchen, where her mother was washing dishes, and asked who Clarice Cohen was. An emotional scene unfolded as Clarice, so shaken with fear that she dropped a glass, admitted that her father had originally been named Cohen. As it turned out, Clarice's mother had been a Gates (and a *Mayflower* descendant) but had married Louis Cohen, a Jew. Clarice had been raised as a Christian, but her father's Jewish name had led to threats of Klan violence against the family in the 1920s and to Clarice's rejection from Ivy League colleges in the thirties due to Jewish quotas. After those and other bruising experiences of anti-Semitism, Clarice as a young adult had legally changed both her and her father's name to Gates. The trauma was still evident years later as she told her daughter the truth. "You mustn't ever tell," she told Mary-Claire. "It's really not safe."[82]

King's discovery of her mother's story was life changing, according to journalist Jon Entine. She switched her college focus from statistics to genetics and went on to conduct ground-breaking work in Jewish genetics. She has also worked with Israeli and Palestinian colleagues to explore congenital deafness among Jewish and Arab children. When asked how her research and family history had influenced her own identity, she sounded as confused as anyone else about what to make of the genetic part:[83]

> If somebody asks me, literally, 'Are you Jewish?' I say, 'It depends on what you mean.' By Jewish law, I am not Jewish. My name, King, is not Jewish. I do not culturally identify as Jewish. . . . I've thought from time to time, if I were not a secular person, would Judaism be closer to my belief set? 'Probably,' is the answer. As a geneticist, I think about that question in the same way that I think about the question of race. We define identity culturally and genetically. Most of us define our identity culturally in qualitative ways like language, religion, and nationality. The qualities have boundaries around them. But when we define our ancestry genetically, there are no boundaries, and it's a lot more complicated. . . . It makes me wonder. Where do you start with a story of history?[84]

WHY A "BLOOD" TEST COULD NEVER WORK

The notion that Jews have heritable traits and tendencies rooted in physical or biological characteristics has deep historical roots. But can we define being Jewish solely on the basis of bloodlines? The answer is no. Like the matrilineal rule, no other ancestry test or genetic test can map the Jewish community accurately: either type of standard would be both over- and underinclusive.

It's easy to imagine a racial test based on ancestry. History suggests any number of ways to set racial standards, as has been done for African

Americans and Native Americans as well as for Jews.[85] But what kind of Jewish ancestry would be required? How many generations back would count? No matter which standard you chose, you'd end up including people like Madeleine Albright, who has the ancestry but not the life history or desire to belong, and you'd exclude converts. Depending on the standard, some descendants of converts might be excluded too.

A test based solely on genetic evidence would have similar drawbacks. Population genetics rests only on correlations. Any test based on DNA sequences might well include some Kurds, Armenians, Italians, and Arabs—that is, people with no Jewish ancestry. It would exclude converts to Judaism. As molecular biologist Robert Pollack succinctly put it, "There are no DNA sequences common to all Jews and absent from all non-Jews. There is nothing in the human genome that makes or diagnoses a person as a Jew."[86]

I must say I'm very glad about this. At the beginning of the chapter I noted my strong visceral aversion to the notion of a Jewish race. Having studied the matter, I am even more persuaded that it would be wrong to base being Jewish solely on bloodlines.

Holocaust echoes aside, bloodlines don't measure the extent to which people identify as Jews or live their lives as Jews. Descent is an element of Jewish identity, but there are more pieces to the puzzle. What is our felt sense of kinship and connection based on? We aren't born knowing what it means to be Jewish. "The central ideas and actions of a Jew have always had to be taught and learned, never inherited," says Pollack.[87]

In the next chapter we'll explore the complex and ever-changing idea of the Jewish "people," focusing on ethnic aspects of Jewish identity that must be learned. What does it mean to be part of the Jewish people, and can "peoplehood" help us define who is a Jew?

5

PEOPLEHOOD

BEING JEWISH HAS a collective dimension: you are part of a group. What's the nature of this group? In the last chapter I rejected the idea that Jews were a *racial* group with distinctive physical or biological characteristics. But the discussion of Jewish identity in America is confusing, in part, because there are other ways of describing the Jewish collective.

The political theorist Michael Walzer has argued that this collective can be described in two different ways. One is as a "community of faith"—a religion. This is a collective of a "familiar kind," Walzer says. "There are many religions, and ours is one among them." The second way is to describe Jews as a "people" who share a nationality or ethnicity, *regardless* of their commitment to the religion. According to Walzer, "The anomaly is that these two collectives are not of the same kind" and, "except in the Jewish case," don't normally "coincide."[1]

I suspect most American Jews identify with both dimensions to varying degrees. "For the most part, Jews have always understood that the two sides of this dual identity—the religious and the ethnic/national—are inextricably intertwined," Professors Steven Cohen and Jack Wertheimer contend.[2] But a significant number identify with only one of these dimensions. Many feel no attachment to Judaism but strongly identify as part of the people. Indeed, the 2013 Pew survey suggests that most American Jews identify *more* with the Jewish people than with the religion.[3] A small number see themselves as Jewish only in religious terms and reject the notion that they are part of a "people" to whom they owe any sort of allegiance. (My cousin Don, for example, told me that for him being Jewish meant only a commitment to Reform Judaism, not belonging to an ethnic group.)

In this chapter we focus on the idea that Jews are a "people" with a sense of shared history, culture, and values. A number of different words have been used to label this collective dimension: in addition to a "people," Jews have been described as a nation, a tribe, an ethnicity, a civilization, and a culture. The idea of "peoplehood" is the most recent and fashionable term used to describe the Jewish collective. Proponents of the term, both in America and in Israel, intend it to be an all-embracing concept that expresses the unity of the Jewish people around the world. It is meant to capture the psychological bond many Jews feel with one another, including a sense of mutual obligation to help one another in times of need.

These aspects of Jewish identity are socially constructed: they are not a biological inheritance. Like membership in a religious community, the sense of belonging to a people may be passed on from generation to generation, largely through the family. In this sense descent and ancestry play a role. But the critical point is that no one is born with a Jewish identity: it must be taught and learned.

How has this notion of a Jewish people evolved, and can it help us define who is a Jew? In the Bible the religious and ethnic aspects were unified—the religion was said to be embedded in a people. The attempt to separate the religious from the ethnic dimension is a modern one, which arose in eighteenth- and nineteenth-century Europe in response to challenges facing Jews at the time. Peoplehood is a twentieth-century American idea, with intellectual antecedents that arose in response to challenges facing *American* Jews. And its meaning has evolved since the 1940s, when it was coined.

In its current form, what is this idea all about? How do its contemporary proponents define it? As we'll see, the term is profoundly ambiguous, which is both a strength and a weakness. The ambiguity lends it rhetorical power: it allows American Jews to feel they "belong." But who gets to be part of the "people"?

HOW ONE JEWISH COLLECTIVE BECAME TWO

As the story of the Jewish people is told in Exodus, Moses's ascent to Mount Sinai marked the birth of a single collective. When Moses received the Ten Commandments, God made a covenant with the "people": the Israelites promised to obey God's laws, and God promised to make them his chosen people.[4] In other words, God made a binding contract with the entire group, not with individuals, and this mutual commitment established the religion as a set of obligations that Jews would forever meet as a group. In Donniel Hartman's terms, "Judaism at its core is a collective enterprise, a religion invested in a people."[5]

For about fifteen hundred years after the Diaspora, the realities of everyday life sustained a unified view of this collective. Jews lived primarily in tightly segregated communities, often as a persecuted minority, and the strands of their lives—religious, cultural, and political—remained interwoven.

The sharp distinction between the two collectives—one a community of faith and the other tribal or ethnic—is a relatively new idea. It emerged in Europe, roughly between 1750 and 1900, as Jews faced new opportunities and threats. New Jewish intellectual movements developed during this period. One school of thought argued that Judaism was simply a religion and that Jews were *not* a distinct people or nation. This claim is associated first with Moses Mendelssohn and the Jewish Enlightenment and later with the leaders of Reform Judaism. Another school of thought, led by the Zionists, made essentially the opposite claim: that Jews were a people who were entitled to their own homeland.

"WE'RE JUST A RELIGION"

In late eighteenth-century Europe, as the ideals of the Enlightenment promoted the rise of the modern nation-state and the idea of citizenship, the fact that Jews lived apart from others and described themselves as a chosen "people" or "nation" became problematic. A pressing political issue of the day became known as the "Jewish Question": Could this "people" be trusted as loyal citizens of France or Germany, or would their primary loyalty remain with their own tribe? The fact that Jews often had transnational ties—economic connections that crossed national borders—magnified this concern.

Jewish emancipation in Europe, sparked by the French Revolution, proceeded in fits and starts amid waves of anti-Semitism.[6] Eager to win citizenship and acceptance in the societies in which they had taken root, some Jewish thinkers tried to persuade Christian Europe that Jews posed no threat to the modern state.

The Jewish philosopher Moses Mendelssohn, born and raised in Germany, was the leading thinker of the so-called Jewish Enlightenment, an intellectual movement that introduced European Jews to secular learning, rationalism, and non-Jewish society.[7] Mendelssohn believed that Jewish life should be less insular and more open to the outside world, that Jews in Germany should learn proper German (instead of the traditional Yiddish) and become educated enough to take part in civil society, and that Jews' entire lives should not revolve around the religion.[8] Accordingly, he and others reframed the role of religion in Jewish life. They argued that there were two different spheres in which Jews could operate with equal loyalty: the private religious sphere and the public secular one.[9] This was a radical splitting of the formerly unified Jewish worldview.

In her book *How Judaism Became a Religion*, Leora Batnitzky suggests that Mendelssohn was the first to promote the idea that Judaism should be thought of as a religion in the modern German Protestant sense: "largely private and not public, voluntary and not compulsory."[10] An observant Jew, Mendelssohn did not seek to modify the religion itself. He simply saw no contradiction between the religious demands of traditional Judaism and the secular demands of the state. A Jew could follow halacha in the private sphere without violating the laws of Germany. He further argued that Jews should be granted civil rights as individuals, not as members of a collective, and that there should be a separation between church and state.[11] In sum, Mendelssohn's work suggested that the Jewish collective should be defined *entirely* as a religion.

In the nineteenth century a new Jewish religious movement went much further and sought to modernize the religion itself. Reform Judaism arose in Germany and central Europe as a direct response to the political and social changes brought about by Jewish emancipation. The movement's primary goal was to make the religion more attractive to Jews who wished both to integrate into European society and remain Jewish—in other words, to avoid the temptation of converting to Christianity.

One of Reform's central tenets was that Judaism was strictly a religion. Reform Jews asserted they were *not* members of a Jewish nation who yearned to return to their biblical homeland but rather "German citizens of the Mosaic faith."[12] In 1845 Reform leaders eliminated from the service the traditional prayers "for the return to the land of our forefathers and for the restoration of the Jewish state."[13] They made the religion easier for Jews to practice and more familiar to Protestants: they got rid of cumbersome halachic practices, held services in a mix of Hebrew and German, and introduced organs and choirs into the service.

In America the Reform movement took root by the mid-nineteenth century, spurred by the arrival of German and central European Jews. Here, too, progressive rabbis rejected the idea that they had any desire to join a Jewish "nation." In dedicating a new synagogue in Charleston, South Carolina, in 1841, the rabbi declared, "This synagogue is our Temple, this city our Jerusalem, and this happy land our Palestine."[14]

In 1869 a conference of American rabbis made a point of restating Judaism's messianic mission: it was no longer to restore a Jewish state in the biblical holy land but instead to build on the prophetic ideals of Judaism for the benefit of all peoples.[15] An even more important conference was held in 1885, when the Reform rabbinate boldly declared as a principle of Reform Judaism in its Pittsburgh Platform: "We consider ourselves *no longer a nation,* but a religious community."[16] By that time Reform was the dominant form of Judaism in the United States.

ZIONISM: "WE ARE A NATION AND WE NEED A HOMELAND"

Zionism took the opposite and equally radical tack, defining the Jewish collective exclusively as a "people" within which religious commitments were optional.

Zionism arose as a political movement in the late nineteenth century as a response to growing anti-Semitism in Europe. The father of Zionism was Theodor Herzl, an Austro-Hungarian journalist from a German-speaking assimilated family. Appalled by the pogroms in Eastern Europe, where Jews were not citizens, he was equally shaken by the Dreyfus Affair in France, where Jews had been citizens for a hundred years. In 1894 Captain Alfred Dreyfus, an assimilated Jewish officer in the French army, was sentenced to life in prison on the basis of false accusations that he had committed treason. Herzl concluded that in Europe emancipation and assimilation would not cure anti-Semitism.

In 1896 he published *Der Judenstaat* (The Jewish State), in which he declared, "We are a people—one people":[17]

> We have honestly endeavored everywhere to merge ourselves in the social life of surrounding communities and to preserve the faith of our fathers. We are not permitted to do so. In vain are we loyal patriots, our loyalty in some places running to extremes; in vain do we make the same sacrifices of life and property as our fellow-citizens; in vain do we strive to increase the fame of our native land in science and art, or her wealth by trade and commerce. In countries where we have lived for centuries we are still cried down as strangers, and often by those whose ancestors were not yet domiciled in the land where Jews had already had experience of suffering. . . . I think we shall not be left in peace.[18]

Until the Jews inhabited and controlled their own land, Herzl believed, they could never fully develop their culture or freely practice their religion.

Secular Jews dominated Zionism in its early phases. Consistent with the nationalist spirit of the times, it stood for the idea that a people with a common ethnic heritage deserved to be self-governing. It urged all Jews to emigrate to Palestine and make *Aliyah* (literally, "elevation" or "going up"). This hoped-for migration, imagined as a reversal of the Diaspora, was often called the "ingathering of the exiles."

The response of European Jews to Zionism was decidedly mixed in the early years. Many Western European Jews, cherishing their hard-won citizenship, were hostile to Zionism because it risked inflaming charges of dual loyalty. For the Jews of Eastern Europe, who in some nations were not citizens, the problem was not simply being accused of dual loyalty and facing discrimination but being persecuted and risking physical attack in a pogrom. Although Eastern European Jews didn't necessarily oppose the idea of Zionism, they did not embrace it en masse. Of those who fled their homes in hordes between 1880 and 1923, about two million emigrated to America,[19] while only about 100,000 heeded the call to Palestine.[20] That pattern changed in the 1920s. The Zionist project received a significant boost when Great Britain endorsed it in 1917[21] and the League of Nations followed a few years later.[22] After 1924, when the United States passed restrictive immigration laws,[23] Jews escaping all parts of Europe found Palestine to be a more welcoming alternative. From 1924 to 1939 some 300,000 European Jews made Aliyah.[24]

American Jews were slower to warm to Zionism.[25] In the early 1900s most American Jews were eager to be accepted as citizens of a nation that promised them unprecedented opportunities. Few found at all enticing the idea of leaving America for Palestine. Many Reform Jews, including rabbis, were staunch anti-Zionists.

The American Zionist movement began to gain traction when Louis Brandeis became its leader in 1914.[26] Under his leadership more American Jews grew sympathetic to the idea of a Jewish homeland as a refuge—not for themselves but for European Jews who were being persecuted.[27]

But troubles within the American movement soon developed. The World Zionist Organization, under the leadership of Chaim Weizmann, came increasingly to demand that Jews of the Diaspora support the eventual creation of a Jewish *state*—a political entity with geographic boundaries under the exclusive control of Jews. Brandeis and his followers balked at this idea, unwilling to support either the idea of a Jewish state or the notion that Diaspora Jews owed "national loyalty to a Jewish peoplehood."[28] A Zionism of this sort, they feared, would never gain widespread support among American Jews and would make it difficult for them to avoid charges of dual loyalty. Instead, Brandeis and his followers continued to support a more modest platform: the economic development of Palestine as a refuge for European Jews.[29]

In 1921 these differences resulted in a schism, in which Brandeis and his followers lost control of the American movement to leaders more committed to Weizmann's views.[30] Membership in the Zionist Organization of America plummeted in the 1920s, from a peak of nearly two hundred thousand in 1919 to eighteen thousand by 1929.[31]

The rise of Nazism, however, galvanized the American Zionist movement. In 1937 the Reform movement reversed its previous stance and explicitly endorsed the idea of a Jewish homeland in Palestine.[32] Organized anti-Zionism lost its influence by the end of the decade. After World War II and the discovery of the full horrors of the Holocaust, nearly the entire American Jewish community had come around to Weizmann's point of view, supporting recognition of Israel as the Jewish state.[33]

THE PEOPLEHOOD IDEA: WHAT DOES IT MEAN?

The term *peoplehood* was a twentieth-century expression first popularized by Rabbi Mordecai Kaplan, a founder of the Reconstructionist movement.[34] In recent years Jewish leaders and organizations have seized upon the term as a rhetorical device to inspire a greater sense of unity for a community that seems fractured. Community Federations (the local umbrella organizations for a wide range of Jewish causes) have sponsored "Peoplehood Commissions" in New York and San Francisco.[35] Jewish fundraisers use "peoplehood" as an organizing concept for philanthropic activities.[36] In the United States, Jewish religious and day schools include the idea of peoplehood as a key part of the curriculum.[37] In Israel, Oranim College has a Department of Jewish Peoplehood.[38]

But what does peoplehood mean? How do its proponents define it? Erica Brown and Misha Galperin recently wrote an entire book about it, entitled *The Case for Jewish Peoplehood: Can We Be One?* They offer many definitions with slightly different shadings. In one passage they say peoplehood is "an overarching loose membership in a tribe, a faith, and an ethnicity that shares a common history, religion, and set of basic values."[39] In another they say peoplehood requires a common cause, "sharing a mission or a purpose with an extended family with whom we have a collective history and a shared language of faith, ritual, and culture." Other Jewish commentators have also tried to pin down the term. Professor Sylvia

Barack Fishman offers this definition: "an ethnic group sharing a common descent, language, culture, and homeland."[40]

As a law professor, I can't resist challenging such amorphous descriptions. "Okay," I'd like to say. "You seem to suggest that a sense of belonging to a group is essential. But what's the nature of this group? Is it a 'tribe,' an 'ethnicity,' or an 'extended family?' Who gets to join? Is the kinship notion based on descent—blood ties—or do common values suffice? You've given me a laundry list that includes history, culture, values, religion, and faith. Which ones are essential? Do members of this collective have to share a mission or purpose, or is any weak sense of connection sufficient?"

This vagueness has led some commentators to declare that peoplehood is an empty concept. Jay Michaelson, a journalist with a Yale Law degree and a PhD from Hebrew University in Jewish studies, claims, "There's No There There."[41]

> I think...peoplehood is better understood negatively—that is by [what] it is not: not a religion, nor a nationality, nor an ethnicity, nor a culture. Peoplehood is none of these things, because many Jews don't identify with them and peoplehood is meant to be universal. Really, peoplehood might be best understood as devoid of *any* meaning at all. It says: "We don't know what this Jewish thing is, but we're here and we're in it together."...There is something appealing about this negative notion. It adds no normative content, and thus excludes no one. We can fill it with a wide range of meanings, and color it with whatever emotional connection we have....Peoplehood embraces it all and, by saying nothing, includes everything.[42]

I think Michaelson overstates the case. The idea of peoplehood is not "devoid of any meaning." I believe there are five central claims on which most contemporary proponents of the concept would agree. Even Michaelson's sharp critique implicitly supports the first two claims.

1. **Inclusiveness.** The collective includes all Jews, no matter which cultural or religious practices they associate with being Jewish.

Although there is no consensus among the three major American Jewish denominations about the requirements of Judaism, the idea of peoplehood includes them all—as well as Jews who have "rejected beliefs and [do] not engage in the practices of the Jewish religion."[43]

2. **Unity.** This idea was central to Herzl's Zionist claim: "We are a people—*one people*."[44] Despite the diversity and disagreements among American Jews, the slogan "We are One" is now found on posters in synagogues around the country.[45] As Professor Noam Pianko observes, such "rallying slogans" are meant to transcend "religious differences, cultural practices, geographic diversity, economic disparity, and political differences."[46]

3. **Shared Past and Future.** The Jewish people are linked not only across space but also time. Brown and Galperin claim that "when people feel a powerful, meaningful connection to a joint past, they feel inspired to realize a communal future."[47] Lord Jonathan Sacks, former chief rabbi of Great Britain, describes this connection as a chain of "vertical links binding us to a history and a hope [for the future]."[48]

4. **Shared Responsibility to Fight Anti-Semitism and Help Jews in Need.** Jews share an obligation to help each other survive. A prime example of this solidarity occurred in the 1980s when American Jews engaged in massive political demonstrations to show support for Soviet Jews, an effort that had a profound effect on President Reagan's foreign policy.[49] This commitment extends to helping Jews in need generally—through charitable contributions to Jewish institutions—even if that need does not arise out of anti-Semitism.

5. **Shared Political and Economic Support for the State of Israel.** Jews worldwide should demonstrate solidarity by supporting the State of Israel, the Jewish "homeland." In America today this support takes many forms, including philanthropy to Israeli institutions and lobbying the American government to support Israel with favorable policies and military aid. Understandably, Israeli proponents believe this is a necessary element of peoplehood. According to the current president of Israel, Reuven Rivlin, "the connection between all Jews, all over the world, is very important to the State of Israel."[50]

Given the diversity and internal conflicts among American Jews, describing the collective as inclusive and unified seems preposterous on its face. So does Brown and Galperin's idea that Jews worldwide share a common mission or a timeless obligation to be a light unto all peoples. Some Jews feel no connection to the collective. Others feel only a slight connection. Still others would reject one or more of the five elements I have identified.

But, in fairness, I suspect that the proponents of peoplehood see the term as embodying their *aspirations* for the Jewish collective rather than as a description of reality.

Moreover, I am not entirely dismissive of the idea.

THE APPEAL OF PEOPLEHOOD

I think the Jewish people is an "imagined community," a concept developed by political scientist and historian Benedict Anderson to describe nationalism and the rise of the modern nation-state. Anderson saw the nation as an "imagined political community" whose members will never know most of their fellow members, where membership is bounded, and where the members have a sense of connection "always conceived as a deep, horizontal comradeship."[51] Peoplehood implies that Jews feel that kind of connection to each other.

Like many American Jews, I feel such a connection to other Jews. It's not intellectual; it is emotional, psychological, and subjective.[52] I wasn't born with it; I absorbed it from my family and community.

Growing up in Kansas City, I lived in a neighborhood and went to schools where Jews were a small minority. Some of my friends were Jewish; many were not. Looking back, I'm struck by the fact that from an early age I was very aware of which of my friends and acquaintances were Jewish. In my kindergarten class, for example, I somehow knew that two of my classmates—Steve Baird and Bruce Adelman—were Jewish. How did I know? Their parents were not friends of my parents. Neither Steve nor Bruce belonged to my temple or were in my Sunday school class. (As I'd later learn, Bruce attended the Conservative synagogue and Steve went to an Orthodox one.) How did I learn at the age of five that we were all

Jewish, and why did that make me feel we were connected? I'm not sure. But the same held true when I was in high school, college, and beyond. Whenever I became acquainted with someone and discovered they were Jewish, I felt some sort of connection, even when I might have had little in common with them. Nor did it matter whether I would ever see the person again. In Professor Chaim Waxman's words, we shared "more of a psychological community than a sociological one."[53]

So I would certainly count myself among those who have a sense of "belonging" to the Jewish people. To varying degrees I can also relate to the five peoplehood elements I identified. I like the broad inclusiveness of this concept, especially the fact that it does not require me to be religious. I like the claim that we are one people, despite our diversity.

I very much relate to the sense of shared responsibility. Through my parents and grandparents I absorbed the idea that being Jewish carried an obligation to other Jews, particularly those who were in need. As a young man my grandfather George Sittenfeld supported a Jewish orphanage in Kansas City; he later served as president of the Jewish Community Center and was a founder of Menorah Hospital, the Jewish hospital. My grandfather Jacob Mnookin was president of his synagogue and started a scholarship fund to send Jewish kids to summer camp. In the years following World War II my father and mother were deeply involved in resettling Jewish refugees in the United States and Israel and in raising money for the new State of Israel. My father was an officer and board member of the Jewish hospital. The example they set became so much a part of me that I, too, devoted time to Jewish causes even during periods of my life when I was not giving much conscious thought to my Jewish identity. In my forties, at Stanford, I was president of the campus Hillel Board of Directors and headed the Jewish Federation's drive on campus. I also served as an international board member and officer of the New Israel Fund.

But I do feel a tension between a special responsibility to my own people and universal obligations to all human beings. Implicit in peoplehood is the notion that you owe greater allegiance to your family than to humanity in general and that other Jews are akin to family. I believe we have both sorts of obligations and that the tension between them must be acknowledged and thoughtfully managed. One can go too far in either direction. Tribalism is indefensible if it leads to favoring a member of your family or tribe in contexts where neutrality is required. At the other extreme are claims like those of philosopher Peter Singer, a utilitarian ethicist, who contends that when we engage in philanthropy, we should essentially ignore all personal attachments. Singer believes that, like Bill Gates, we should presume "all lives have equal value" and should, thus, direct our philanthropy to where our contributions will have the greatest positive impact.[54] I disagree. In allocating charitable efforts, I think it's entirely ethical to honor any special bonds one feels with people and institutions with which one identifies.

I relate to the peoplehood claim that we must support Israel, but only up to a point. If peoplehood requires political support of *all* Israeli government policies, I can't sign on. As I will explain in a later chapter, I am appalled by certain major policies of the Israeli government. But I do feel an emotional connection to Israel, and I am deeply committed to its survival as a Jewish *and democratic* state.

What appeals to me most about Jewish peoplehood is the idea that I'm involved in a collective enterprise larger than myself that existed long before my birth and will, I hope, survive long after my death. As part of the Jewish people, I'm part of a project that has a rich heritage, thousands of years in the making, that aspires to help heal the world now and long after I am gone.

That is how I respond to the idea of peoplehood emotionally. Now, here's how I see it analytically.

"Peoplehood" Doesn't Answer the Boundary Question

The central question of these first seven chapters is: Who should be counted as a Jew, and what's the role of descent? The concept of peoplehood dodges these questions. Peoplehood proponents talk endlessly about "inclusiveness," but they're vague about what the boundaries are. Of course, I understand why they avoid the subject: they're trying to be inclusive. They don't want to alienate anyone, especially the Orthodox, by pushing the boundaries beyond those set by traditional Jewish law. But underneath all their embracing and including and unifying, the issue of descent lurks as surely as a shark under water.

As noted above, Fishman offers a definition of peoplehood that includes "sharing a common descent." I commend her for at least acknowledging the issue that everyone knows is there, even if she doesn't specify what kind of descent—matrilineal or otherwise—she has in mind. Other commentators avoid the word *descent* entirely, but as I've said, such evasions demand probing.

Must all members of a tribe or extended family share a common descent? Obviously not. Tribes and extended families include those who become members by marriage, as the Israelite tribes did in biblical times. Is my son-in-law Cory Olcott part of the Jewish people? If not, can he join if he wants to? Would he have to undergo a religious conversion, or are there other options for membership?

Moreover, what are today's children of intermarriage to make of all this ambiguity? If they are patrilineal Jews, are they part of the people? If not, can they choose to join? What if they have "dual loyalties"—emotional connections to the religions of both parents?

"Peoplehood" Alone, Without Religion, May Not Sustain American Jewish Identity

The idea of the Jewish people is a notion that still appeals powerfully to many American Jews today. But social scientists suggest that if it's defined only as an ethnic or cultural collective, it may not offer enough substance for future generations to grab onto.

According to the 2013 Pew study 75 percent of American Jews report having a "strong sense of belonging to the Jewish people," with only modest generational differences: 84 percent of those age sixty-five or older responded yes, compared to 70 percent of those between eighteen and forty-nine.[55] They also respond strongly to the idea of mutual assistance. When asked whether they agree that Jews "have special responsibility to care for Jews in need," 67 percent of the older group and 61 percent of the younger group replied affirmatively.[56] Moreover, the difference between age cohorts doesn't necessarily mean that these beliefs are ebbing with each generation; instead, it may reflect the fact that people often feel less connected to their heritage when they are young and more so as they grow older.

However, "for peoplehood to be a meaningful term that is truly engaging," say Brown and Galperin, "peoplehood must demand a greater threshold of intensity than other sentiments that vie for our attention."[57] That is a very high standard of engagement. It implies that unless a sufficiently large number of Jews make being part of the "people" quite central to their lives, the idea of peoplehood won't have much impact.

How likely is this aspiration to become a reality? When Pew asked respondents whether being Jewish was "very" important in their lives, only about half (54 percent) of the oldest group agreed, compared to only one-third of the youngest group.

Two broad social trends in America, which historians and sociologists have observed for decades, suggest that peoplehood advocates face an uphill battle.

The Decline in Ethnic Identity. The first trend is that ethnic identity is declining in America for all white ethnic groups, including Jews. The further one gets from the immigrant generation, the weaker one's connection to the collective is likely to be. Sociologist Herbert Gans observed this phenomenon in the 1970s among third-generation descendants of the original Jewish and Catholic New Immigrants.

In a pathbreaking 1979 article Gans wrote that these descendants had adopted a new form of ethnic identification that he called "symbolic ethnicity"[58]—a loose connection to their heritage that was "more of a leisure-time activity" than a way of life.[59] Although proud of their roots, they no longer lived in tight ethnic clusters in which their ethnic identity determined who their friends were, how they earned a living, and how they conducted their daily lives; instead, these acculturated Americans had found new ways of expressing the ethnic identity they still *felt* but was no longer instrumental in their lives.

Gans said that most of them "look for easy and intermittent ways" of expressing this identity, "for ways that do not conflict with other ways of life. As a result, they refrain from ethnic behavior that requires an arduous or time-consuming commitment, either to a culture that must be practiced constantly, or to organizations that demand active membership."

For third-generation Jews, he noted, that might mean celebrating some Jewish holidays and rites of passage, such as bar or bat mitzvahs, without feeling the need to engage on a regular basis with any Jewish organization, religious or not. They might enjoy Passover and Hanukah and eating lox and bagels with family and friends, but being Jewish didn't affect their everyday lives. "Because people's concern is with identity, rather than with cultural practices or group relationships, they are free to look for ways of expressing that identity which suit them best," Gans observed.[60] That might include joining a Jewish organization if it "enhances the feeling of being ethnic,"[61] but such membership wasn't essential. Symbolic ethnicity allowed people to choose from a smorgasbord whatever tidbits appealed to them.

Gans was skeptical that symbolic ethnicity would ensure the survival of the Jews as an ethnic group in America beyond the fifth or sixth generation. By the seventh generation, he predicted, some people might still practice the *religion* of their immigrant ancestors, but "their secular cultures will be only a dim memory."[62]

Gans's idea of symbolic ethnicity is a reasonably accurate description of changes that have occurred and may still be occurring within the American Jewish community. If his prediction is right, American Jews connected to the religion will continue to feel connected to the people because the religion is *defined* as membership in a people. But Jews who lack a substantial connection to the religion will need to work harder to find ethnic and cultural supports for their Jewish identity.

For members of my generation, two elements of the secular culture have offered strong anchors for Jewish identity. I was born in 1942 and grew up with the knowledge that anti-Semitism during my lifetime had led to two epochal events: the Holocaust and the founding of the state of Israel. These realities—and the ongoing need to fight anti-Semitism and support Israel—provided many of us with a political mission that had little to do with religion. These events also provided the intensity that Brown and Galperin say is necessary for a shared sense of peoplehood.

But things have changed a lot for Jews since then. What will my grand-children's generation make of the idea of peoplehood?

I suspect at least two of its five central claims may not resonate with them. One is the shared responsibility to combat anti-Semitism. My grandchildren's generation is growing up with no personal experience of anti-Semitism. As I will argue in Chapter 8, anti-Semitism no longer rep-resents a substantial threat to American Jews. Unless Jews elsewhere in the world suddenly face a dramatic crisis, akin to the Six Day War or the persecution of Soviet Jews, the idea of fighting anti-Semitism is not likely to motivate this generation.

The second central claim is the obligation to support Israel. As I will show in Chapter 9, Israeli government policies are currently a source of bitter division among American Jews. If Jewish peoplehood is said to demand blind loyalty to Israel, many young American Jews are likely to flee in the opposite direction. To remain relevant to that generation, any claim involving Israel will need to tolerate strong differences of opinion.

Intermarriage. The second social trend that imperils the idea of peo-plehood is intermarriage, a subject we'll explore in depth in Chapter 10. In a nation where mixed marriages are becoming the norm, individuals with hybrid ethnic identities have more freedom than ever to choose which ones, if any, to express. If they want to reject an ethnic strand entirely, they can. (Erik Erikson, in an earlier era, did exactly that: on his natural-ization application in 1939 he identified his race as "Scandinavian.")[63]

This, too, may not bode well for the kind of intensity Brown and Gal-perin call for. Children of intermarriage may not want to put their Jewish identities first.

The intellectual historian David Hollinger has coined the term *post-ethnicity* to address this phenomenon, calling for an appreciation of multiple, overlapping identities as more relevant to our era than the old single-ethnicity model. As Hollinger writes, "A postethnic social order would encourage individuals to devote as much—or as little—of their energies as they wished to their community of descent, and would discourage public and private agencies from implicitly telling every citizen that the most important thing about them was their descent community."[64] In other words, people should be free to choose which strands of their identity to emphasize.

Scholars are divided on what this means for the future of the Jewish collective. Shaul Magid, a scholar of Jewish studies, agrees with Hollinger about the importance of choice in a post-ethnic world, and he doesn't think it spells the end of the Jewish collective. He acknowledges that ethnicity is no longer the "stable anchor" it was in the past but declares that reports of its demise are exaggerated.[65] He sees a great flourishing of Jewish identification among young adults; it just looks different from before. Many children of intermarriage "have not abandoned Judaism or Jewishness," he argues. "Quite the opposite."[66]

Other commentators fear that the post-ethnic approach is a disaster for Jewish continuity. Professors Cohen and Wertheimer acknowledge the reality of intermarriage, but they reject the idea that being Jewish should be a matter of choice. "Those of us who wish to build a strong and authentic Jewish life dare not communicate to our children that everything is up for grabs, that their Jewish descent is non-binding, and that Jewish living is merely one option among a broad array of lifestyle choices," they write with palpable alarm. Cohen and Wertheimer do not celebrate intermarriage or any trend in which multi-faith, multi-ethnic Jews are free to pick and choose among religious or ethnic commitments. Such an approach "puts us at risk of abandoning a critical aspect of our 'thick' Jewish culture, our obligation and familial ties to the Jewish people in Israel and around the world—in effect, trading our Jewish birthright for a thin gruel."[67]

I share Magid's optimism, and I agree that many children of intermarriage will still identify as Jews. My concern is more specific: that the elements of peoplehood that mean the most to me—inclusiveness, unity, and shared past and future—may not resonate with children of intermarriage unless they are raised to be Jewish and are actively embraced by the community.

On the bright side, the vagueness and plasticity of the peoplehood idea make it highly adaptable. It has potential. But the story of peoplehood won't be complete until we explore how Israel has struggled with the descent issue. As you might imagine, it's a very different story from ours in America, but the question is the same: Who gets to be part of the people?

6

WHO IS A JEW IN ISRAEL?

FASTEN YOUR SEAT belts. I am about to take you on a wild and challenging ride. This chapter deals with the *legal* conflicts within Israel over who is a Jew.

For most American readers this will be a journey into unfamiliar territory. It's hard to imagine Congress passing a law defining who counts as a Jew and even harder to imagine how such a law would pass constitutional muster.

But Israel is different. There, a person's status as a Jew affects issues central to civic life: whether she can come to Israel and become a citizen, whether and how she can marry and divorce, how she must register with the state her nationality and religion, and where she can be buried.[1] For Americans, who treasure respect for religious pluralism and a constitutionally mandated separation of church and state, the status of religion and state in Israel is complicated and difficult to understand.[2]

The central tension that drives this story is between secular Israelis, who have typically favored flexible interpretations of who counts as Jewish, and Orthodox Jews, who have pressed for narrow halachic definitions. These two groups have been fighting for control of the steering wheel since Israel's founding, and the conflicts have involved every branch of government.

The reason to examine Israel's experience is because there is much to learn from Israel's struggles in trying to decide who is entitled to membership in the tribe. It is not because Israel has found a single right answer to who a Jew is—it hasn't. Nor can Israel's answers provide a model for America. Nevertheless, I've discovered some lessons in Israel's struggles that I've found useful in developing my own standard.

THE LEGAL FRAMEWORK

As a first step in our journey, let me describe the three different contexts in which the question "Who is a Jew?" matters in Israel. These three contexts constitute the legal framework that has been in place since the state's early days.

1. Homecoming and Citizenship. At the heart of the Zionist project was the notion of the "ingathering of the exiles" (*Kibbutz Galuyot*)—the idea that the Jewish people deserved a state of their own as a refuge from discrimination and hostility.[3] Israel's Declaration of Independence boldly stated this purpose: "THE STATE OF ISRAEL will be open for Jewish immigration and for the Ingathering of the Exiles." Consistent with this idea, the 1950 Law of Return gives "every Jew" anywhere in the world a right to immigrate to Israel as an *oleh* (someone who makes Aliyah, the migration to Israel). Under the 1952 Citizenship Law any oleh qualifies for citizenship automatically and is eligible for resettlement subsidies. Non-Jews, by contrast, face a much more onerous process: they must receive permission to immigrate, and they have no automatic right to become citizens. Among other things, they must learn Hebrew and live in the country for at least three years before they can even become eligible.

2. Personal Status Issues. In matters of marriage and divorce, all Jews—whether observant or not—are subject to the exclusive jurisdiction of the Rabbinical Courts, manned by Orthodox rabbis who apply traditional religious law.[4] To marry in Israel, the couple must satisfy the rabbinate that both are Jewish, and a rabbi must officiate in a religious ceremony. There is no civil marriage. As a result of these restrictive rules, many Israeli Jews either get married outside of Israel or simply live together without marriage.[5] One's halachic status as a Jew also controls whether one can have a Jewish funeral and where one can be buried.[6]

Let's pause a moment to appreciate the contradictions here. Given the secular roots of the Zionist movement[7] and the large number of nonobservant Jews in Israel, how in the world did the Orthodox rabbinate get control of marriage, divorce, and burial? The explanation lies in history: a political deal that David Ben-Gurion, soon to become the first prime minister of Israel, made in May 1947, shortly before the new State of Israel was formed.

In 1947 the UN was considering dividing Palestine to create a Jewish state and an Arab state. The UN Special Committee on Palestine sent representatives to the region to investigate whether the Jewish and Arab communities were each capable of establishing an independent state. Ben-Gurion wanted the various Jewish groups in Palestine—religious and secular—to present a united front to the UN representatives.

A tiny ultra-Orthodox religious party, Agudat Yisrael, didn't seem fully on board with Ben-Gurion's plan. Its members worried that if a new Jewish state were formed, it would be so secular that it would erode the role of religion. Ben-Gurion feared that without some sort of deal, this religious minority might undermine his delicate negotiations with the UN. To buy off this small political party, Ben-Gurion wrote a letter promising to maintain the "status quo"[8] with respect to certain issues. Among other things, Ben-Gurion promised that once the new state was established, it would retain the so-called millet system used by the Ottoman Empire and continued by the British, which delegated control over marriage and divorce standards to the religious communities (Jewish, Christian, and Muslim).[9]

The implementation of this so-called status quo deal was to produce, in the words of the Hartman Institute's Micah Goodman, "a spectacular irony: the state created by secular rebels now enshrined religious legislation; the state conceived as a revolt against religion betrayed elements of religious coercion."[10] As we shall see, this concession, which may have seemed modest to Ben-Gurion at the time, would have significant repercussions.

3. Registration and Identity Cards. In 1949 Israel enacted the Registration of Inhabitants Ordinance, which required every person, citizen or not, who lived in Israel for more than thirty days to register his or her nationality, religion, marital status, and other personal details. Each resident received an identity card containing this information.[11]

The meaning of *nationality* in Israel is a direct product of Zionism. It refers to one's ethnicity or people, not citizenship. Jew, Arab, and Druze are among the different choices. This notion of nationality is a pre-modern one, foreign to Americans. If I were asked my nationality, I would never say Jew. I would say "American" because I am a US citizen. In Israel no one is allowed to register his nationality as Israeli.[12]

Religion is a separate matter—for example, Jew, Christian, or Muslim. In other words, for registration purposes in Israel, being a Jew is both a religion and a nationality.[13]

IN ISRAEL'S EARLY DAYS all three sets of laws used the word *Jew*, but none of them defined it. For personal status issues, since the rabbinate was in charge, it was commonly understood that the rabbis would apply the matrilineal standard, which required a Jewish mother or conversion to Judaism. But the two secular laws, the Law of Return and the Registration Ordinance, which reflected Zionist notions of a Jewish people, left the issue open to administrative interpretation. I suspect the Knesset, the Israeli national legislature, hoped to avoid the inevitable conflict that would arise if this sensitive issue had to be addressed head-on. That hope would be in vain.

THE EARLY YEARS: AN UNWRITTEN STANDARD

The Ministry of the Interior had the task of administering the two secular processes: immigration and registration. During Israel's first decade the Ministry adopted an informal policy of simply accepting as Jewish virtually anyone who declared himself or herself a Jew. If you stated on an application that you were Jewish, that was good enough for the Ministry—no questions asked.

The effect of this lenient policy was to allow families of mixed heritage to enter and become fully integrated into Israeli society. For example, a Jewish man who was a Holocaust survivor could come to Israel with a non-Jewish wife and their children, and all of them could register as Jews. After the tragedy of the Holocaust, "bickering about 'who is a Jew?' appeared tasteless and inappropriate," according to the scholars Asher Cohen and Bernard Susser.[14] Israel was eager to expand its Jewish population, and if a

person was willing to throw his or her lot in with the "young state struggling with difficulties and hurdles," as the distinguished Israeli law professor Ruth Gavison puts it, he or she was welcome to do so.[15]

For several years this system worked without much controversy. But
in 1957 a bureaucrat in the registration department of the Ministry of the
Interior—a member of the National Religious Party (NRP), composed of
religiously observant Zionists—objected to simply taking an applicant's
word that he or she was Jewish. This low-level administrator thought that
an immigrant's claim to being Jewish should be subject to proof that the
applicant had a Jewish mother.[16]

The Minister of the Interior, Israel Bar-Yehuda, disagreed with this
suggestion. Bar-Yehuda issued a formal directive spelling out the policy
on nationality: "An individual who in good faith declares that he is a Jew,
will be registered as a Jew, *and no additional proof will be required*."[17] Particularly controversial was a second aspect of the directive, which provided that all parents, including intermarried couples, could register their
child's nationality and religion based on the parents' own declaration.[18]
In issuing this directive, the Interior minister relied on an opinion of
the Israeli attorney general (at the time Haim Cohn, who later became
a Supreme Court justice), which explicitly acknowledged that the definition of a Jew under secular statutes did not have to match the religious
law definition. "It is inevitable," the attorney general had written, "that at
times the religious determination will be different in content and nature
from the secular determination."[19]

Once the registration policy was set in black and white, it provoked a
political firestorm.

A CRISIS THAT CHANGED THE STANDARD

The Orthodox religious groups objected to the self-declaration policy for
obvious reasons: it was inconsistent with traditional religious law. Without
a Jewish mother, according to halacha, a person can become Jewish only
through a formal religious conversion controlled by a rabbi. Bar-Yehuda's
directive made explicit the possibility that a person could be registered

as having a Jewish nationality and thereafter claim to be Jewish when, according to halacha, they were not. The Orthodox feared this approach would divide the Jewish people into two groups: one group would meet the halachic standard but the other would not. No longer could any Jew assume he or she was free to marry any other Jew. Indeed, the Orthodox groups argued, the government's willingness to register as Jewish a person without a Jewish mother risked legitimating intermarriage.[20]

Two members of the NRP, who were ministers in Ben-Gurion's cabinet, demanded that the standard for Jewish nationality be debated in a cabinet meeting. They got their debate but not the result they wanted. Only one uncontroversial clause was added to the directive: that to be registered as a Jew, you could not be a "member of another religion."[21] In protest, the two NRP ministers withdrew their support for Ben-Gurion's government, prompting a political crisis.

Ben-Gurion managed the conflict as best he could. He appointed a cabinet committee to draft guidelines for the registration of children of mixed marriages. That effort produced no agreement. Hoping to find a path forward and perhaps provide some political cover, Ben-Gurion's government next asked a cabinet committee to consider "statements of opinion by Jewish scholars in Israel and abroad."[22]

In October 1958 Ben-Gurion wrote a letter seeking advice from eminent rabbis, scholars, and jurists drawn from both Israel and the Diaspora. The goal, he wrote in lofty language, was "to formulate registration rules 'in keeping with the accepted tradition among all circles of Jewry, orthodox and non-orthodox of all trends, and with the special conditions of Israel, as a sovereign Jewish State in which freedom of conscience and religion is guaranteed, and as the center for the ingathering of exiles.'"[23] Ben-Gurion's letter posed the following specific question: "How to register under the heading of 'Religion' and 'Nationality' children born of mixed marriages, when the father is a Jew and the mother is not a Jewess and has not become converted as a Jew...but both she and the father agree that the child shall be Jewish?"[24]

An impressive cast of fifty luminaries responded, including Isaiah Berlin, the Latvian-British social and political theorist; and Rabbi Mordecai

Kaplan, a founder of the American Reconstructionist movement. It was, of course, preposterous to think anyone could come up with registration rules "in keeping with the accepted traditions *among all circles of Jewry.*" Remember the expression, "Ask two Jews, get three opinions"? The views from this group were all over the lot.

But the effort did produce a clear majority view, if not a consensus. Most respondents suggested relying on traditional Jewish law for the answer: for both nationality and religion, a child should be registered as a Jew only if the child's mother was Jewish, absent a religious conversion.[25] This outcome wasn't surprising given the composition of the group: nearly half the respondents were rabbis, and all but one favored the traditional standard.

A spirited minority argued against that view.[26] On what ground? They really struggled to articulate a secular standard for nationality. Some argued that because Israel was a modern secular state, a religious law standard was not necessary and flexibility on the issue was desirable. Berlin fell into this camp.[27] A few supported the self-declaration standard on the ground that parents should have the right to decide the nationality of their children.[28] Others, including Kaplan, insisted that children of mixed marriages be registered as Jews, perhaps under a new category of "Jewish resident."[29]

Once the results were in, Ben-Gurion conceded defeat on the issue and the Interior minister's directive was canceled. In December 1959, after an election, Ben-Gurion formed a new government and appointed a member of the NRP as minister of the Interior,[30] essentially handing control of the issue to the religious right. The new Minister of the Interior moved quickly to make the matrilineal definition official. A month after he was appointed, in January 1960, he issued a new directive: for registration purposes, a Jew was "one who was born to a Jewish mother and did not belong to another religion, or who has converted according to Halacha."[31]

THE ISRAELI SUPREME COURT TIES ITSELF IN KNOTS

There was still plenty to fight about, however. The directive did not change the underlying statutory language relating to registration, nor did it apply to the Law of Return or citizenship standards. So it was only a matter of time before somebody sued. In the 1960s the matter of who was a Jew went to the Israeli Supreme Court in two controversial cases. The first involved a Catholic priest, born a Jew, who desperately wanted to be considered a Jew for purposes of both the Law of Return and registration of nationality. The second case involved the registration of children with a Jewish father but a non-Jewish mother. As a result of these decisions, the Knesset would be forced into action.

THE BROTHER DANIEL CASE

Brother Daniel was a Catholic priest with a perfect Jewish bloodline: both of his parents were Jewish. He was also a Holocaust survivor. Had he simply been an atheist—that is, a Jew with no religious convictions—he would have sped through the citizenship and registration processes without a hitch. But before reaching Israel he had converted to Catholicism and even become a priest. For purposes of citizenship and registration, could he still be a Jew? This was the issue posed by *Oswald Rufeisen v. Minister of the Interior*, commonly called the Brother Daniel case.[32] It was the first legal challenge to both the Law of Return and the Registration of Inhabitants Ordinance.

Oswald Rufeisen was born in 1922 in Zadziele, a village in southern Poland. His parents kept a kosher home. His parents spoke German at home and sent him to a Jewish school where classes were taught in German.[33] As a teenager he became fervently involved in the Zionist youth movement and made plans to become a "pioneer" who would help build a new Jewish state in Palestine. When he was seventeen, however, those plans were interrupted by the German invasion of Poland.

He survived the war by relying on his wits and his fluency in German. He was arrested by the Gestapo but escaped. Using forged documents, he began to pass himself off as a Christian of Polish nationality and German ethnicity. He found work with the police chief of the city of Mir, Belarus, who was working under Nazi direction and needed a translator.[34] Later Rufeisen became the official secretary of the police station, where he took advantage of his position to gather information and help Jews. When he learned of the Nazis' plans to wipe out the city's Jews, he organized a massive escape from the ghetto: around three hundred Jews fled with his help, armed with German weapons he had smuggled to them.[35] The Germans discovered his treachery and arrested him, but he escaped once again, this time taking refuge in a Catholic convent.

While at the convent Rufeisen converted to Catholicism. As he later told his biographer, a spiritual need to make sense of the Holocaust inspired his conversion. In Jesus, he said, he saw "a crucified Jew who through his crucifixion offers redemption."[36] In 1943 he left the convent to join the Polish partisans fighting the Nazis.

After the war Rufeisen returned to the monastery and became a Carmelite monk—Brother Daniel—and then a priest, officially ordained in 1952. After serving in a parish, he returned to a Carmelite monastery. But Brother Daniel never stopped thinking of himself as a member of the Jewish people. He publicly identified himself as both Jewish and Catholic and remained a devoted Zionist.[37]

Brother Daniel yearned to go to Israel to help build the Jewish state. After becoming a priest, he periodically applied to Church authorities to be transferred to a Catholic monastery in Israel, but his requests were denied. The determined priest didn't give up. Finally, in 1958, the Church authorities authorized his transfer to a Carmelite monastery in Haifa.[38]

With the Church's transfer in hand, his next challenge was to secure an exit visa from the Polish government. This was no easy task because the Communist government severely restricted foreign travel. But in the late 1950s, eager to rid itself of its few remaining Jews, Poland was facilitating Jewish emigration.[39] Brother Daniel applied for an exit visa, writing that he loved Poland "with all my heart,"[40] but because of his Zionist upbringing, he considered it his duty to go to Israel and help build a state for his Jewish people.[41] The Polish authorities allowed him to leave Poland *as a Jew*, but only on condition that he give up his Polish citizenship.[42]

The final hurdle was to get permission from the Israeli ambassador to Poland to immigrate to Israel as a Jew. The ambassador said, "I cannot give you a visa as a Jew," citing uncertainty and disagreement in Israel

over whether a Catholic convert would qualify.[43] Instead, the ambassador eventually arranged for a temporary visa allowing a one-year stay in
Israel.[44] Thus, in the hope of living permanently in Israel, Brother Daniel
took the perilous step of severing his links to Poland, becoming stateless,
and entering Israel on a temporary visa.

Once in Israel, Brother Daniel applied to immigrate as a Jew under the
Law of Return and to be registered as a Jew by nationality and a Catholic
by religion. The Ministry of the Interior refused both the immigration
and registration requests, pointing to its directive on registration that to
be a Jew, one could not be "a member of another religion."[45]

Brother Daniel appealed to the Israeli Supreme Court, making three
arguments: (1) that the Law of Return contained no legislative definition
of who was a Jew, (2) that he *was* a Jew under traditional Jewish law, and
(3) that he had demonstrated a lifelong commitment to the Jewish community, the Zionist project, and the State of Israel.[46]

In 1962 a divided court ruled against Brother Daniel, four to one, holding that neither the Law of Return nor the Registration Ordinance could
embrace a Jew who had converted to Christianity.[47]

Two members of the majority were clearly distressed by the outcome.
Justice Moshe Silberg, the author of the majority opinion, wrote that the
case caused him "great psychological difficulty"[48] because he felt "deep
sympathy and great sense of obligation"[49] to Brother Daniel, who had
demonstrated an abiding commitment to the Jewish people and Israel and
a desire to be "identified with the people which he loves."[50] Justice Zvi
Berenson expressed similar admiration for Brother Daniel:

> An exceptional man, for whom material comforts and worldly pleasures
> have no attraction, he is a Jew by birth and as a Jew he grew up, suf-
> fered and conducted himself. Even after embracing Christianity, he did
> not spurn his people. Of himself he says, and his deeds prove it, that in
> consciousness he remained a Jew in the national sense, and he claims
> that nothing in the Christian faith which he has embraced prejudices
> his belonging nationally to the Jewish people.... Even after he became
> a Christian he never ceased both by inner conviction and in external

manifestation to regard himself as a national Jew bound heart and soul to the Jewish people.[51]

Justice Berenson added that if he had felt free to "follow my own inclination" rather than interpret the law, he would have ruled in Brother Daniel's favor.[52]

For those who wonder how the court could have ruled against Brother Daniel, the justices' reasoning provides a glimpse into the fluid world of legal interpretation. Four justices wrote opinions in this case, and each opinion reveals a different approach to interpreting the meaning of a word that had not been explicitly defined in the statutes.

The first issue the court had to decide was whether, for purposes of the Law of Return and the Registration Ordinance, the word *Jew* should be interpreted according to religious law standards. All five justices agreed that religious law standards should not control because the laws in question related to secular matters. Unless the Knesset stated a clear intention to apply religious law to such legislation, the justices said, the court lacked the authority to do so.[53]

If halacha did not control, the more difficult issue was: How should the word *Jew* be interpreted? The justices were in uncharted territory now; the Knesset had never offered any guidance on the matter. Although four justices managed to agree on the result, their paths differed and their struggle is evident.

Justice Silberg favored an "ordinary meaning" standard: What would the Jew on the street think? Silberg thought the answer was "sharp and clear—a Jew who has become a Christian is not deemed a 'Jew.'"[54] In reaching this conclusion, however, Silberg offered no evidence of such a consensus: no poll, no survey, not even an indication that Silberg had put the question to his neighbor. To bolster his argument, Silberg cited what I consider to be a non sequitur: the historic persecution of the Jews by the Catholic Church. "Although the Church has both in theory and in practice ceased to be our mortal enemy," he wrote, "it can no more deny its past than we can deny ours, and a Jewish Catholic will forever remain a contradiction in terms."[55]

Justice Berenson agreed with Silberg that the term *Jew* should be interpreted according to its "popular meaning"—again without offering any evidence of consensus. A Jew who has changed his religion is "lost to the nation," Berenson wrote dramatically. "His family mourn for him, rending their clothes, as they would for someone who had really died. All ties with him are broken as if he were indeed dead."[56] Most Jews would agree, Berenson said, that "a Jew and a Christian cannot reside in one person and certainly not a Jew who is a Catholic priest—to them that would be a contradiction in terms."[57]

Justice Moshe Landau took a different approach, somewhat akin to a heresy argument applied to ethnicity. By converting to Catholicism, Landau wrote, Brother Daniel had deliberately "denied his national past" and "erected a barrier between himself and his brother Jews."[58] Landau also scoffed at the idea that Jewishness might be based solely on a good-faith declaration: "It was certainly never intended by the Legislature that any person might declare himself to be a Jew for purposes of the Law of Return and, at his pleasure, be a Jew or cease to be a Jew according to his ever-changing mood."[59]

The lone dissenter was Justice Haim Cohn, who argued that Brother Daniel should have prevailed on both the immigration and registration issues. Cohn began by asserting that because the Law of Return didn't explicitly *exclude* converts to other religions, the law "must be construed and applied as it stands literally, without attributing to the term 'Jew' any religious significance or qualification."[60] Absent an explicit legislative definition, Cohn claimed, a *good faith* self-declaration should suffice because the Knesset had not excluded this possibility. He further argued that it is not the job of Interior Department bureaucrats to investigate the basis of the applicant's claim or assess their good faith. He concluded that, on the facts of this case, there could be no doubt that Brother Daniel's declaration that he was a Jew had been made in good faith. (However, the opinion never addressed how the "good faith" of other immigrants could be assessed if authorities could never look behind the declaration.)

If I had been on the Israeli Supreme Court, I would have dissented but on different grounds. First, as American law professor Marc Galanter has pointed out,[61] the majority opinion did not address which "ordinary usage" of the word *Jew* should apply to Brother Daniel. (Indeed, the majority didn't even acknowledge that more than one "ordinary usage" might exist.) As the responses of Jewish intellectuals to Ben-Gurion's letter had demonstrated, contemporary Jews had many different views on who should count as Jewish. Whose view should count, and why? Second, like Galanter, I am troubled by a logical inconsistency in the ruling. Under religious law a Jew by birth who has *no* religious beliefs is still a Jew. If beliefs are irrelevant, then why should a Jew by birth be disqualified for having the "wrong" sort of religious beliefs?[62]

My approach to this problem would have been to ask: What was the purpose of the Law of Return? What was the Knesset's goal in keeping the definition of Jew wide open? As I mentioned in the previous chapter, one goal—the bedrock purpose of Zionism—was to offer any Jew, anywhere in the world, a refuge from persecution. Another goal was to encourage Jews to move to Israel—instead of, say, the United States—by offering them a fast-track immigration process that included interfaith couples, their children, and virtually anyone else with ties to the Jewish people. Did Brother Daniel qualify as a Jew for either of these purposes? I think he qualified for both. If the Nazis had discovered Brother Daniel's Jewish heritage, they would have killed him. He had strong ties to the Jewish people: he was ethnically Jewish, he was a lifelong Zionist, he had bravely risked his life to save Jews during the Holocaust, and he had given up his Polish citizenship to move to Israel. The only question left: Was his conversion to Catholicism such a grievous offense that it should negate all these factors? I see no logical reason to set up the "Jew on the street" as some kind of secular authority on immigration law, much less to assume that Israeli social norms precluded Brother Daniel from being classified as ethnically Jewish.

I acknowledge, of course, that Israel, as a sovereign state, has the right to decide for itself who qualifies for special immigration rights and nationality. It pleases me that in the end Israel allowed Brother Daniel to become a citizen—not as a Jew under the Law of Return but under the standard for naturalization. However, Brother Daniel was never fully satisfied with this outcome. As he once said, rather bitterly, "I am just an Israeli. Jewish national belonging was denied to me.... In my identity card, opposite to the word 'nationality' it says 'turn to page 10' where the all-powerful official wrote 'Nationality: Not clear.'"[63]

Brother Daniel spent the rest of his life at Stella Maris, a Carmelite monastery in Haifa. There he always introduced himself as a "Jew of Catholic religion."[64] This didn't make life easy for him. He never completely fit in at the monastery, where he was considered "the convert," and although he was warmly embraced by a large group of survivors who had fled the Mir ghetto and made it to Israel,[65] the larger Jewish community never fully accepted him. He spent the rest of his life trying to create a bridge between Judaism and Christianity. He conducted Mass in Hebrew and supported Hebrew-speaking Christians, including the spouses of Jews. Once, when asked whether he would ever return to Judaism, he replied, "But how can I return? I never left!"[66] He died in 1998, leaving a will in which he had included this parting note: "I don't know if I am to be doomed or spared, but from all the things you may know about me, I would like you to remember that I was born a Jew, and died a Jew."[67]

THE CASE OF BENJAMIN SHALIT: CHILDREN WITH A JEWISH FATHER AND A NON-JEWISH MOTHER

Not many Jews convert to Catholicism, become priests, and publicly declare they are Jews.[68] A much more common situation involves a mixed marriage where a child with a Jewish father but no Jewish mother wants to be identified as a Jew. This was the basis of the Shalit case, which, unlike the Brother Daniel case, was seen as a profound threat to the matrilineal standard. The case led to an unexpected Supreme Court ruling that provoked an intense political controversy.

Major Benjamin Shalit, a naval officer in the Israeli military, was born in Israel to Jewish parents. In 1958, while in Europe, Shalit met and subsequently married Ann Geddes, a Scottish woman with a non-Jewish mother and a Jewish father. Geddes never converted to Judaism and did not identify with any religion. The couple moved to Israel, where they had two children. Because both children were born in Israel and their father was Israeli, they automatically acquired Israeli citizenship.

Ann and Benjamin considered themselves atheists. In 1968 the Shalits tried to register their children's nationality as Jewish while leaving the religion category blank. The Ministry of the Interior was willing to leave the religion category blank, but it rejected their application with regard to nationality. Citing the directive of 1960, the Ministry ruled that neither child could register as a Jew because their mother was not Jewish; instead, "nationality" should be left blank for each child.

Shalit challenged that decision in the Israeli Supreme Court. It was the first legal challenge to the directive's narrow religious standard for nationality. Given the court's reluctance to give an expansive definition of Jew in the Brother Daniel case and the clarity of the directive, one might have expected a short, straightforward ruling in which the court simply affirmed the Ministry's decision.

Instead, the court split five to four in Shalit's favor, ignoring the directive and ordering the Ministry to register the children as having a Jewish nationality. It was a stunningly liberal result, but not because the majority held liberal views on who was a Jew. To the contrary, the Court was in complete disarray, producing nine separate opinions, none of which represented the views of a majority. The closest the Court could come to agreement was this conclusion by three justices: that only the Knesset—not the Ministry—had the power to require that religious law be applied to a secular statute.[69] The five-man majority agreed only on the result, not the reasoning.

THE KNESSET TAKES ACTION

The Shalit ruling did not stand for long. In 1970, prompted by the NRP, the Knesset amended the Population Registry Law. As a result, the Shalit's third child, born in 1972, could not be registered as having a Jewish nationality because the child was not "born of a Jewish mother." The Shalits tried to appeal the Ministry's decision, but this time the Supreme Court, citing the amendment, declined to hear the case.

At the same time, the Knesset amended the Law of Return. As a result, both secular laws contain the same explicit language: a Jew is "a person who was born of a Jewish mother or has become converted to Judaism and who is not a member of another religion." But at the same time as it narrowed the definition of Jew, the Knesset added new categories to the Law of Return to welcome family members who would not otherwise qualify. These categories included spouses of Jews, children of Jews (and their spouses), and grandchildren of Jews (and their spouses). Indeed, the amended Law of Return in one respect adopted a Nazi definition—a person with one Jewish grandparent (and no other connection to the Jewish world) qualifies under the Law of Return.

To this day the standard for immigration and automatic citizenship under the Law of Return remains far broader than the traditional religious law definition of a Jew. These important rights are extended to persons who have significant familial ties to the Jewish people, even though they do not themselves qualify as Jews by birth under the matrilineal rule. Why did Israel do so? Presumably because these persons have a sufficient connection to and identification with the Jewish community to be welcomed.

ANYONE WHO LOOKS TO the State of Israel for a neat and coherent answer to the question of "Who is a Jew?" will be disappointed. On the one hand, Israel was unable to develop a secular definition of Jew. On the other hand, the religious right has not always gotten its way. The Orthodox rabbinate and the religious political parties have achieved some successes, but so have secular forces. The story involves more than a one-way trend from the flexible self-declaration test to a strict halachic standard. Stubborn social realities have made it impossible for religious law standards to be applied in every case. Israel is not a theocratic state.

With regard to personal status issues, for example, Israeli law initially appeared to recognize only religious marriages and to give the rabbinical courts a monopoly in this realm. But over time the secular courts have created more liberal options by recognizing civil marriages performed outside Israel and cohabitation outside of marriage.[70]

The push and pull between secular and religious forces has played out in the other contexts as well. In its approach to the Law of Return, Israel has managed to broker a grand compromise. Since 1970 the law has included a definition of Jew that satisfies the rabbinate while also embracing family members who don't meet halachic standards. Since 1989 this solution has allowed Israel to welcome more than a million immigrants from the former Soviet Union, about 25 percent of whom would not be considered Jewish by the Orthodox rabbinate. Some have since converted to Judaism, but many have not.

Israel now counts among its citizens several hundred thousand "non-Jewish Jews"—those who lack a Jewish mother, have never undergone an Orthodox conversion, and who remain nonreligious. They are well integrated into the large nonreligious Jewish segment of Israeli society. They think of themselves—and are widely accepted—as loyal citizens of the Jewish state. Their day-to-day lives are no different from those of secular Israeli Jews, who number in the millions.[71]

Now let's return to the question of who should count as a Jew in America. In no sense should the Israeli experience be seen as controlling; I'm not about to suggest that the matrilineal principle should win out in our country. Israel and the United States are too different politically and socially for one to serve as a map for the other. In Israel, even the most secular Jew lives in a country where Hebrew is the national language, Jewish holidays are national holidays, and citizens are called upon to risk their lives to defend the continuing existence of the Jewish state. There, the fundamental challenge is political: how to remain a Jewish state with democratic values in the face of severe security threats. In America, by contrast, where most Jews don't live in a "thick" Jewish environment, the core challenge is social and personal: how to maintain a thriving Jewish community and a strong individual Jewish identity in a culture where Jews are a tiny, well-integrated minority, intermarriage has become the norm, and religious commitment is thin.

But four lessons from the Israeli experience are worth noting.

- The meaning of the word Jew can vary by context and change over time. Being Jewish for some purposes can be defined differently from how it is defined for other purposes.
- Even in Israel, the Jewish homeland, halachic standards for who is Jewish are not fully controlling.
- Public self-identification was for a time treated as a legitimate test of who counts as a Jew.
- Ethnic identity may be different from religious identity; a Jew by birth might continue to identify with the Jewish people even after converting to another religion.

7

WHO IS A JEW IN AMERICA? A TWENTY-FIRST-CENTURY STANDARD

I'VE JUST SPENT the last six chapters finding fault with the best-known ways of describing the tribe and its boundaries. I've expressed impatience with them all. So what's my answer?

Let me begin, in rabbinic fashion, by answering a question with another question. For American Jews, is it possible or even desirable to agree on a common boundary? Some scholars argue that a collective *must* define itself by establishing clear boundaries. Moshe Halbertal has written, "The manner in which a community establishes the identity of its members is expressed in the ways it constructs the rules that govern how members are admitted into and removed from the community. The concepts of a community's identity are honed at its edges, in its rites of passage and exclusion ceremonies, its admission demands and exclusion procedures."[1]

Donniel Hartman, in his brilliant book *The Boundaries of Judaism*, contends, "As a collective identity, by definition Judaism cannot be determined solely by the actions of or decisions of individuals, but must entail *some shared common notion of boundaries which serve to demarcate the space which all who are Jews agree to share*."[2]

I disagree with Hartman. In America today there is no "shared common notion of boundaries which...all who are Jews agree to share." No single boundary is accepted by all American Jewish institutions. With a community as diverse as ours, it's impossible to draw just one bright line that neatly divides Jews from non-Jews and captures what it means to "be Jewish" for all purposes that "all who are Jews agree to share."

Instead, I propose a new two-part standard. One part defines the boundary for the American Jewish community as a whole—what I call the "Big Tent."[3] The second part relates to the particular groups or institutions under the Big Tent and their right to impose their own boundaries.

Under this standard, as you'll see, a person may qualify as a Jew for purposes of the community as a whole but not for a particular subgroup. This approach reflects an idea we saw illustrated in the examples from Israel: the word *Jew* can have different meanings in different contexts. To explore the richness of this idea before I lay out the new standard, the law professor in me cannot resist using a famous problem employed to teach first-year law students about legal interpretation.

THE "VEHICLE" IN THE PARK PROBLEM

Suppose a city enacts a rule that provides, "No vehicle is permitted in any public park," with a $100 fine for any violation.[4] What counts as a "vehicle" for purposes of this ordinance?

I sometimes use this as a hypothetical in my contracts course. I typically begin the discussion by asking, "Would driving an automobile in the park violate the ordinance?" This invariably elicits a resounding yes from the students. I then follow with: "How about a motorcycle?" Another "yes" chorus. "What about riding a bicycle through the park?" Fewer yeses than before. "What about a parent pushing a baby in a stroller?" "Suppose a veterans group wants to build a war memorial that involves a military truck fixed to a pedestal?"[5] "Can a child bring a toy truck into the park?"

By this point the room is silent.

The goal of this exercise is to teach students that words don't have a fixed meaning; they must be interpreted in context. The Israeli Supreme Court faced this problem in interpreting the word *Jew* in the Brother Daniel case. There are many different approaches to interpreting words in statutes and other legal rules. One approach is simply to give a word its "plain meaning"—what an ordinary person would say the word means. But how does one establish that meaning? For a common word like *vehicle*, does one go to the dictionary? The *Merriam-Webster* dictionary defines vehicle as "a machine that is used to carry people or goods from one place to another."[6] A car and a motorcycle clearly fall within this definition. But so does the stroller. Fining a parent for pushing a stroller through a park seems perverse.

As I've said, I favor an interpretive approach that asks what the purpose of the rule was. Why did the city council enact this ordinance? What problem did it hope to solve? If the purpose was public safety, to protect pedestrians from injury, that offers guidance. The car, the motorcycle, and the bike pose clear hazards to pedestrians; the stroller, the toy car, and the stationary truck don't.

But even when the purpose of the rule is clear, you might still have borderline cases. How about someone walking a bike through the park? Or a small child riding a tricycle? These fit the dictionary definition of vehicle, but they create only minimal risks. A public park has a *purpose* of providing recreational space for adults and children.[7] If I were the judge in this case, I would rule that walking a bike in the park does not violate the statute, but riding a bike does. I would be aware that this approach might be seen as inconsistent: in one context I treat a bicycle as a vehicle and in the other context I don't. But given what I see as the purpose of the ordinance, this approach makes sense to me. So does the result.

A BIG-TENT STANDARD

In developing my own standard for who is a Jew, what are my purposes? For the first part, which relates to the American Jewish community as a whole, I want a standard that is broadly inclusive, emphasizes individual choice, and does not require people to express their Jewishness in any particular way. In short, I want to welcome into the American Jewish community those who choose to be included but not those who don't.

For the second part, my purpose is to respect the right of subgroups to develop and apply their own standards for membership and participation. I do not want to infringe on their liberty.

Therefore, my proposal is this:

Public Self-Identification. For the American Jewish community as a whole, the standard should be public self-identification. Are you willing to identify yourself publicly as a member of the Jewish people? If so, you're welcome under the Big Tent of the American Jewish community. You'll find a huge variety of organizations and groups here. Some are religious. Others focus on social justice or the needs of Israel. There are educational programs, community centers, museums, and film festivals. Come explore.

Local Discretion. Each organization or group under the Big Tent may set its own boundaries for membership and participation. An Orthodox synagogue, for example, can exclude from its congregation anyone who doesn't meet halachic standards. A Reform congregation can have different standards for membership and participation. A Jewish day school can set its own criteria for admission. But no institution has the right to dictate the standard for any other.

IN DEFENSE OF AN INCLUSIVE STANDARD

I think the first part of this standard, which I'll call the Big-Tent standard, is necessary for two reasons. First, it recognizes that there are many different dimensions to being Jewish, and it accepts them all: self-identification, ancestry, religious beliefs and observance, participation in Jewish community activities, and social networks of friends and family. It doesn't try to draw an arbitrary line that favors one factor over the others.

Second, the Big-Tent standard minimizes the importance of descent and makes membership in the American Jewish community a matter of individual choice. This reflects my own ideological preferences as an American; individualism and choice are values to which I attach great importance. It also reflects the fact that, as the intermarriage rate has skyrocketed, an increasing number of Americans have Jewish family connections but don't meet the matrilineal standard. I want to embrace as many of these people as possible—without requiring them to convert to Judaism. By being more inclusive, our community will be greatly enriched.

Now let me be specific about the people I want to embrace—if they want to be included. They fall into five categories, which I'll identify in order of importance.

Children of Intermarriage

This is by far the largest group, and it's growing quickly. These are the people I worry about. Many of them don't feel fully included as Jews, especially if they haven't been raised in a welcoming Jewish community. I'll discuss this issue further in Chapter 10.

The Big-Tent standard would include them regardless of which parent is Jewish, whether they're practicing the religion, or where they fall on the spectrum of intensity. But they must choose to identify.

Note that this standard is broader than the Reform standard, which only conditionally embraces children of mixed heritage. At least on paper, the Reform standard requires them to work to earn their credentials: to demonstrate some affirmative commitment to Judaism, such as attending Sunday school, becoming a bar or bat mitzvah, or being confirmed. Although I doubt this requirement is being much enforced in practice, the Reform approach does treat children of intermarriage differently from those who have two Jewish parents. The Big-Tent concept would eliminate this double standard.

Non-Jewish Spouses Raising Jewish Children and Participating in a Jewish Community

This is another large and growing group. Many gentile spouses make significant contributions to the tribe, not only by raising Jewish children but often by paying temple membership dues and making other financial sacrifices. I want to include those who wish to self-identify as Jewish, even if they have no desire to convert to Judaism.

Let me illustrate with a story. Beth Andrews, the wife of a colleague and friend, was a prime example of someone who made a Jewish journey. Beth was raised as an Episcopalian. She married my good friend David Hoffman, a Reform Jew. After their children were born, they provided their children with a religious education by joining Kerem Shalom (Vineyard of Peace), a liberal Reconstructionist congregation in Concord,

Massachusetts. They attended High Holy Days services together and participated in the congregation's community life. Their children celebrated a bar and bat mitzvah. The family celebrated Passover and Hanukah every year; Beth loved cooking *latkes* and other sorts of Jewish food. But she never converted.

Beth was diagnosed with cancer when she was fifty-eight. Four years later David and Beth started making plans for hospice care. The hospice nurse, after asking about Beth's health history and treatment preferences, asked about her religion. Beth hesitated, initially suggesting that maybe the answer was "none." But then she said, "If you need to put down something, you can say I'm Jewish." This declaration brought tears to David's eyes. Beth died six weeks later. Her memorial service was celebrated at Kerem Shalom.

Here is someone who never converted to Judaism but who raised Jewish children and was actively engaged with a Jewish congregation. Near the end of her life she identified herself as Jewish. In my view Beth was an integral part of the American Jewish community and deserved to be recognized as such.

Indeed, gentile spouses like Beth are already being accepted to a substantial degree. They are not considered Jews, but the Reform and Reconstructionist movements embrace them as active participants in their congregations, albeit with limits that vary among congregations.[8] Some Conservative congregations are also becoming more accepting.[9]

The difference between those approaches and mine is that for the American Jewish community as a whole, the Big-Tent standard would accept these spouses *as Jews*, if they wanted to be so included, without requiring conversion. Under the second part of my standard, each synagogue would still have the right to set its own rules.

People with No Jewish Parent but a Jewish Grandparent

In America there are probably tens of thousands of people who fall into this category, which may grow over time because of intermarriage. Some of these individuals may love and admire a Jewish grandparent and become interested in exploring their Jewish heritage. How can we encourage them to have a Jewish journey and participate in the Jewish community? They can convert in, of course. But why not provide another option? I would say, "If you choose to identify yourself as a Jew, I would embrace you as a Jew."

The astute reader will note that individuals who fall into any of these first three categories would qualify to emigrate to Israel and automatically become citizens under the Law of Return, as amended in 1970. The Big-Tent standard simply goes a bit further—or, as some might say, a lot further—and allows them all to qualify *as Jews*.

PEOPLE WITH REMOTE JEWISH ANCESTRY

I think it's arbitrary to draw the line at having a Jewish grandparent. How much Jewish heritage should it take to be considered a Jew? I find it distasteful to quibble over percentages; to me it seems racist. Moreover, because so many European Jews converted to Christianity under duress, people with remote Jewish ancestry constitute a sizable group. Some of them may discover this ancestry as adults, and a few may be strongly drawn to explore their Jewish heritage.

Doreen Carvajal is a wonderful example. She is an American journalist who lives in Paris and has worked as a correspondent for the *International Herald Tribune* and now the *New York Times*. Born and raised as a Catholic in the San Francisco Bay Area, she is descended from a Spanish family that settled in Costa Rica in the sixteenth century. She grew up with no idea that her ancestors might have been Jewish. But in her career as a journalist, her byline sometimes caused people to comment on the name Carvajal; some told her it was an old Sephardic Jewish name, and one reader wrote to ask, "Do you know that your last name is the same as a family of secret Jews burned at the stake in Mexico in the sixteenth century?"[10]

Carvajal became obsessed with tracing her family's Sephardic roots. Her search went back sixteen generations to the Spanish Inquisition and included archival research, interviews with relatives in Costa Rica, and even moving her family to a small village in Spain "for my own personal right of return—to recapture what might be a homeland, to salvage beginnings and an identity that my family forgot."[11] She wrote a book about her search in which she explored the culture of secrecy that the conversos and their descendants typically maintained for generations. As an adult, from her cousins, Carvajal learned that her great-aunt Luz had kept a menorah in a bedroom dresser and had told family members that they were descended from "Sefarditas," the Costa Rican word for Sephardic Jews.[12]

When I interviewed Carvajal in 2014 she told me she was no longer a practicing Catholic and had become completely nonobservant. She had attended Yom Kippur services and Passover Seders and felt she "need[ed] an education" in Judaism. When I asked about her religious identity, she suggested that she was perhaps on the path to conversion, "step by step."[13]

This is someone who has taken a significant Jewish journey—which is still unfolding—and whose strand of Jewish identity has become very important to her. I would certainly welcome her into the tribe if she chooses to identify herself as Jewish.

ADULTS WHO ARE JEWS BY BIRTH AND CONSIDER THEMSELVES ETHNICALLY JEWISH BUT ALSO HAVE TIES TO ANOTHER RELIGION

As we've seen, Brother Daniel fell into this category. A more famous example was Cardinal Jean-Marie Lustiger (1926–2007), the "Jewish Cardinal" who rose to become the archbishop of Paris. Lustiger's parents were Polish Jews who had moved to Paris around World War I. Lustiger himself was born in France and converted to Catholicism at the age of thirteen, over his father's objections. He became a priest and rose in the Church hierarchy until Pope John Paul II appointed him the archbishop of Paris in 1981. Like Brother Daniel, Lustiger always insisted that he remained ethnically Jewish.[14] On being appointed archbishop of Paris, he declared, "I was born Jewish and so remain, even if that is unacceptable for many. For me, the vocation of Israel is bringing light to the goyim. That is my hope, and I believe that Christianity is the means for achieving it."[15]

Lustiger's Jewish ancestry would be hard for any Jew to discredit. His Jewish mother died at Auschwitz. He fought anti-Semitism all his life. He also helped negotiate the resolution of a bitter conflict between Jewish groups and Carmelite nuns who had built a Carmelite convent at Auschwitz.

Brother Daniel and Cardinal Lustiger claimed to believe the tenets of both religions. The strongest argument that such individuals are not Jews, in my view, is that Catholicism and Judaism are in direct conflict with each other on a major point of theology: whether Jesus is the Messiah. A person cannot believe both "yes" and "no" at the same time. I think this conflict might be relevant to a synagogue trying to decide whether to accept such a person as a member. But if a Jew by birth identifies as an *ethnic* Jew—part of the people—while practicing a different religion, I wouldn't exclude him from the Big Tent. His Jewish strand is clearly salient. Moreover, Catholicism is only one religion to which a Jew by birth might be drawn. American Jews are often attracted to other religions, such as Buddhism.[16]

CRITIQUES, QUESTIONS, AND ANSWERS

When I've discussed the Big-Tent standard with friends, colleagues, students, and others, the reactions of some have ranged from bafflement to indignation and disbelief. Here are their key objections and my responses.

It's ridiculously overbroad. If anyone can join, are there any boundaries? Is there anyone you'd leave out?

Yes, there are people I'd leave out: those who don't publicly identify with the tribe and don't want to belong—in other words, people who are Jews by birth but don't consider themselves Jewish. Erik Erikson and Madeleine Albright are good examples. Choice is essential in both directions. If a person wants to leave the tribe or never join it in the first place, I respect that choice.

As one of my inquisitors demanded, "What if a Minnesota farmer, descended from Norwegian immigrants, wakes up one day and decides he wants to be Jewish? He goes out to the cornfield and declares to the sky, 'I'm a Jew!' Are you seriously going to accept him as part of the tribe?"

I'm not worried about the Minnesota farmer. If that happens, it will be rare. If he comes into the Tent wanting to look around, I certainly won't object. Whether he finds a subgroup willing to accept him is another story. The religious groups would require him to convert, but he might find secular groups happy to educate him and welcome his contributions.

Nor am I concerned about, say, an opportunistic college student with no Jewish background who declares he is Jewish in order to get a free Birthright trip to Israel. Under the Big-Tent standard, nothing would prevent the Birthright organization from imposing a stricter standard.

It has no content, no sense of shared mission. If self-identification is enough, that's a pretty thin definition.

You're right, it's extremely thin. But there *is* no consensus in America about the mission.

I wish I could in good conscience require more than public self-identification—for example, some sort of active participation in the Jewish community. All of us, whether we're born Jewish or join the tribe in other ways, should express our choice through action in our lives and service to the collective. As a nonobservant Jew, I've given a lot of thought to how I express that in the world.

But I'm not about to tell people that their way of being Jewish is not good enough. As a liberal, I don't want to presume to tell people how to express being Jewish. In America there's an extraordinary range of ways you can do it. I don't think there is one right way.

Another reason to keep my minimum requirement light—or, as critics might say, "lite"—is that I want to welcome *marginal* Jews: people whose Jewish identity is weak and who may even have one foot out the door.

As Herbert Gans suggested in his theory about symbolic ethnicity, many Jews might say they're proud to be Jewish, especially when researchers for the Pew Report come around, but what does that really mean? For many, being Jewish has little effect on their daily lives. They don't know much about Jewish history and aren't participating in the community.

The Jewish community is divided on how to deal with this category of Jews. One approach is to ignore them and focus only on Jews who are willing to be very actively engaged. The other approach is to reach out to them and hope to light a spark.

I fall into the latter camp. I want to invite them to participate more—especially if they're young. I don't accept that they're a lost cause. Even if the Jewish strand of their identity is very thin at this point in their lives, it may become more important at a later time, as it did for me. I want the door to be wide open.

You can't maintain a "tribal dimension" without blood ties. If you eliminate the descent requirement, the psychological bond among Jews will disappear.

I have several thoughts on this. First, the tribe has never been defined exclusively by descent. In biblical times non-Jews were welcome to join the tribe simply by marrying in. Beginning in the Roman era the method of entry changed to religious conversion. What I'm suggesting is an additional way for people to join the tribe: self-identification.

Second, the descent aspect is central to Judaism and always will be, whether we define it narrowly or broadly. Even if we make it easy for people with no blood or spousal ties to join the tribe, such members will be rare. Virtually all the people I'd like to welcome or reabsorb have a Jewish family connection of some sort.

My third point goes to the question: How will we maintain our psychological bond? As I've noted, the mere fact of having Jewish ancestry doesn't create that bond. It's what we are taught and what we choose to make of it. Moreover, Jews will always be a tiny minority in this country. It's that minority status, combined with the importance of descent and *what we do to express our Jewishness* that will keep us bonded to each other.

For those without some sort of familial Jewish connection, why not require religious conversion?

This is a fair question. Suppose the Big-Tent standard—public self-identification—applied only to individuals who had at least one Jewish grandparent or were married to a Jew, and all others had to convert? As a practical matter, the "all others" category would be very small.

My response is that being Jewish does not require "born Jews" to be religiously observant, so it shouldn't require that of others either. For many American Jews (perhaps a majority) their primary identification is with the ethnic/cultural collective. I want a way for others to join this collective without facing an unduly burdensome process. Formal religious conversion is a formidable barrier to entry.

One way of mitigating this problem is to relax the standards for religious conversion. I'd certainly favor that. In principle I would also favor creating some method of secular conversion. It might require learning about the Jewish religion, history, and culture. One might need to pass a test. There have been discussions within the Jewish community about creating such an option, but the idea has never come to fruition, in part because there is no institutional mechanism for bringing it about.

There is no American Jewish community as a whole. The Big Tent doesn't exist. There are only diverse subgroups with different standards of admission.

Daniel Elazar, an Israeli-born political scientist who spent much of his time in the United States, has made this argument:

> The American Jewish community is built on an associational base to a far greater extent than that of any other in Jewish history. In other words, not only is there no external or internal compulsion to affiliate with organized Jewry, but also there is no automatic way to become a member of the Jewish community. Nor is there even a clear way to affiliate with the community as a whole. To participate in any organized Jewish life in America one must make a voluntary association with some particular organization or institution.[17]

The "American Jewish community," and my notion of a "Big Tent" are metaphors. There is no gatekeeper, akin to a night-club bouncer, for the community as a whole. American Jews don't have a formal umbrella organization that speaks for the entire community. But most Jews do feel connected to some sort of collective enterprise that is not simply religious, and the various subgroups seem to acknowledge some link with each other. I want to keep this tribal dimension alive but to make it a tribe of choice.

It's unworkable. Mnookin, who are you kidding? Many Jews, especially those who are traditionally observant, will not accept many of your "Jews" as "really Jewish."

This is no doubt true. Many Jews think the matrilineal principle should be the *only* standard, for all purposes. That's why my standard has two parts. Under the second part, traditionally observant Jews can impose this boundary for those organizations they control.

Where do I end up?

The challenge of deciding who counts as Jewish has no simple answer. What I'm really arguing for is greater tolerance for ambiguity. The Jewish community has evolved for thousands of years and is still evolving. The American community is increasingly diverse. Conflicting standards already exist. The intermarriage rate is exploding. Instead of fighting this trend, which I think is futile, we should find a productive way to address it.

My biggest quarrel is with the Orthodox, both here and in Israel, who purport to be gatekeepers for the entire community. I do not want the religious authorities, either here or in Israel, to decide who gets to be part of the family—especially in America. I'm not asking the Orthodox to give up the way they interpret Jewish law; they can set the standards for their own community of worship. I'm asking them to be more tolerant.

For example, I'd like them to stop telling people, "You're not Jewish." When they meet a self-identified Jew who doesn't meet their standards, I would frankly hope they'd say nothing. But if they feel compelled to make a comment, I hope they'd say something like, "By my standard you are not Jewish, but I recognize that you see it differently." And to say it with respect.

What I'm trying to get at is a level of generosity. A recognition that there is no standard that neatly solves all problems. An acknowledgment that, as a practical matter, American Jews do have the gift of individual choice. Let's reach out to those who might be reachable. Welcome everyone who wants to come in.

8

CAN WE SURVIVE ACCEPTANCE?

EVERY YEAR THE American Jewish Committee polls Jews and asks, "In your opinion, is anti-Semitism currently a problem in the United States?" In 2017 more than eight in ten respondents (84 percent) said yes, and about half of those characterized it as a "very serious problem."[1] At first glance this may seem surprising.

Jews are more accepted and better integrated in America today than they have ever been, in any time or place in a Diaspora community. Since World War II, institutionalized anti-Semitism has virtually disappeared. Jews no longer face discrimination in employment, education, housing, and other areas, and they are thriving in virtually every field of public life. Indeed, if Americans are guilty of bias toward Jews, it is arguably in the form of *philo*-Semitism: according to the Pew Research Center, Jews are the nation's most highly regarded religious group.[2] And yet most American Jews still see anti-Semitism as a problem.

This paradox lies at the heart of this chapter.

To be sure, anti-Semitic attitudes and stereotypes have not been eradicated in America. The white supremacists who marched in Charlottesville, Virginia, in 2017 provided dramatic proof that hate groups such as neo-Nazis still exist—and are speaking out more boldly than at any time since the 1940s. Nor was Charlottesville an isolated event. A spike in anti-Semitic incidents in 2016 and 2017 seemed to confirm the worst Jewish fears: that anti-Semitism may be poised for a serious comeback.

Although I'm troubled by this increase in anti-Semitic incidents and rhetoric, I don't share the fear that Jews are in danger of renewed persecution in this country, certainly not of the pervasive sort they suffered in earlier times. *Structural* barriers to Jewish success have disappeared, and they're not coming back. Although hate groups have recently been more active than they had been in many decades—spewing venom not just against Jews but also blacks, gays, immigrants, liberals, Muslims, and others—they do not seem to represent the views of many. When their attacks occasionally command media attention, leaders across the political spectrum broadly condemn them as "un-American." Although it's too soon to predict the impact of the alt-right movement, I don't think it has the power to reverse sixty years of civil rights legislation and jurisprudence. Nor do I think it has the power to persuade most Americans to hate Jews.

Does this mean that Jews who see anti-Semitism as a problem in America are just being irrational? I don't think so. I've come to the conclusion that they are expressing a central aspect of Jewish identity: belonging to a minority group that has been hated and persecuted for two thousand years. Our long history of persecution, culminating in the Holocaust, cultivates a keen sensitivity to potential threats. Repeated oppression in Europe—even after many Jews believed they had successfully assimilated—indelibly shaped our culture of vigilance. In America anti-Semitism peaked during the first half of the twentieth century, and many Jews alive today have experienced it firsthand.

The irony, however, is that today the *decline* of anti-Semitism may pose the greater challenge to Jewish identity. Many Jews in my daughters' generation have never experienced a single act of anti-Semitic discrimination. For my grandchildren's generation, anti-Semitism is largely an artifact of history. As the memory of the Holocaust recedes, American Jews may lose this reason to identify as Jewish—and the community may lose an important source of social cohesion. How will we adapt to the fact that few Americans hate us anymore? We have long survived affliction. Can we survive acceptance?

SOURCES OF AMERICAN ANTI-SEMITISM

No one is born hating Jews—it must be learned. For most of American history Jews have made up less than 1 percent of the population (never more than 4 percent and only about 2 percent today). Yet many Americans—even those who have never met a Jew—have harbored anti-Semitic attitudes. How did these beliefs and stereotypes become part of American culture?

According to historian Leonard Dinnerstein, Christianity provided the most important foundation. "It cannot be emphasized too strongly," he writes, "that all aspects of American antisemitism are built on this foundation of Christian hostility toward Jews."[3] Beginning in the early Christian era, he notes, "animosity toward Jews was not only encouraged [by Christian leaders] but also lauded as a religious virtue."[4] The Europeans who settled America brought this prejudice with them.

Of course, not all Christians throughout history were anti-Semites, and other factors contributed too: economic crises, wars, and waves of immigration, for which the Jews were often blamed. But "without the underlying base of deeply ingrained and culturally accepted Christian teachings to build on," Dinnerstein writes, "none of the other factors would explain a prejudice that has lasted for almost two thousand years."[5]

The most insidious Christian teaching was the charge that "the Jews" were responsible for killing Jesus.[6] The New Testament provides abundant support for this accusation. The Gospel of John refers nine times to "the Jews" as those who urged or aided in Jesus's execution. The Gospel of Matthew states, in a key passage, that Pontius Pilate gave a crowd of Jews the choice of releasing either Jesus or the notorious criminal Barabbas. According to Matthew, the Jews chose Barabbas and said of the condemned Jesus, "His blood be on us and on our children."[7] To many Christians this passage justified the idea that the Jews deserved the subsequent fate God imposed on them: the destruction of their Temple, the loss of their homeland, and eternal punishment, with conversion to Christianity their only hope of salvation.[8]

The Jews' second crime, in Christian eyes, was their refusal to accept Christ as their savior. Christian animosity "arose out of the religious conflict between Judaism and Christianity, which was focused on the rejection of the Christian Messiah by the Jews."[9] By the eleventh century most of Europe was Christian, and the conversion of the Jews became an obsession. As a result, Christians demonized Jews as "devils from Hell, enemies of the human race."[10]

Christian folklore—stories, jokes, songs, and proverbs—also fostered negative stereotypes of Jews.[11] Three ideas have been especially damaging.

The Blood Libel. Originating in the twelfth century, this was the long-lived accusation that Jews killed Christian children to obtain blood for ritual purposes. One common variant was that Jews required human— and preferably Christian—blood to bake matzo for Passover. There have been about 150 recorded cases of blood libel, most in the Middle Ages. "In almost every case, Jews were murdered, sometimes by a mob, sometimes following torture and a trial."[12] Even modern Americans were not immune to this calumny. In 1928 a four-year-old girl went missing in Massena, New York, two days before Yom Kippur. A rumor spread that Jews had killed her, and a state trooper questioned the local rabbi about Jewish ritual practices involving blood. The girl was found alive and unharmed a few hours later.[13]

The Greedy Jew. The image of the Jew as a scheming, blood-sucking usurer also dates to the Middle Ages. In the eighth century Jews began to specialize in trade and moneylending in the Muslim world, where Muslims were prohibited from charging interest on loans. When Jews brought these skills to medieval Christian Europe, where the Catholic Church also banned usury, they became targets of mistrust and resentment.[14] Christian mythology portrayed the Jew as a "vastly powerful, manipulative, corrupt, devious, cunning, greedy, tricky, materialistic, dishonest, shrewd, grasping, and close-fisted man who would do anything to acquire and hold onto gold."[15]

No literary figure embodies this caricature better than Shylock, the Jewish money lender in Shakespeare's *Merchant of Venice*, who demands a pound of flesh as payment for a loan. Shylock has few redeeming qualities, although Shakespeare did give him a moving speech suggesting that Jews are no different from Christians and deserve empathy as well. ("Hath not a Jew eyes?")[16] The play's "happy ending" involves Shylock's daughter Jessica's marriage to a Christian and abandonment of her father, followed by Shylock's own forced conversion to Christianity.[17] Whatever

Shakespeare's intention, anti-Semites, including the Nazis, have used the play to reinforce stereotypes against Jews.

The International Jewish Conspiracy. A third strand of anti-Semitic folklore portrays the Jews as a powerful cabal trying to destroy Christian civilization and control the world. This myth typically emphasizes the Jews' status as a separate "people," loyal only to each other, and their dominance in economic sectors such as banking and the media.

The *Protocols of the Elders of Zion* exemplifies this enduring fear of Jewish conspiracy. The *Protocols*, first printed in Russia in 1903, purported to be the minutes of a late nineteenth-century meeting where Jewish leaders plotted world domination through control of the press and the world's economies, the undermining of Christian morals, and the subversion of national governments. The *Protocols* remained rather obscure until after the Russian Revolution, when they gained broad circulation and were used to blame the Jews for the revolution.

In fact, the *Protocols* were a fraud. No such meetings ever took place. Much of the text was plagiarized from several earlier texts. The forgery was first exposed in 1921 by Philip Graves, a reporter for *The Times* of London,[18] and followed by other proof,[19] but this had little impact on those who wanted to believe in a Jewish conspiracy. The believers included Henry Ford, the American auto magnate and industrial hero, who said, "The only statement I care to make about the *Protocols* is that they fit in with what is going on."[20] To this day the *Protocols* are cited in the Middle East—by the Hamas Covenant of 1988[21] and the Saudi Education Ministry[22]—to prove the existence of a Jewish conspiracy.

These teachings and folklore are woven into the story of Jews in America. The history of American anti-Semitism can be roughly divided into three periods: the colonial era to about 1880, when Jews encountered some prejudice but also found great opportunity; 1880 to 1945, when anti-Semitism peaked; and 1945 to the present, when hatred of Jews was replaced by extraordinary acceptance. We will also see that no matter how much prejudice Jews met in America, they still fared better here than their counterparts did in Europe.

COLONIAL PERIOD TO 1880

The first Jewish settlers in the New World immediately faced anti-Semitism. In 1654 twenty-three Dutch Jews arrived in New Amsterdam (later New York). Their ancestors had originally fled the Spanish and Portuguese Inquisitions, found a haven in Holland, and later settled in the Dutch colony of Recife, Brazil. The twenty-three refugees had fled Recife because it had just been taken over by Portugal. Fearing the Portuguese would establish the Inquisition in Recife, this tiny group of Jews had sailed to the nearest Dutch colony in search of religious tolerance.

Instead they encountered Peter Stuyvesant, the director-general of New Amsterdam, who wanted to expel them immediately. Stuyvesant, a devout member of the Dutch Reformed Church, the colony's only recognized faith, wrote to the Dutch West India Company for permission to expel the Jews, calling them a deceitful race, repugnant, "hateful enemies and blasphemers of the name of Christ."[23]

The refugees, desperate and nearly penniless, got word to the Jewish community in Amsterdam, which took action. Jewish merchants in Amsterdam wrote a letter to the Dutch West India Company, which governed the colony, urging that the refugees be allowed to stay. (Among other arguments, the merchants pointed out that some Jews were principal shareholders in the company.)[24] The directors granted the request and ordered Stuyvesant to stand down. Later that year the settlers established Congregation Shearith Israel, a congregation that continues in New York to this day.[25]

Few Jews came to America in the colonial period. Those who did were permitted to practice their religion and could own property, but they were a long way from gaining religious equality or full political rights. Jews, Catholics, Baptists, Presbyterians, Quakers, and other religious minorities were *tolerated* by the majority Puritans and Anglicans but not exactly welcome; in most colonies they were denied the right to vote or hold public office.

When the United States was formed, the Jewish presence was minuscule. In 1790 there were only about fourteen hundred Jews.[26] "By the onset of the American Revolution, six congregations"—in New York, Philadelphia, Richmond, Charleston, Newport, and Savannah—existed, and they "were geographically isolated from each other."[27]

In 1790 George Washington, the first president, provided Newport's synagogue with reassurance about the new nation's commitment to religious freedom. While visiting Newport on a tour to drum up support for the Bill of Rights, Washington was greeted by prominent members of the community, some of whom read aloud letters of welcome. Among the greeters was the president of the Jewish congregation in Newport, who expressed the Jews' anxiety by raising the issue of discrimination.[28]

A few days later the president personally replied in a letter that one scholar calls "perhaps his most eloquent and famous pronouncement on religion."[29] Assuring the Jews that religious freedom was one of their "inherent natural rights," Washington continued, "Happily the Government of the United States, which gives to bigotry no sanction, to persecution no assistance, requires only that they who live under its protection should demean themselves as good citizens, in giving it on all occasions their effectual support."[30] With a flourish, the president displayed his fluency in the language of the Old Testament: "May the children of the fine stock of Abraham who dwell in this land continue to merit and enjoy the good will of the other inhabitants—while every one shall sit in safety under his own vine and fig tree and there shall be none to make him afraid."[31]

Washington's vision of peace under the fig trees, however, did not mean that Jews in the United States had complete political equality. The US Constitution, adopted in 1788, gave Jews and other religious minorities citizenship rights at the federal level.[32] That alone was a milestone. As historian Stanley Chyet notes, it was the first time in sixteen hundred years that a national government had granted citizenship to Jews.[33] At a time when the Jewish Question was still being bitterly debated in England and Europe, American Jews suddenly possessed greater political rights than Jews anywhere else in the world.

But at the time Washington wrote his reassuring letter, Jews were still second-class citizens under many state constitutions and would remain so until well into the nineteenth century. Most Americans believed that the country was a Protestant nation and that political rights should be reserved for Protestants or Christians.[34] In many states Jews could not hold office or vote. By 1840 twenty-one of the twenty-six states had granted Jews full political equality.[35] However, the issue of state citizenship was not fully settled until the Fourteenth Amendment was adopted in 1868.

Meanwhile, the anti-Semitism of Christian culture "festered beneath the surface."[36] Although individual Jews often fared well and were treated cordially by their Christian neighbors,[37] most Americans had never met a Jew and therefore had no personal knowledge to counteract the stereotypes. The result was a "pervasive tension between the 'mythological Jew,' that cursed figure of Christian tradition, and the 'Jew next door' who seemingly gave the lie to every element of the stereotype."[38]

Jews as a group were routinely denounced from Christian pulpits for refusing to accept Christianity.[39] Children's schoolbooks portrayed Jews as evildoers responsible for killing Christ.[40] As one children's book, published in 1848, stated, "The Jews are to be seen in every land. What is the reason for this? Why do they not live in a country of their own as we do? The reason is that they were disobedient to God."[41]

Despite such hostility toward Jews, during the first half of the nineteenth century Jews still fared better as a group than Irish Catholics and far better than Native Americans or African Americans.[42] As Jews spread throughout the country, many of them starting out as peddlers and later becoming successful merchants, they mixed socially with gentiles and, in some cities, attained positions of political power.[43] Still, the Jewish presence in America remained inconspicuous, at only about 0.5 percent of the population in 1860.[44]

The Civil War, however, brought anti-Semitic prejudice to a high boil.[45] There were Jews on both sides of the divide, as soldiers and civilians. Also on both sides were Jewish peddlers and merchants, who were reviled as profiteers and blamed for the economic upheaval of the period.[46] One newspaper attacked Jews as a "tribe of gold speculators" and "hooked nose wretches" who profited from disaster and "chuckled" as they "put money in their purse."[47]

Against this backdrop Union general Ulysses S. Grant committed a flagrantly bigoted act that he later regretted. Grant became convinced that Jewish profiteers were to blame for the booming black market in Southern cotton. In 1862 he issued General Order No. 11, which expelled all Jews "as a class" from Kentucky, Tennessee, and Mississippi—the entire area under his command.[48] It was "one of the most blatant official episodes of anti-Semitism in 19th-century American history."[49]

Grant's order did not have a substantial impact because President Lincoln revoked it a few days later—thanks to prompt action by the Jewish community. In Paducah, Kentucky, Jewish merchants immediately sent a telegram to Lincoln condemning the order as an "enormous outrage" and the "grossest violation of the Constitution."[50] Paducah merchant Cesar Kaskel then sped to Washington, joined up with a congressman, and met with Lincoln.[51] Because of slow communication between Grant's headquarters and the White House, Lincoln had not yet seen the order and was "surprise[d] that such an order should have been issued."[52] When he read Kaskel's copy, he instantly told the Army to revoke it.[53]

Grant went on to become a Civil War hero and then the Republican Party's presidential nominee in 1868. American Jews were sharply divided on whether to vote for Grant; some couldn't forgive him for Order No. 11.[54] In all events, before his inauguration Grant apologized for the order by allowing a private letter to be published in the newspapers. "I have no prejudice against sect or race, but want each individual to be judged by his own merit," the letter read. The order "never would have been issued if it had not been telegraphed the moment penned, without one moment's reflection."[55]

As president, Grant atoned further by taking significant actions in support of Jews. He appointed more Jews to government offices—and to higher posts—than any previous president.[56] He opposed a movement to make America officially a "Christian nation" that swore "allegiance to Jesus Christ."[57] He spoke out against the persecution of Jews in Russia and Romania.[58] When he died in 1885 he was mourned in synagogues across the country.[59]

According to historian Jonathan Sarna, Grant's presidency (1869–1877) was a brief "golden age" for Jews.[60] As they built new synagogues and temples across the country and became more socially integrated with gentiles, many Jews "optimistically assumed that prejudice against them would in time wither away."[61]

Social Segregation Among the Elite: 1880–1900

The "golden age" for Jews—to the extent it existed at all—ended in 1877 with an incident involving banker Joseph Seligman.

Seligman by then was a very wealthy and well-known financier. A German immigrant, he had begun his career as a peddler, built a successful clothing firm with his brothers, founded an international banking house, and become friends with Presidents Lincoln and Grant.[62] He supported the Union cause and helped found New York's elite Union League Club.[63] After the Civil War he was instrumental in retiring the national war debt.[64] Grant even asked him to become secretary of the Treasury, but Seligman declined.[65]

Seligman and his family summered every year in Saratoga Springs, a resort town favored by wealthy New Yorkers. For ten years the Seligmans had stayed at the posh Grand Union Hotel. But in June 1877 the family was turned away by the hotel's new "No Israelite" policy.

The episode caused a furor. The *New York Times* reported the story under the headline: "A sensation at saratoga."

> [Seligman's] family entered the parlors [of the hotel], and Mr. Seligman went to the manager to make arrangements for rooms. That gentleman seemed somewhat confused, and said: "Mr. Seligman, I am required to inform you that [owner] Mr. Hilton has given instructions that no Israelites shall be permitted in future to stop at this hotel."
>
> Mr. Seligman was so astonished that for some time he could make no reply. Then he said: "Do you mean to tell me that you will not entertain Jewish people?" "That is our orders, Sir," was the reply.

Before leaving the banker asked the reason why Jews were thus persecuted. Said he, "Are they dirty, do they misbehave themselves, or have they refused to pay their bills?"

"Oh, no," replied the manager, "there is no fault to be found in that respect. The reason is simply this: Business at the hotel was not good last season, and we had a large number of Jews here. Mr. Hilton came to the conclusion that Christians did not like their company, and for that reason shunned the hotel. He resolved to run the Union on a different principle this season, and gave us instructions to admit no Jew."[66]

The *Times* quoted the hotel's owner, Judge Henry Hilton (unrelated to Conrad Hilton), as saying the Jews "have brought the public opinion down on themselves by a vulgar ostentation, a puffed-up vanity,...and a general obtrusiveness that is frequently disgusting, and always repulsive to the well-bred."[67]

The incident drew wide press coverage, with editorials largely siding with Seligman.[68] But as the Saratoga affair played out, it emboldened other hotels and resorts to bar Jewish guests, with signs such as "No Jews or Dogs Admitted Here."[69] In 1879 railroad baron Austin Corbin announced that Jews were not welcome at his Coney Island hotels. "We do not like Jews as a class," he told one newspaper. "If this is a free country, why can't we be free of the Jews?"[70]

During the 1880s this social exclusion of Jews spread "like wildfire" within elite institutions.[71] In New York, Jews were banned from the Union League Club (despite the founding role of Joseph Seligman and his brother Jesse) and from the boards of directors of the Metropolitan Museum of Art and the New York Public Library, positions that represented the apex of New York society.[72] The pattern soon spread throughout the country to social clubs, country clubs, and private secondary schools.[73] These social limitations on Jews would persist in various forms for more than a hundred years.

This new form of bias translated anti-Semitic stereotypes into more pervasive social discrimination against Jews. To people like Judge Hilton, Jews were unwelcome not because they drank Christian blood but because they were nouveau riche, loud, and uncultured. Twentieth-century American literature contains many such portrayals of Jews. The stereotype of the vulgar Jew would find its way into many American novels of the early twentieth century, including Edith Wharton's *The House of Mirth*, F. Scott Fitzgerald's *The Great Gatsby*, and Ernest Hemingway's *The Sun Also Rises*.

IMMIGRATION MAKES THINGS WORSE: 1880–1945

Just as this sinister trend was unfolding, the massive wave of southern and Eastern European immigrants began to wash over America. To understand the enormity of this event, consider that by 1890 only about 15 million immigrants had come to the United States in the hundred years since the revolution. Fewer than 2 percent were Jews. By contrast, between 1890 and 1914 about 16.5 million immigrants arrived—most of them poor, uneducated, non-Anglo-Saxon, and non-Protestant. About 10 percent were Jews.[74] As a result, the Jewish population rose from a mere 250,000 in 1877 to more than 4 million in 1927.[75]

This influx, combined with the upheavals of World War I and the Bolshevik Revolution, spurred a vicious nativist backlash. Scientific racism and the eugenics movement swept the country, promoting the idea that these New Immigrants—especially the Jews—were of inferior racial stock and threatened the country's well-being.[76] Loud calls for immigration restrictions followed.

The passage of the National Origins Immigration (Johnson-Reed) Act of 1924 had tragic repercussions for Jews worldwide. The act not only kept Jewish families apart during the interwar years, but "when Jews most needed refuge, following Adolf Hitler's ascension to power in 1933, they found America's doors virtually barred."[77]

During the period between 1900 and 1945 Jews suffered more intense hostility than at any other time in American history. The venom took many forms, including physical attacks, demonization in the press, and institutional discrimination.

One notorious incident involved a lynching. Leo Frank was a Jew who managed a pencil factory in Atlanta, Georgia. In 1913 one of Frank's employees, thirteen-year-old Mary Phagan, was found strangled and dumped in the factory basement. Frank was tried, convicted, and sentenced to death as mobs outside the courthouse shouted, "Hang the Jew!"[78] After Frank's sentence was commuted to life in prison in 1915, a mob abducted him from the state penitentiary and lynched him. In fact, Frank was innocent. Almost seventy years later an eyewitness revealed that the killer was a janitor who had been the key witness against Frank.[79] The state of Georgia posthumously pardoned Frank in 1986.[80]

In the press Jews were vilified as scheming monopolists who would soon control the economy. The speed with which Jewish immigrants built successful businesses raised alarm; in 1913 an article in *McClure's Magazine* warned that "there is not the slightest doubt that in a few years the Jews will own the larger part of Manhattan Island" and that Jews would soon control so many trades and industries that they would financially take over the country.[81]

Henry Ford amplified these stereotypes and conspiracy theories, using his wealth to spread anti-Semitic propaganda through his weekly newspaper, *The Dearborn Independent*. In the 1920s the paper published a series called *The International Jew: The World's Problem*, which borrowed heavily from the *Protocols of the Elders of Zion* and claimed that Jews were plotting to take over the world.[82] The series was enormously influential, even beyond the United States.[83] At its peak Ford's newspaper boasted a circulation of seven hundred thousand—close to that of New York's *Daily News*, then the country's largest daily newspaper.[84]

The Great Depression inflamed this form of anti-Semitism even further. One sign of this was the immense popularity of Father Coughlin, who used dog-whistles like "international bankers" to attack Jews on his radio show. A Catholic priest who increasingly warmed to Nazism, Coughlin inveighed against the "evils of Communism, capitalism, labor unions, Wall Street, 'the international money-changers in the temple,' and dozens of other targets."[85] By the late 1930s "Coughlin learned to utilize the new medium and won an audience estimated at some 30 million. Even if only 10 million listened, this would still have been the largest radio audience in the world."[86]

Jews also had to deal with institutionalized anti-Semitism that resulted in pervasive discrimination in education, housing, and employment.

Although educational quotas had begun in private secondary schools in the late nineteenth century, many universities adopted them en masse in the 1920s. Harvard president A. Lawrence Lowell worried about a "Jewish problem" when the percentage of Jewish undergraduates reached 21.5 percent in 1922—an overrepresentation by a factor of ten.[87] Lowell stated that "the main problem caused by the increase in the number of Jews comes... from the fact that they form a very distinct body, and cling, or are driven, together, apart from the great mass of the undergraduates." He feared that an invasion of Jews "would mean the departure of the sons of the Protestant upper and upper-middle classes whom Harvard most wished to enroll."[88] Other university leaders shared this fear. Columbia College dean Frederick Paul Keppel warned that too many Jews might make the campus "socially uninviting to students who come from homes of refinement."[89] Apart from Harvard, the schools that subjected Jews to quotas included Yale, Columbia, Princeton, Duke, Rutgers, Barnard, Adelphi, Cornell, Johns Hopkins, Northwestern, Penn State, Ohio State, Washington and Lee, as well as the Universities of Cincinnati, Illinois, Kansas, Minnesota, Texas, Virginia, and Washington.[90] As Dartmouth president Ernest Hopkins explained, "Any college which is going to base its admissions wholly on scholastic standing will find itself with an infinitesimal proportion of anything else than Jews eventually."[91]

Jews also found themselves unwelcome to live in some of the country's best neighborhoods, where developers added restrictive deed covenants to prohibit sales to Jews and blacks.[92] In 1924 my grandfather George Sittenfeld bought a home at 801 Westover Road, in the heart of Kansas City's upscale "Country Club District." But he could do so only with the help of a gentile friend, who served as a "straw purchaser" who then transferred the deed to my grandparents.

Employment discrimination was rampant in white-collar jobs, from medicine and law to universities, banks, factories, and publishing houses. Newspapers ran "Help Wanted" ads indicating that "Christians only" should apply. As one factory owner put it, with unintentional irony, "We try to have only white American Christians in our factory regardless of religion."[93]

Notwithstanding pervasive discrimination, American Jews were remarkably resourceful. They created their own subeconomy and alternative institutions. They built their own law firms, hospitals, country clubs, fraternities and sororities, hotels, resorts, and neighborhoods. They flocked to colleges that would accept them, especially to City College of New York, which became known as the "Jewish Harvard."[94]

They also developed permanent defense organizations to fight prejudice and discrimination. The American Jewish Committee (AJC), founded in 1906, was headed by Louis Marshall, who would later broker an apology from Henry Ford for his series on "The International Jew" and effectively shut down the *Dearborn Independent*.[95] The Anti-Defamation League of B'nai, B'rith (ADL) was founded in 1913, the same year Leo Frank was convicted of murder in Atlanta.[96] The American Jewish Congress was founded in 1922, initially to promote Zionism as well as fight discrimination.

Until World War II these institutions mainly worked behind the scenes, afraid that strenuous public advocacy of Jewish interests would invite retaliation.[97] As Professor Steven Windmueller has written, "There was major debate among the main Jewish defense organizations about what strategies to take toward the rise of the Nazis in Germany. The American Jewish Congress advocated a highly public campaign, whereas the American Jewish Committee favored low-key diplomatic initiatives."[98] But during the war, as evidence of the Holocaust became apparent, American Jewish organizations became more forceful in fighting discrimination in the United States.[99] After World War II these organizations would begin to have a far-reaching impact.

BARRIERS FALL

World War II ended with Japan's surrender on September 2, 1945. Six days later Bess Myerson, the daughter of a Bronx house painter, was crowned the first—and, so far, only—Jewish Miss America. In an era when the Miss America pageant defined American femininity, Myerson's victory struck many Jews as a hopeful sign of acceptance. As historian Edward Shapiro observed, "Not only did it vindicate their pride in being

Jews, but it was also [a] reproach to those who questioned their status as Americans."[100]

Over the next few decades American attitudes toward Jews underwent a profound shift. Anti-Semitic comments became socially unacceptable in public. Major economic barriers in education, employment, and housing virtually disappeared, and, to an extraordinary degree, Jews became integrated.

How did so much change take place so quickly? Many factors contributed. After the war a booming peacetime economy led to a surge of optimism, reducing the need for ethnic scapegoats.[101] The knowledge of the Holocaust curbed anti-Semitic commentary, at least in public; after 1945 few Americans wanted to be compared to the Nazis.[102] Indeed, anti-Semitism came to be viewed as "un-American." President Harry Truman provided leadership by calling for civil rights legislation banning discrimination in higher education, employment, and other areas.[103]

Jews played an active role in this change, "founding and funding of some of the most important civil rights organizations."[104] Jews worked alongside African Americans to pass the Civil Rights Act of 1964, the Voting Rights Act of 1965, and the Fair Housing Act of 1968.

To understand these changes and their effect on American Jews, it's helpful to distinguish between anti-Semitic *behavior* and anti-Semitic *attitudes*.

THE DECLINE OF INSTITUTIONALIZED DISCRIMINATION AGAINST JEWS

By the late 1960s educational quotas limiting Jewish enrollment in colleges and professional schools had disappeared, even at the most elite institutions.[105]

Discrimination at resorts and hotels also declined quickly. By 1964 about 90 percent of resort hotels welcomed Jews.[106] The rest were soon forced to do so by the passage of laws such as the federal Civil Rights Act of 1964, which explicitly prohibits discrimination in "public accommodations" based on race, religion, or national origin.[107] All but five states have enacted similar public accommodation laws.[108]

Housing discrimination was dealt an early blow in a 1948 Supreme Court decision, *Shelley v. Kraemer*, which declared restrictive covenants unenforceable in court.[109] By the 1960s new federal and state laws banned "gentleman's agreements" and other tacit forms of housing discrimination, but widespread change took decades, especially in easing housing discrimination against African Americans.[110]

Economic factors sometimes provided an extra catalyst. The wealthy beachside community of La Jolla, California, largely excluded Jews until about 1960. Though state law had banned restrictive housing practices in 1959,[111] informal and unwritten practices only broke down when the University of California decided to open a campus in San Diego. As Roger Revelle, a prominent local scientist, later recalled, "You can't have a university without having Jewish professors. The Real Estate Broker's Association and their supporters in La Jolla had to make up their minds whether they wanted a university or an anti-Semitic covenant. You couldn't have both."[112] The brokers voted with their wallets.

Employment barriers against Jews subsided unevenly. Beginning in the 1950s some law firms, hospitals, and university departments that had been closed to Jews began to open, but only to a limited degree. Corporate America took longer to hire and promote Jews, especially to executive positions.[113] In 1965 fewer than 1 percent of the executives in heavy industry were Jews, although Jews made up 25 percent of Ivy League graduates.[114] Like other forms of institutional bias, discrimination in conservative sectors—banks, public utilities, insurance companies, and other large corporations—may have been reinforced by social discomfort. As a labor economist explained in 1978, "the upper echelons in American business were not so much anti-Semitic as they were ill-at-ease with Jews in their midst; they found them 'too intellectual.' "[115]

But progress was made. In 1973, when Irving Shapiro became CEO of DuPont, the news made national headlines.[116] By the 1980s even the WASPy commercial banking sector began to welcome Jews.[117]

Universities moved slowly in hiring Jews for the very top administrative positions. In 1966 fewer than 1 percent of the nation's university presidents were Jews.[118] That, too, changed in the 1980s and 1990s, when more than fifteen Jewish university presidents were appointed,[119] including Michael Sovern (Columbia 1980), Harold Shapiro (Princeton 1988), and Richard Levin (Yale 1993). Larry Summers became the first Jewish president of Harvard in 2001.[120] Today the Jewish identity of many university administrators is an unremarkable distinction—and a factor irrelevant to their appointments.

Private social and country clubs proved most resistant to dropping restrictive practices. The AJC started tracking this issue in the 1950s, and in 1965 it identified social clubs as the "last citadel" of discrimination.[121] The AJC took such segregation seriously not only because it perpetuated bigotry in general but also because corporate promotion often depended on belonging to the right club.[122] Many WASP clubs—and their Jewish counterparts—did not drop their exclusionary practices until the 1980s and 1990s. When they did, it was largely due to a mix of public pressure (mostly related to race and gender discrimination),[123] state laws (revoking tax exemptions and liquor licenses for clubs that discriminate), financial necessity (in cases of declining membership), and the distaste that a younger generation felt for self-segregated clubs.

When I was growing up in the 1950s no Jewish families were members of our city's most elite country club—the Kansas City Country Club. That remained true until 1990, when the golfer Tom Watson resigned from the club after Henry Bloch, a founder of the tax-preparation firm H&R Block, was denied membership, reportedly because he was Jewish. Watson is not Jewish, but his then wife and two children are, and he said the club's failure to admit Bloch was "something that I personally can't live with."[124] Watson's resignation was widely reported in the national press, and the club admitted Bloch a week later as its first Jewish member.[125]

The Decline in Anti-Semitic Attitudes

Although new laws make a difference, institutional change rests on cultural change. With respect to Jews, one of the biggest cultural shifts occurred in public discourse. Within twenty years of World War II overt anti-Semitic comments became unacceptable and all but disappeared from public discourse.[126]

A variety of factors nudged progress along. In the immediate postwar period anti-Semitism was for the first time identified and openly discussed as a social problem. A profusion of books, many by Jewish authors, featured sympathetic Jewish characters and "condemned antisemitism as un-American."[127] One example was *Gentleman's Agreement* (1947), a best-selling novel by Jewish author Laura Z. Hobson that was made into a popular, Oscar-winning movie of the same name.[128]

The movie features a gentile journalist, Phil Green (played by Gregory Peck), who poses as a Jew, "Phil Greenberg," in order to write a magazine exposé on the anti-Semitism then pervasive in WASP America. While masquerading as a Jew, Phil experiences social insults: he is turned away from a fancy hotel because he is a Jew, and his young son is called a "dirty Jew" at school. Phil's secretary reveals that she is Jewish but changed her name to get the job (after being rejected under her real name). Phil's childhood friend, also Jewish, cannot find a landlord who will rent to him. In 1947 such portrayals in the movies were new and influential.[129]

Another important factor was the initiative Christian leaders took to acknowledge and denounce the anti-Semitic stereotypes long promoted in Christian teachings. In 1964 the House of Bishops of the Episcopal Church in the United States rejected the charge of deicide against the Jews and condemned anti-Semitism.[130] The following year the Second Vatican Council of the Catholic Church issued its own historic statement repudiating collective Jewish guilt in the death of Jesus Christ. The Vatican also denounced all forms of anti-Semitism, embraced the Jewish roots of Christianity, affirmed God's covenant with the Jews as his chosen people, and prohibited religious teachings that portrayed the Jews as "accursed."[131] In later years other Christian denominations issued similar statements.[132]

When anti-Semites did engage in public discourse—for example, shouting anti-Semitic rhetoric at rallies organized by neo-Nazis or the Ku Klux Klan—they were considered part of the extremist fringe and universally condemned.

In fact, negative stereotyping of Jews became so politically incorrect that when individual Jews became involved in economic scandals and disasters, the public reports did not attribute their behavior to them being Jewish. Consider the insider-trading scandals of the mid-1980s, featuring Wall Street investment bankers Ivan Boesky and Michael Milken; the investment fraud of financier Bernard Madoff, whose massive Ponzi scheme was uncovered in 2008; and the global financial crisis that began in 2008, in which many American Jewish investment bankers were implicated. In each case many American Jews braced themselves for an anti-Semitic backlash. Some Americans did blame "the Jews" in private. According to a survey of almost three thousand Americans published in the *Boston Review* in 2009, researchers found that a "strikingly high" number—about 25 percent—of non-Jewish respondents blamed "the Jews" at least a "moderate" amount for the 2008 financial crisis, and almost 40 percent attributed at least some blame to the group.[133] But despite what some Americans were thinking in private, no public backlash occurred.

WHERE ARE WE TODAY?

Jews are now so well integrated into American life—with three Supreme Court justices, thirty members of Congress,[134] scores of university presidents, and legions of corporate CEOs—that their Jewish heritage often goes unmentioned. In politics this change has been especially marked. When Joseph Lieberman, an Orthodox Jew, became the Democratic vice presidential candidate in 2000, his heritage was widely cited as a sign of Jewish progress. In 2016, when presidential candidate Bernie Sanders's Jewish background was barely noted in the press, that was celebrated as a sign of even *greater* progress. "It's the lack of attention to Sanders's Judaism that Jewish leaders find most exciting," *The Atlantic* noted, and it quoted a rabbi as saying, "It's the most wonderful anti-climax in American Jewish history."[135]

By one measure Jews may be the most highly regarded religious group in the country. In 2017 the Pew Research Center asked Americans to rate religious groups on a "feeling thermometer" ranging from 0 (coldest) to 100 (warmest). Jews had the warmest overall rating of any religious group, at 67 degrees.[136]

Despite this generally very positive picture, many American Jews have been reluctant to accept the good news. Consider this example from 1985. In an informal poll San Francisco–area Jews were asked whether they thought a Jew could be elected to Congress from San Francisco. One-third said it could not be done. At the time all three members of Congress from the city and its contiguous districts were Jewish.[137]

Are today's Jews similarly out of touch with objective facts? As I mentioned above, every year the AJC asks, "In your opinion, is anti-Semitism currently a problem in the United States?" In 2017, 41 percent characterized it as a "very serious problem" and 43 percent as "somewhat of a problem."[138] This view was consistent with decades of earlier surveys. Twenty years earlier the results were even more pessimistic, with 95 percent of respondents saying anti-Semitism was a problem.[139]

As I've shown, the most pernicious form of anti-Semitism—institutionalized discrimination—is gone, and I think most Jews would agree with that. What are they really worried about? Today, as I write this book, many Jews are alarmed by the election of President Trump, the divisiveness of the public discourse, the ascendancy of the alt-right, and the growth of hate speech on the internet. Jews were shocked by the march in Charlottesville, at which white nationalists and neo-Nazis shouted anti-Semitic slogans. Many fear that Charlottesville is just the start of a much more serious trend in which anti-Semitism infects broader political movements, perhaps even the Republican Party. There is also concern that some leaders on the political left unfairly criticize Israel and minimize the pervasive anti-Semitism that still exists outside of America.

When I started writing this book in 2015 I was confident that fears of a sharp resurgence of American anti-Semitism were unwarranted. With the recent rise in anti-Jewish activity, I am less certain. Let's take a closer look at three phenomena that seem to provoke the most fear among Jews: hate crimes (and other hostile incidents), private prejudice, and criticism of Israel.

HOSTILE BEHAVIOR TOWARD JEWS: HATE CRIMES AND ANTI-SEMITIC INCIDENTS

Two agencies, the FBI and the ADL, make it their business to track anti-Semitic activity in the United States. The FBI data strongly suggest that anti-Semitic activity has *decreased* over the past twenty years; the ADL's reports do not.

Since 1990 the FBI has collected data on hate crimes: those that "manifest evidence of prejudice based on race, religion, sexual orientation or ethnicity."[140] These broad surveys, despite their methodological limitations,[141] offer a way to assess how Jews compare to other targets of hate crimes. Blacks are by far the most frequent victims: 29 percent of all reported hate crimes are directed at them. Whites are the second most frequently targeted group (12 percent), followed closely by Jews (11 percent) and gay males (10 percent).[142]

Notably, crimes against Jews follow an unusual pattern: whereas most hate crimes against other groups involve physical violence and intimidation, most anti-Jewish crimes are aimed at property. Killings motivated by anti-Semitism are extremely rare; in most years none are reported.[143] Assaults are infrequent. In 2016 the most recent year for which statistics are available, the FBI reported only seventy-three assaults motivated by anti-Jewish bias.[144] Most hate crimes against Jews involve vandalism and other property damage.[145] Moreover, over the past twenty years, despite yearly fluctuations, *the total number of FBI-reported anti-Semitic crimes has dropped by about 38 percent.*[146]

The ADL has been tracking anti-Semitic "incidents"—a much broader category than hate crimes—since 1979.[147] In addition to criminal acts, the ADL counts behavior that is lawful: public demonstrations by hate groups, insults, threats, hate mail, and "distribution of hateful materials."[148] It compiles data from not just law enforcement agencies but also community leaders and individuals, which is why its numbers are higher than the FBI's.

The ADL's numbers climbed during the 1980s and early 1990s, partly due to increased reporting of hate crimes by law enforcement, and hit a peak of 2,066 incidents in 1994.[149] This is a small number—and again, physical assaults were rare; the vast majority of incidents related to vandalism and harassment. Over the next three years the totals dropped by 24 percent. "The way it stands now," Spencer Blakeslee wrote in 2000, "the probability of any of America's nearly six million Jews being directly involved in an antisemitic incident approaches the infinitesimal. Jews have never been safer in America than they are today."[150] The number of yearly incidents hit a low of 751 in 2013.

But beginning in 2016 the ADL's numbers increased substantially: to 1,267 in 2016 and to 1,986 in 2017.[151] The biggest increase was in the category of vandalism. Incidents at K–12 schools and college campuses also surged, involving both harassment and the drawing of swastikas.[152] (The number of assaults fell.) The ADL attributed this rise to the divisiveness of the 2016 presidential election[153] and a "rising climate of incivility" that had emboldened hate groups generally.[154]

This recent spike in activity, however, doesn't explain why many American Jews think anti-Semitism remains a serious problem. This worldview among Jews has persisted for decades, and I believe three factors can explain it.

One factor, as I've mentioned, is our history. Given centuries of persecution and the trauma of the Holocaust, our anti-Semitic "Geiger counters" are extremely sensitive.

Another factor is that the most dramatic incidents are conspicuously reported in the press, even when the perpetrators' intentions are not known, making it hard for Jews to put individual events in perspective.

In early 2017, for example, 163 bomb threats were made against Jewish community centers across the country. No bombs were found, but the centers had to be temporarily evacuated. The threats were alarming but not, it turned out, evidence of anti-Semitism.

The person responsible for the vast majority of these threats was a Jewish teenager, age eighteen, who lived in Israel with dual citizenship and, according to his lawyer, suffered from "a brain tumor that could affect his behavior."[155] Such so-called telephone terrorism can't be considered evidence that American anti-Semitism is a "very serious problem" or that hate crimes against Jews are on an upward trajectory.

A few months later, in the summer of 2017, the New England Holocaust Memorial in Boston—consisting of six glass towers—was vandalized twice, two months apart. In both incidents the perpetrator threw rocks at the memorial and shattered huge panes of glass. These widely reported incidents were similarly painful to Jews but not evidence of anti-Semitism. One culprit turned out to be a homeless twenty-one-year-old with a history of mental illness. The other was a seventeen-year-old whose motive was not known.[156] Although neither incident was reported to the FBI as a hate crime, the press reports were deeply jarring to many Boston-area Jews—especially the second incident, which occurred just three days after the rally in Charlottesville.

The vivid television images broadcast from Charlottesville, of course, offered real evidence of hatred: hundreds of white supremacists marching at night with torches, chanting "Jews will not replace us" and Nazi slogans like "Blood and Soil." What does such an incident mean?

It's too soon to tell whether the rally augurs significant growth in anti-Semitic hate groups. I'm certainly more cautious in my outlook than I was before. According to the Southern Poverty Law Center, the number of hate groups overall has risen from 892 in 2015 to 954 in 2017. Within the white supremacist movement the number of neo-Nazi groups rose by 22 percent (from 99 to 121) in 2017 alone.[157]

On the positive side, the Charlottesville rally was a public relations disaster for white supremacy. With the notable exception of President Trump, political leaders were unanimous in lambasting the white nationalists who brawled with counterprotesters.[158] When President Trump responded tepidly to the event and then commented that there were "very fine people" on both sides, he was bombarded with criticism. CEOs quit the president's business councils in such large numbers that the groups were disbanded.[159] Lawmakers from both parties assailed him for failing to respond appropriately. In fact, Congress passed a unanimous resolution calling on Trump to condemn hate groups, which he signed. I believe most Americans deplore hate-based behavior and will continue to do so.

A third factor in Jewish assessment of these incidents may be the alarmist approach adopted by Jewish advocacy organizations, especially the ADL. The ADL plays an important role in keeping both Jews and policymakers aware of the risks of anti-Semitism, both in America and worldwide, but it often exaggerates those risks in language that the mainstream media typically quotes verbatim.

Take, for example, the headline on this ADL press release: "Anti-Semitic Assaults Rise Dramatically Across the Country in 2015." As it turns out, in the entire nation the ADL found there were twenty more assaults in 2015 than in 2014. Does a national increase from thirty-six assaults to a still-minuscule fifty-six assaults qualify as dramatic?

Even more striking was the ADL's approach to the 163 bomb threats in 2017. Although virtually all of them had been attributed to the disturbed Jewish teenager in Israel (who has since been indicted), the ADL included them in its "harassment" statistics for 2017 and insisted they were evidence of anti-Semitism. "The motive may have been unclear, but the impact was crystal clear," Jonathan Greenblatt, chief executive of the ADL, told the *New York Times*. "These were acts that terrorized a community just because of their faith."[160] By including these threats in its 2017 report, the ADL was able to claim a dramatic 41 percent spike in harassment cases in just one year instead of a less dramatic 18 percent without those cases.[161] As the report explained, "ADL included the bomb threats in the total count because, regardless of the motivation of any specific perpetrator, Jewish communities were repeatedly traumatized by these assaults on their institutions and threats to their safety."

I reject such reasoning because it ignores the motivation of the perpetrator. The word "anti-Semitic" has everything to do with the actor's motivation, in my view, and not with the impact on Jews. There was no evidence that a hatred of Jews motivated this troubled Jewish teenager: he has also been charged with making bomb threats against airports and selling his threat services on the internet.[162] Much as I value the ADL's role as a watchdog, I don't believe the Jewish community is well served by such hype.

Hostile Attitudes Toward Jews: Negative Stereotypes

Aside from the small number of hate groups and individuals who engage in threatening behavior, Jews also worry about private attitudes held by the broader public. Some Jews fear that anti-Semitic stereotypes haven't so much declined as gone dormant, apt to reawaken at any moment. This fear causes some Jews to experience a situation or remark as anti-Semitic even when they don't know the speaker's intent.

What does the data show?

Anti-Semitic attitudes are notoriously difficult to measure accurately, but what polling data we have suggests a substantial decline. For many years the AJC asked a sample of Americans: "Have you heard any criticism or talk against the Jews in the last six months?" Between 1946 and 1951 those responding "yes" dropped sharply from 64 percent to 16 percent.[163]

Poll Question: Have you heard any criticism or talk against the Jews in the last six months? (*percentage*)

	Yes	No
1940	46	52
1942	52	44
1944	60	37
1946	64	34
1950	24	75
1951	16	84
1953	21	79
1954	14	86
1955	13	87
1956	11	89
1957	16	84
1959	12	88

Source: Leonard Dinnerstein, *Antisemitism in America* (New York: Oxford University Press, 2004), 151.

Another AJC poll asked gentile respondents to name "any nationality, religious, or racial groups in this country that are a threat to America." In 1946, 18 percent cited Jews. In 1954 barely 1 percent did.[164]

The best-known data on attitudes toward Jews is collected by the ADL, which has conducted national telephone surveys since 1964. These surveys ask gentile respondents to answer "probably true" or "probably false" to the following eleven statements:[165]

1. Jews stick together more than other Americans.
2. Jews always like to be at the head of things.
3. Jews are more loyal to Israel than America.
4. Jews have too much power in the United States today.
5. Jews have too much control and influence on Wall Street.
6. Jews have too much power in the business world.
7. Jews have a lot of irritating faults.
8. Jews are more willing than others to use shady practices to get what they want.
9. Jewish business people are so shrewd that others don't have a fair chance at competition.
10. Jews don't care what happens to anyone but their own kind.
11. Jews are (not) just as honest as other business people.

The ADL uses these statements as a "key index" to assess the extent to which the American public has "anti-Semitic propensities."

For each respondent the ADL counts the number of "probably true" answers. Respondents who agree with zero or one of the key statements are considered "essentially free" of prejudice toward Jews. Those who agree with two to five statements are considered "neither prejudiced nor unprejudiced." Those who agree with six or more statements are considered the "most anti-Semitic group of Americans"—that is, to have anti-Semitic "propensities." For this last group the ADL provides demographic information related to age, race, and education.

On this basis, the data suggests a striking improvement in American attitudes over time. Between 1964 and 2016 the proportion of those with anti-Semitic propensities has dropped by half—from 29 percent to 14 percent.[166]

The 2016 report contains other encouraging data: 58 percent of respondents were "remarkably free of anti-Semitic views" and an additional 28 percent were "neither prejudiced nor unprejudiced." But the survey does suggest that the remaining 14 percent (about one in seven Americans) hold anti-Semitic beliefs.

There are good reasons to view this 14 percent figure skeptically. One problem is the survey's structure. For each statement respondents are given only two options: "probably true" and "probably false." Respondents are not allowed to say "I don't know" or indicate how strongly they hold each view.

Second, some of the statements do not, in my view, necessarily reflect anti-Semitic attitudes. Take the assertion: "Jews are more loyal to Israel than America." About 30 percent of Americans consistently agree with this statement. The sentiment obviously stems from the old stereotype that Jews are loyal only to their own people. But the statement doesn't say: "Jews are *disloyal* to the United States because their only commitment is to Israel." I would consider that belief anti-Semitic. But this statement is more ambiguous. Many Americans may think it is "probably true" without being anti-Semitic.

Some of the other propositions also strike me as being neutral. If Jews "stick together more than other Americans," is that a negative trait? If a respondent agrees that "Jews always like to be at the head of things," is that a compliment or a criticism? How about "Jews have a lot of irritating faults?" Compared to whom? The index can't measure these subtleties.

A third problem stems from the method of identifying "anti-Semites" as those who respond yes to six statements. *Any* six statements. This aggregation is arbitrary because it treats each statement as equally anti-Semitic. The statements about "too much power" and "shady practices" in business deserve far more weight than the others.

Finally, the survey can't—and doesn't claim to—assess the relationship between what the respondents believe and how they might *behave*. "All of the opinion surveys in the world have never been successful in deciphering who among a population of respondents is ever likely to take action on his beliefs, or at what point in time, or under what provocation," Blakeslee observes.[167]

Methodological flaws aside, some Jews may find these survey trends more unsettling than I do. Pessimists may argue that if 14 percent of Americans have anti-Semitic propensities, that represents millions of people and poses a real danger to Jews. Pessimists would probably be even more alarmed by another finding in this survey: as of 2016, 30 percent of the respondents still believe that "Jews were responsible for the death of Christ."[168] I would counter that negative stereotypes don't predict behavior. Moreover, more than two-thirds of the respondents *don't* believe this claim is true, even though I suspect nearly all respondents are aware of it.

Stereotypes are notoriously hard to erase completely. They exist for all groups. Claude Steele, a distinguished social psychologist who was my Stanford University colleague, argues that nearly all Americans could "take out a piece of paper, write down the major stereotypes" for various groups—Jews, gays, women, African Americans, WASPs—and "show a high degree of agreement."[169] That doesn't mean most Americans believe the stereotypes, just that they're aware of them.

Because Jews are highly sensitive to these stereotypes, we may experience an offensive remark as an anti-Semitic attack, even when the speaker does not mean to offend. This happened to me some years ago when Jack Jones, a brilliant software expert with whom I was working, nonchalantly said that someone had "Jewed him down."

I was offended and gave him a startled and disapproving look. Jack immediately apologized. If the ADL had polled me that year, I might have reported this as an anti-Semitic incident. But Jack Jones was no anti-Semite. We worked together for more than a decade, and I got to know him very well. We became close friends. He had been raised in rural Iowa, and I came to the conclusion that he had absorbed the phrase by osmosis and used it unthinkingly. I didn't hold the remark against him, and he never used it in my presence again.

HOSTILE ATTITUDES TOWARD ISRAEL: THE BDS MOVEMENT

Many American Jews view criticism of Israel, especially opposition to the idea of a Jewish state, as evidence of anti-Semitism. One example is the way Jewish institutions have responded to a movement called BDS, which stands for Boycott, Divestment, and Sanctions. BDS is a global Palestinian-led nonviolent movement, modeled after the South African anti-apartheid movement, which seeks to end Israel's occupation of the West Bank, stop discrimination against Israel's Palestinian citizens, and win for Palestinian refugees the right to return to Israel.[170]

The BDS movement rejects the idea of a Jewish state. In other words, it is anti-Zionist. It is most active on university campuses, and its campaign is extremely broad. It calls for boycotts of Israeli products, people, and academic institutions; it asks universities, churches, and unions to eliminate from their investment portfolios stock in "all Israeli companies" and from "international companies involved in violating Palestinian rights," and it asks international organizations and foreign governments to issue sanctions against Israel such as ending military trade, stopping free trade agreements, and excluding Israel from international forums and activities, including sporting events.[171]

Not surprisingly, the Israeli government vehemently opposes BDS, as do most American Jews. But some American Jews go further: they don't just oppose BDS; they call it anti-Semitic.

The ADL, the primary American Jewish institution aiming to combat anti-Semitism, is a prime example. Its website states, "Many of the founding goals of the BDS movement, including denying the Jewish people the universal right of self-determination . . . are anti-Semitic. Many individuals involved in BDS campaigns are driven by opposition to Israel's very existence as a Jewish state."[172]

I reject this broad argument. Opposition to Israel as a Jewish state is anti-Zionist because it opposes the central Zionist claim that Israel should be a refuge for persecuted Jews. But individuals can criticize Israel and even oppose Zionism without hating Jews. *Some* BDS supporters may be motivated by a general hatred of Jews and want to spread that prejudice. If so, they are anti-Semites and should be condemned as such. But many people who support BDS want to pressure the Israeli government in a nonviolent way to end the occupation and recognize what they see as legitimate Palestinian rights. That is not anti-Semitism, nor does it mean that the movement's core goals are anti-Semitic.

Another argument used to support the charge of anti-Semitism is the "double standard" argument: that BDS is applying a standard of conduct only to Israel and not to other countries whose abuses may be far more egregious. The idea is that any organization that singles out Israel for criticism and economic pressure may be motivated by general hostility toward Jews. There's some power to this argument. As Larry Summers has pointed out, "We live in a world where there are nations in which the penalty for homosexuality is death, in which women are stoned for adultery, in which torture is pervasive, in which governments are killing tens of thousands of their own people each year. But the proponents of Israeli boycotts, divesture and sanctions do not favor any form of pressure against countries other than Israel."[173] Both Summers and I agree with a State Department document that suggested that "while criticism of Israel cannot automatically be regarded as anti-Semitic, rhetoric that...applies double standards to Israel crosses the line of legitimate criticism."[174]

Where I differ with Summers is on an argument he first made in 2002, when he was president of Harvard. At the time BDS was circulating petitions at Harvard and MIT, calling on the universities to sell their stock in Israeli companies. Summers gave a well-publicized speech arguing that those who supported BDS were "advocating and taking actions that are anti-Semitic in their effect if not their intent." He later expanded on his ideas in 2015.[175]

What is the meaning of "in effect"? Maybe it means that many American Jews emotionally experience a verbal attack on Israel as an attack on Jews in general. That statement is probably true, but it doesn't mean that BDS supporters are *motivated* by anti-Semitism; indeed, Summers seemed to acknowledge as much ("in their effect *if not their intent*").

One of the core skills in conflict resolution is to differentiate between the *intent* of a speaker and the *impact* of her words on someone else. The two are not necessarily the same. For example, most of us have said or done things with good intentions, only to find (to our surprise) that our action had a negative impact on someone else. All too often the person we've offended assumes we *intended* to hurt or offend them; they accuse us of wrongdoing, we respond defensively, and conflict escalates. When the situation is reversed and a person's action has a negative impact on us, we often assume they *intended* to have that effect on us—and attribute all sorts of evil motives and character flaws to them, forgetting that we don't actually know what they intended.[176] This conflating of intent and impact is a major cause of misunderstanding and conflict. By characterizing BDS as anti-Semitic "in effect," Summers conflates the two.

There is a second possible meaning to the notion that an action may be anti-Semitic "in effect." Criticism of Israel may embolden hardcore anti-Semites to engage in truly anti-Semitic conduct: defacing schools with swastikas, shouting "Blood and Soil," and the like. If this link could be shown, it would be a matter of real concern. But nowhere does Summers—or others who equate anti-Zionism with anti-Semitism—make this factual showing.

Perhaps by "in effect" Summers means that the consequences of BDS and economic and political pressure would be "harmful" to Israel or, more broadly, the Jewish people. In the 2015 publication he states, "Note I did not label anyone an anti-Semite. I said instead that the effect of the actions they favored—singling out Israel for economic pressure—if carried out would be anti-Semitic—in other words, in opposition to the Jewish people."[177]

American philosopher Judith Butler, who is Jewish, wrote an essay critical of Summers, suggesting that to equate criticism of Israel with anti-Semitism was to undermine academic freedom. She claimed it would inhibit some faculty from supporting BDS for fear of being labeled anti-Semites.[178] Summers responded in 2015, saying he opposes "any form of speech code or ban on hate speech" because he believes it is an attack on academic freedom. Moreover, he said he opposed "any limitation on the right of faculty or students to invite any speaker they wish to hear from as long as there is no implied university endorsement of the speaker or the speaker's views." But he went on to acknowledge that his characterization of "anti-Semitic in effect" might cause some people on campus "to be much more hesitant about supporting divestiture and the like...because they did not want to be embroiled in controversy" and associated with anti-Semitism. Summers indicated that this was his intention and he had hoped it would have that effect: "Academic freedom does not include freedom from criticism."[179] Fair enough. But by conflating criticism of Israel with anti-Semitism, Summers is implicitly attacking the character of BDS supporters rather than meeting their arguments on their merits.

In short, "anti-Semitic" is an easy label to fling around, but I would urge Jews to use it carefully. To me "anti-Semitic" does not mean "critical of Israel" or "opposed to the Zionist project"; it means having prejudice against or hatred of Jews. The BDS movement may include some people who hate Jews, but it also includes many others who instead wish to support Palestinian aspirations for political autonomy. Rather than relying on name calling, it would be far better to address their claims on the merits.

WHY HAS AMERICA BEEN BETTER FOR JEWS?

To keep things in perspective, Jews need to understand that if the United States "has not been utter heaven for Jews, it has been as far from hell as Jews in the Diaspora have ever known."[180]

Drawing on Sarna and other historians, let me briefly describe why, compared to other nations, the Jewish experience in America has been so favorable.

NATIONAL CITIZENSHIP FOR JEWS FROM THE START

The United States was the first modern nation to grant Jews full political equality. In Europe Jews had to struggle for emancipation. They won political equality in France in 1791, but not until the nineteenth century in Switzerland, Great Britain, Italy, Germany, and Sweden, and not until the early twentieth century in Spain, Portugal, and Russia.

No Established National Church and a Tradition of Religious Liberty

Unlike some European nations, the United States has never had an official national religion. Although the populations of the original thirteen colonies were overwhelmingly Protestant, they were of different denominations. Once the nation was formed, the First Amendment to the Constitution prohibited the establishment of a national religion.

Another source of protection for Jews was the First Amendment's guarantee of "free exercise" of religion. Even in colonial times Jews were generally allowed to practice their religion without governmental interference. This tradition and constitutional provision safeguarded Jews from a variety of efforts to impose elements of Christianity on religious minorities. For example, Jews and others have successfully challenged state and local laws requiring all students to recite Christian prayers in public schools.[181]

A Nation of Immigrants—Not an Ethno-National State

America has long viewed itself as a nation of immigrants from many *different* countries and cultures. This feature of American ideology has mitigated a tendency to see Jews as not "real Americans."

Most European nations are ethno-national states in which a single indigenous ethnic group—with a shared ancestry, language, culture, and sometimes religion—has dominated for centuries. A Jew may be a citizen in Germany, France, or Norway, but he or she is unlikely to be considered ethnically German, French, or Norwegian. In the United States, by contrast, "American" is not an ethnic label; it includes all citizens. Groups of "native-born" Americans and political leaders have periodically expressed hostility to immigrants and tried to inhibit immigration. Nonetheless, the descendants of Jewish immigrants have been accepted as fully American, along with the descendants of other immigrant groups.

ANTI-SEMITISM VIED WITH OTHER AMERICAN PREJUDICES

In Europe anti-Semitism was often the dominant form of discrimination. In America prejudice against African Americans dwarfed anti-Semitism. As we have discussed, although American Jews were subjected to prejudice, some of it "racial" in nature, they were always considered white.

Because of America's ethnic diversity, anti-Semitism "has always had to compete with other forms of animus," Sarna notes, including hatred of Quakers, Catholics, Masons, Mormons, Asians, and Communists. With so many forms of prejudice brewing, "no group experiences for long the full brunt of national odium."[182]

AMERICAN JEWS USED THEIR POLITICAL AND ECONOMIC INFLUENCE TO FIGHT ANTI-SEMITISM

Although a small proportion of the total population, American Jews have been remarkably effective in fighting anti-Semitism. "Where European Jews prided themselves on their 'forbearance' in the face of attack, Rabbi Isaac Mayer Wise boasted that he was a 'malicious, biting, pugnacious, challenging, and mocking monster of the pen,'" notes Sarna, referring to the nineteenth-century American Reform leader.[183] Other American Jewish leaders may have been more diplomatic but were equally effective. In this chapter we've seen Jewish assertiveness achieve some striking successes: persuading Lincoln to rescind Grant's order during the Civil War, forcing Henry Ford to shut down his Dearborn newspaper, and helping secure passage of landmark civil rights legislation.

AS I WRITE THIS in early 2018, the remarkable decline in anti-Semitism since World War II strikes me as a significant challenge for Jews in America. Although I'm aware that some anti-Semitism remains, I see acceptance of Jews as a bigger challenge for American Jewish continuity. My advice to American Jews is as follows.

First, maintain perspective. Recognize that America is different from other countries and that the nature of anti-Semitism here—episodic, on the fringe—does not pose a "serious" threat to Jewish well-being. By all means, be vigilant and fight bigotry wherever it appears. That will always be important work. But don't allow your feelings about past persecution to mislead you about the healthy status of American Jews today.

Second, confront what this means for the future of American Jewish identity. For today's young Jews, being a member of a persecuted minority is not a strong foundation on which to build a Jewish identity. They have never personally experienced persecution, and our tragic history is not a good reason to *choose* to be Jewish today. We should teach that history to our children and grandchildren so they can appreciate the exceptional conditions in which they live, but we should not ask them to build a Jewish identity on a collective memory of genocide. Nor should we expect the American Jewish community to remain united on that basis. If Americans of Jewish heritage are going to identify as Jewish, it will need to be for *positive* reasons.

9

THE CHALLENGE OF ISRAEL

I HAVE COME to feel an emotional attachment to Israel, a feeling that has grown both stronger and more complicated over the years. I am not alone in this. Most American Jews (about 70 percent) say they feel a similar attachment. Indeed, the 2013 Pew survey suggests that "caring about Israel" is an element of what we think being Jewish means.[1]

In earlier chapters we've seen some of the reasons for this emotional bond. For some the attachment is religious and spiritual, a desire to reconnect with the biblical land. For many more, I suspect it has to do with peoplehood, a sense of ethnic kinship that implies mutual responsibility. Before World War II not many American Jews thought of themselves as Zionists. America was our homeland. But once the scope of the Holocaust was discovered, few American Jews have been able to resist the power of the Zionist claim that a Jewish state was necessary to provide a refuge for Jews facing persecution elsewhere in the world. Over time a number of American Jewish families came to have Israeli relatives.

Ethnic pride has also played a role. In Israel's early years some Americans admired Israel's pioneering spirit in making the dessert bloom. For many more Americans, Jewish pride was sparked by Israel's extraordinary victory in 1967 in the Six Day War and reinforced by Israel's remarkable achievements ever since: its resilience in the face of regional hostility and terrorist attacks; its scientific, technological, and economic accomplishments as a "startup nation"; its cultural and academic vibrancy; and its success in providing a haven for hundreds of thousands of Jews facing persecution throughout the world, including in Russia and Ethiopia.

It was once thought that pride in and support for the State of Israel would serve to unite a diverse American Jewish community and buttress

Jewish identity in this country. Today I fear the opposite is becoming true. Certain present-day policies of the Israeli government now fuel intense conflicts among American Jews and reinforce deep divisions within the American Jewish community. In the words of Professor Dov Waxman, "Israel used to bring American Jews together. Now it is driving them apart."[2]

At issue are two aspects of Israeli government policy: first, the Israeli-Palestinian conflict and the continued Israeli military occupation of the West Bank, and second, the exclusive role of the Orthodox rabbinate in defining for Israel what is authentic Judaism. Both are political issues that illustrate what I see as Israel's core challenge: managing the tension between being Jewish and democratic in the face of serious security concerns. In recent years the political center of gravity in Israel has shifted to the right on both issues, favoring increasingly ethno-nationalist and expansionary policies with regard to the West Bank and the treatment of Palestinians there as well as increasingly Orthodox views on Judaism.

The political and religious center of gravity in America is very different, meaning that our Jewish community is no longer well aligned with Israel's, at least on these two contentious issues. A substantial majority of American Jews—some 70 percent—are politically liberal. Many are troubled by Israel's continued military occupation of the West Bank, its continued expansion of Jewish settlements, and its discriminatory treatment of Palestinians. Few American Jews are traditionally observant, while most Israelis are. Most American Jews belong to the Reform or Conservative denominations, which are not officially recognized in Israel and are often derided. In Israel the Orthodox religious establishment delights in claiming that Reform Jews hardly—if at all—count as being Jewish.

These tensions could have adverse long-term effects on the American Jewish community for two reasons. First, they reinforce a serious rift between the Orthodox and everyone else. The Orthodox, who make up only 10 percent of American Jews, tend to agree with the Israeli right wing on both issues. Second, these tensions threaten to weaken many American Jews' emotional attachment to Israel, a psychic bond that in the past has bolstered American Jewish identity. This is particularly true for young

Jews, who tend to be more politically liberal than their elders, more critical of Israel's policies toward Palestinians, and less tolerant of Orthodox religious views, especially those on intermarriage.

Internal rifts within the American Jewish community about Israel are nothing new, but I find the current dynamic troubling and unhealthy. Particularly with respect to the Israeli-Palestinian issue, too many American Jews are afraid to express publicly their unease with Israeli policies. For reasons I will explain, I think it is essential that they find their voice.

THE ISRAELI-PALESTINIAN CONFLICT

As a scholar involved in dispute resolution, I have devoted considerable energy to the Israeli-Palestinian conflict. I have provided negotiation training and advice to Israelis and Palestinians involved in the conflict, organized and facilitated "off-the-record" confidential meetings between Israeli and Palestinian leaders, and written articles about the barriers that have prevented a negotiated resolution.[3] In the process I've come to appreciate the complexities of this seemingly intractable conflict.

I don't intend to explore these complexities fully here but instead to provide a brief summary of the current situation before discussing its impact on American Jews.

In resolving the Israeli-Palestinian conflict, the core question is: Should an independent and sovereign Palestinian state be established alongside the State of Israel? A "two-state solution" would mean that Israel would remain the Jewish national homeland and Palestine would become the Palestinian homeland. To achieve such an agreement—and eventually end Israel's military occupation of the West Bank—five so-called final status issues were identified almost twenty-five years ago as part of the Oslo Peace Process, and President Bill Clinton outlined the parameters for resolving each issue in December 2000.[4]

1. *What would be the **border** between Israel and the new Palestinian state?* Israel has no internationally recognized eastern border. In 1949 the United Nations established a "Green Line," which marked the cease-fire in Israel's War of Independence. The conflict ended not with a peace

treaty but with an armistice. The Green Line became a "provisional border" between Israel and the West Bank territory, which was then occupied by Jordan.[5] For the next eighteen years Jordan controlled the West Bank, including East Jerusalem, but never annexed it. In 1967, as a result of the Six Day War, Israel captured the West Bank territory from Jordan. For more than fifty years now, Israel has exercised military control over the West Bank but, with the exception of metropolitan Jerusalem, has never annexed the territory or claimed sovereignty over it.

Under a two-state solution, according to the conventional wisdom, the border between Israel and the new Palestinian state would be based on the 1967 borders, with "land swaps" that would allow incorporation into Israel of large Jewish settlements that lie close to the Green Line. This would mean that a two-state deal would not require a substantial majority of Jewish settlers to be displaced.

2. *What would happen to the **Jewish settlements** that lie within the new Palestinian state?* Since the Six Day War about five hundred thousand Jewish settlers have established homes in some 120 settlements in the West Bank.[6] These settlers are citizens of Israel and subject to Israeli law.

In order to create a contiguous Palestinian state, any settlements that lie within the new Palestinian borders would be dismantled, and Israel would reabsorb the Jewish settlers.

3. *How would **Israel's security** be maintained?* Israel's vital interest in security provides its primary justification for continued occupation of the West Bank. Historically, the occupation provided strategic territorial depth against the risk of an invasion from Arab countries to the east. Today the greater risk to Israel is thought to be terrorism emanating from Palestinians who live in the West Bank.

Under a two-state deal the new Palestinian state would be demilitarized; the Palestinian government would pledge not to enter into a military agreement with any country that does not recognize Israel, and it would agree not to allow any foreign army to enter its territory.

4. *What rights would be guaranteed to **Palestinian refugees** displaced by the conflict?* During what the Israelis call the War of Independence and what Palestinians call the *Nakba* (Disaster), about 750,000 Palestinians

fled or were expelled from their homes and became refugees. Today they and their descendants number in the millions, many of whom remain in refugee camps in Gaza, the West Bank, Lebanon, Syria, and Jordan. A key Palestinian claim is that these refugees and their descendants have rights to the property they lost, including a "right of return" to what is now Israel.

A two-state solution would provide Palestinian refugees with a modified right of return consistent with a two-state approach. The new Palestinian state would be the focal point for Palestinians who choose to return to the area, and monetary compensation might also be provided.

5. *What would happen to **Jerusalem** generally and the holy sites in particular?* Both Israel and the Palestinians claim Jerusalem as their capital. Important Jewish, Christian, and Muslim religious sites are located throughout the Old City. Shortly after the 1967 war Israel annexed East Jerusalem (previously controlled by Jordan) and announced that the "reunited" Jerusalem was now the capital of Israel.

Most nations in the world do not recognize the validity of the Israeli annexation and do not recognize Jerusalem as Israel's capital. Instead, the international consensus is that the status of Jerusalem should be resolved only through negotiations between the Palestinians and Israelis as part of any final status agreement.

Under the two-state solution long envisioned by its proponents, Jerusalem would be divided and declared the capital of both countries. The areas of Jerusalem inhabited primarily by Jews would become the Israeli capital, while the areas of East Jerusalem where Palestinians live would be the new Palestinian capital. For the holy sites, a special regime—perhaps under international control—might be created.

On December 6, 2017, President Donald Trump stunned the world by announcing that the United States would recognize Jerusalem as Israel's capital. In May 2018 he moved the American embassy from Tel Aviv to that city. Other nations and the United Nations broadly condemned this decision. In the announcement, however, the president claimed, "This decision is not intended in any way to reflect a departure from our strong commitment to facilitate a lasting peace agreement," including the possibility of a two-state resolution. Thus, he left open the chance that someday, through negotiations, Jerusalem might also become the capital of a new Palestinian state.[7]

ASSUMING A RESOLUTION ALONG the lines outlined above, polling data has suggested that a majority of both Israelis and Palestinians would accept a two-state solution if they thought the other side was really prepared to implement it. Yet despite mediation efforts by the Clinton, Bush, and Obama administrations, Israeli and Palestinian leaders have not achieved a negotiated resolution. Why has so little progress been made?

There are many barriers to agreement,[8] including the distrust created by a long history of violence between the two sides. But my own view is that the most significant barriers are *internal conflicts* among Israeli Jews on the one hand and Palestinians on the other.

For Israelis the most divisive issue is the future of the settlements.[9] As a practical matter, the creation of a contiguous Palestinian state in the West Bank would require the relocation of tens of thousands of Jewish settlers, at great cost to them and the Israeli government. As an ideological matter, it would also mark the end of the Eretz Israel (Land of Israel) project, the dream of some religiously observant Israelis to reclaim biblically significant lands for the Jewish state. These Israelis, known as National Religious settlers, have long pursued settlements as a way of restoring Israel to its ancient contours. There is some fear within Israel that a negotiated two-state deal that destroys this dream might provoke violence from these settlers.

Among Palestinians the most divisive issue is the right of return.[10] The Palestinian National Liberation Movement has always defined itself as a refugee movement, and Palestinian leaders have long insisted that the Palestinian people, both collectively and individually, have the right to reclaim the land and property that once was theirs. But beneath the surface there lurks a profound internal conflict among Palestinians about the scope and meaning of the right of return. Privately, many Palestinians acknowledge it's unrealistic to expect that Israel would ever accept the immigration of millions of Palestinian refugees. Moreover, some polls suggest that many refugees would rather receive compensation and citizenship rights in a new Palestinian state—or in some other country of their choosing—than in Israel. But the same polls indicate that a sub-stantial minority of refugees and their descendants want to return to their original homes in what is now Israel. There is concern among Palestinians that any negotiated two-state solution that extinguishes the right of return to Israel proper could provoke violent opposition from those refugees.

DIVISIONS AMONG AMERICAN JEWS

Like the Israelis and the Palestinians, American Jews are deeply divided on how to approach the conflict. Whereas a clear majority favors a two-state resolution in the long run, only about half favor it "in the current situation."[11]

American Jews are also divided on the issue of settlements. Most American Jews consistently support dismantling at least some Jewish settlements in the West Bank, but "a significant minority"—35 to 45 percent—"opposes the dismantling of *any* settlements."[12]

To some degree these divisions reflect denominational differences. American Orthodox Jews, who tend to be politically conservative and Republican, are much more likely to oppose the creation of a Palestinian state and the dismantling of any settlements. Non-Orthodox Jews, who are overwhelmingly liberal and Democratic, are more likely to support a two-state solution and cutbacks on settlements.

There's also a generational divide. Younger American Jews grew up long after the Holocaust and are less strongly shaped by it than their par-ents and grandparents. As I've mentioned, they tend to be more politically liberal and more critical of Israel.[13]

These conflicts have led to a fractured political landscape marked by anguished discourse and frequent intolerance of different perspectives. Before I try to illuminate this landscape, let me tell you where I stand.

I believe that only a comprehensive two-state solution can both pro-vide for Israel's security *and* allow Israel to remain both Jewish and dem-ocratic. I believe that unless the settlement expansion is stopped soon, a two-state solution will become politically impossible. Even now it's not clear whether any Israeli government would have the political will to end the National Religious settlers' dream of Eretz Israel and relocate tens of thousands of settlers. The strategy of the National Religious settlers has long been to create "facts on the ground" in the West Bank that would make it impossible for any Israeli government to require evacuation. Many fear it may already be too late.[14]

I don't think it's too late, but I think the window of opportunity is closing. For that reason I think it's essential that the US government, which has long explicitly opposed settlement expansion, put serious pressure on the Israeli government to stop the expansion of those settlements that would not be covered by the land swap. The most significant "action" of the Obama administration involved inaction—its decision on December 23, 2016 (days before President-elect Trump took office) not to veto a UN Security Council Resolution declaring the illegality of Israeli West Bank settlements.[15] Settlement expansion must end if the two-state solution is going to remain a viable option.

My point of view represents only one position on a broad spectrum of American Jewish opinion that ranges from far right to far left. To understand this range, let's examine four organizations that illustrate the most distinct and influential points of view.[16]

On the far right is the Zionist Organization of America (ZOA), founded in 1897. The ZOA vehemently opposes any two-state resolution of the conflict. Instead, it favors a one-state solution in which the West Bank would be incorporated into Israel proper. For that reason, it enthusiastically supports Jewish settlement activity in the West Bank, which includes the biblical lands of Judea and Samaria that the National Religious settlers hope to reclaim. The ZOA believes Israel should make no territorial concessions and Palestinians should be satisfied with some degree of personal autonomy under Israeli political jurisdiction. Indeed, the ZOA often stands to the right of the Israeli government and openly criticizes Israeli actions it views as unwise concessions to the Palestinians.[17] As its name suggests, the ZOA is deeply committed to the notion that Israel must remain a Jewish state.

I reject this position because it embodies a demographic time bomb that the ZOA fails to address. If Israel absorbs the entire West Bank territory and its millions of Palestinian residents, Israel risks eventually losing its Jewish majority. To retain its character as a Jewish state—with special immigration rights for Jews, national celebrations of Jewish holidays, and the like—it would be forced to limit the political rights of the Palestinians. The ZOA has never acknowledged the obvious: that if its hoped-for single state is to remain Jewish, it cannot remain a democracy.

On the far left is Jewish Voice for Peace (JVP), founded in 1996. Standing at the opposite end of the political spectrum, JVP might be characterized as anti-Zionist. It sees Zionism as outdated and questions the legitimacy of a Jewish state that privileges Jews and Judaism. It calls for an immediate end to the Israeli occupation of the West Bank, condemns the settlements as illegal, and characterizes Israel's disparate treatment of West Bank Palestinians as creating an "apartheid state." JVP joins with Palestinian groups in supporting the use of BDS to pressure the Israeli government to withdraw from the West Bank and recognize the rights of Palestinian refugees under international law. It favors cutting off all American military aid and arms sales to Israel.

I reject this position because it, too, ignores the complexity of the problem. Although JVP calls for "any solution" that would provide peace and equality for both Israelis and Palestinians, it fails to grapple with how that might be achieved. Officially, JVP favors neither a one-state nor a two-state resolution; apparently its membership is divided.[18] I suspect many JVP supporters would prefer a one-state resolution in which the state was entirely secular and democratic.[19] But Israeli Jews would never accept such a deal because it would mean the end of the Jewish state. A two-state resolution would be equally problematic, given JVP's position on Palestinian refugee rights. For example, the JVP appears to support the Palestinian claim that Palestinian refugees must be allowed to return to Israel proper if they so choose. Israel is a rich, prosperous country with low unemployment and high wages. The new Palestinian state would likely be very poor in comparison. Given the choice, many Palestinians—perhaps millions—would flock to Israel, which would create a Palestinian majority there. As an Israeli friend suggested to me, the result would be not one, but two Palestinian states.

The American Israeli Public Affairs Committee (AIPAC), established in 1963, is representative of the center right. AIPAC is the preeminent lobbying group concerned with US government relations with Israel. A large organization with more than one hundred thousand dues-paying members and annual revenues of $70 million, AIPAC wields enormous political clout.[20] It is staunchly Zionist and believes that Israel must remain a Jewish state. It doesn't oppose a two-state resolution of the conflict, but it insists that any resolution should be the result of negotiations between the two parties—*not* the result of outside pressure. It strenuously objects to American pressure on the Israeli government to promote such negotiations; instead, it essentially backs the position of the Israeli government on all issues relating to the Israeli-Palestinian conflict and suggests that anyone who criticizes Israel is, in effect, harming Israel. This stance is sometimes referred to as "Israel right or wrong." In recent years AIPAC's top priorities have been maintaining US aid to Israel and backing the Netanyahu government's position with respect to Iran's nuclear program.

My problem with AIPAC is its determined silence on the continued expansion of the settlements and its view that all supporters of Israel should follow its lead. I don't minimize Israel's security concerns or the political difficulty of the settlement issue. As long as the Israeli government can postpone making tough choices on the settlements, it will. Indeed, the Netanyahu coalition seems to prefer the status quo to any negotiated agreement. That's why I consider silence from American Jews and the US government to be so dangerous: it tacitly condones the status quo. By failing to speak out on the settlement issue and trying to prevent others from doing so, AIPAC is making the situation worse.

On the center left is J Street, founded in 2007. J Street, like AIPAC, is a lobby organization in Washington that considers itself firmly Zionist. But that is where the similarities end. J Street (named after the street missing from the Washington, DC, grid) is the only organization of the four that publicly and strongly advocates a two-state resolution. It views the creation of a Palestinian state as vital to Israel's long-term survival as a Jewish and democratic state, and it doesn't hesitate to criticize Israel for actions it sees as hampering that goal.[21] It views the settlements as a serious obstacle to peace and of questionable legitimacy. It supports US government pressure on Israel to curb settlement expansion and take more active steps toward a negotiated resolution. It considers the need for action urgent. I stand squarely with this group.

AN EXAMPLE OF CONFLICT AMONG AMERICAN JEWS

For decades AIPAC was virtually the only significant American Jewish lobby in Washington. When J Street emerged in 2007 and began to criticize the policies of the Netanyahu government, it was immediately attacked from the right as an irresponsible upstart. Israel's ambassador to the United States, Michael Oren, refused to speak at J Street's annual convention,[22] and the ZOA characterized J Street as traitorous.[23] As J Street's influence grew, conservative Israeli and American Jewish elements intensified their efforts to depict the organization as disloyal to Israel and not part of the American Jewish mainstream.

The conflict came to a head in 2014 when J Street applied for membership in the Conference of Presidents of Major American Jewish Organizations. This umbrella group, whose members head some fifty diverse organizations, has long purported to be the most broadly representative voice of the American Jewish community. By 2014 J Street was a major organization,[24] far bigger and more influential than some of the conference's other members.[25]

AIPAC and the ZOA led the opposition to J Street's admission and successfully blocked it. There were seventeen votes in favor of admission, twenty-two against, and three abstentions.

The vote caused an immediate uproar among members who saw the rejection of J Street as a disgrace. Because every member organization had one vote, regardless of size, the results arguably did not represent the views of most American Jews. All the organizations representing Reform and Conservative Judaism, who together represent more than half of America's Jews, voted in favor. After the vote Rabbi Rick Jacobs, president of the Union for Reform Judaism, said, "It is clear that the Conference of Presidents, as currently constituted and governed, no longer serves its vital purpose of providing a collective voice for the entire American Jewish pro-Israeli community."[26]

Despite the conference's decision, J Street has demonstrated its growing influence in Washington. In 2015 J Street achieved a striking victory in connection with President Obama's nuclear weapons deal with Iran. Netanyahu's government vehemently opposed the deal and characterized it as creating an existential threat for Israel. AIPAC and other main-line American Jewish institutions fell into line behind Netanyahu, spent millions of dollars on television ads criticizing the deal, and lobbied Congress hard to scuttle it. J Street vigorously defended the deal as being in the security interests of both Israel and the United States.

In the congressional review process that followed, J Street's view prevailed; AIPAC and its Jewish establishment allies failed to block the deal. According to Ambassador Wendy Sherman, the chief American negotiator of the deal, "Getting through the congressional review process took an enormous effort both inside and outside of government. Without a doubt J Street was a key organization in demonstrating to Congress [that] strong support for the agreement also existed within the American Jewish community."[27]

It was a rare defeat for AIPAC and a stunning success for J Street. "It used to be that AIPAC could deliver votes in a situation like this by emphasizing the political cost of going against them," said Jeremy Ben-Ami, J Street's executive director. "That no longer works as well as it used to, with Democrats in particular, who recognize that the majority of their supporters in the Jewish community support this deal.... The days of AIPAC being able to present itself as the sole voice of American Jews on these issues are over."[28]

Indeed, polls suggested that, by a slight majority, American Jews *supported* the deal, despite the vehement opposition of the Israeli government and nearly all the major American Jewish organizations.[29]

THE DILEMMA FOR MOST AMERICAN JEWS: "AMBIVALENT CENTRISM"

Most American Jews are not engaged with any of these political organizations, and they are in a real bind. When it comes to Israel, most are centrists, according to polls.[30] Indeed, Waxman claims most American Jews are "ambivalent centrists." By this he means that "they want peace and favor some Israeli territorial concessions, but they also worry about Israeli security and are highly suspicious about Palestinians' intentions." They fear Israel would face a security threat if it withdrew from the West Bank, but they also worry about the "major demographic threat to Israel's future as a Jewish and democratic state if it continues to hold onto this territory and effectively rule over the Palestinian population within it."[31]

This ambivalence causes deep discomfort for many American Jews and paralysis for some. Most want Israel to remain both Jewish and democratic. Most are distressed by the occupation of the West Bank, which has gone on much longer than anyone anticipated in 1967. Most are distressed by the seeming intractability of the conflict and the position in which it puts Israel as an occupying power. They are ashamed of Israeli treatment of Palestinians in the West Bank and think Israel is failing to live up to its democratic ideals. They don't think either side is doing all it can to achieve a two-state solution.

But many do not speak out on these issues. They are silenced by a multitude of factors, including their own ambivalence. Some don't feel well enough informed to voice an opinion. Some dislike conflict. Some find the problem hopelessly complicated and don't know how to articulate a coherent stance, especially when challenged by passionate arguments from the right or left. Some are uncomfortable being publicly critical of Israel because of the security issue. They tell themselves, *I'm not living there, so I don't have to live with it. Who am I to judge?* Some have been cowed by the AIPAC stance that being pro-Israel means "no public criticism"; they don't want to do anything that would hurt Israel.

As a result, many have decided they don't want to be involved and have disengaged from the issue.

Nowhere is this problem more acute than on university campuses, highly politicized environments where the Israeli-Palestinian conflict often comes up in the context of BDS petitions circulated by student pro-Palestinian groups. Since 2000, BDS has focused most of its efforts on college campuses. Its petitions call on American universities to divest the stock of companies doing business in or with Israel and to boycott Israeli academic institutions. BDS also seeks endorsements from student groups and academic associations.[32] Palestinian or Muslim student groups often lead these efforts and typically attempt to form coalitions with other progressive student groups, such as students of color, LGBTQ groups, and women's groups.[33]

This means that Jewish students often encounter BDS through fellow students whose progressive views they may largely share on other issues. They may find some aspects of BDS appealing, especially its emphasis on nonviolent resistance and human rights. When they're approached by fellow students asking them to support BDS, many of them feel caught. BDS rejects the idea of a Jewish state, but most Jewish students don't want to go that far. They want to support Israel but not uncritically, and they fear that whatever they say, they might be attacked and not know how to respond. Many Jewish students don't want to argue about Israeli politics at all, so they avoid the subject.[34]

J Street entered this fray in 2009 with a campus organizing arm known as J Street U, hoping to provide a voice to precisely those Jewish students who were sitting out the fight: those who support Israel's continued existence as a Jewish and democratic state, oppose settlement expansion and continued occupation, and want help articulating a coherent point of view. J Street U hoped to achieve this goal by promoting educational student programs such as speakers on Israel-related topics. It soon found itself embroiled in campus controversies that mirrored its battles with the Jewish community at large.

On most college campuses the primary Jewish organization is Hillel. It is the key ally for any Jewish group hoping to flourish on campus. Hillel is the world's largest Jewish college student organization, with 550 local affiliates.[35] It fosters Jewish campus life through a variety of religious and cultural activities—Sabbath and Jewish holiday services, Passover Seders, lectures, discussion groups, and other programs. The umbrella organization is Hillel International, and each local chapter enjoys substantial autonomy. Jewish groups are eager to affiliate with the campus Hillel because it provides a space to hold events, a ready audience, and economic support.

For most of its history Hillel has been nonpolitical, taking no particular position on Israeli politics and tolerating a wide range of views.[36]

But during the Second Intifada (2000–2005), as BDS became a presence on American college campuses, Hillel began to see its role as not just education and Jewish identity building but also pro-Israel advocacy. As BDS has gained traction among students, "many in the Jewish world and Israel [have come to] view college campuses as the state of Israel's latest battleground."[37]

In 2010, just after J Street U entered the campus scene, Hillel International made an unprecedented move to ensure that Hillel's name would not be associated with anti-Zionist or BDS points of view. It adopted the Standards of Partnership, a new addition to the "Hillel Israel Guidelines" that prohibits hosting or partnering with any speakers or groups that "delegitimize" or "demonize" Israel or support BDS.[38] Any local chapter that defies these rules would presumably be subject to some sort of sanction from Hillel International.

This highly political move outraged some Hillel students, who saw it as a form of censorship and launched a protest campaign called Open Hillel, which rejects the Standards of Partnership and aims to eliminate them. So far, the Standards have served mainly to prevent Jewish student groups from using Hillel buildings to hold events that are cosponsored by groups that support BDS.[39]

As J Street U tried to make itself a presence on campus, it sometimes got caught in the crossfire between Hillel International and BDS. Although J Street U was accepted as an affiliate by many local Hillels, there were several instances of rejection that illustrated how fraught the political atmosphere had become.[40]

In some cases the rejection was based on J Street's alleged positions on Israel. These arguments were often hyperbolic, claiming that J Street "endorses anti-Israel, anti-Jewish narratives" and "contribute[s] to anti-Israel biases and misinformation"[41] and that its positions "weaken the State of Israel and inspire anti-Semitism." There were also claims that J Street's funders and advisers "opposed Israel" and even had "ties with Arab governments that have been consistently hostile to Israel."[42] But when I interviewed students who had knowledge of the reasons for these rejections, I also heard a second argument: they did not want Hillel to become "politicized" by admitting J Street.[43] Hillel's Berkeley student president reported that many students want the Jewish Student Union "to stay a place they feel comfortable saying they love Israel."[44] The message I took from that astonishing statement was that some Jewish students would *not* be comfortable hearing from an affiliate group that both loved Israel and criticized it.

Notwithstanding the misgivings of some Jewish students, by 2015 J Street U claimed to have activities on nearly sixty campuses, involving several thousand student members. It, too, opposed the Hillel International guidelines.

The tension between J Street U and Hillel International reached a crisis in March of 2015, when J Street held a national conference in Washington, DC. Eric Fingerhut, the CEO of Hillel International, had initially agreed to speak at the national student group meeting. But he later withdrew and issued a statement expressing "concerns regarding my participation amongst other speakers who have made highly inflammatory statements about the Jewish state." In other words, the leader of Hillel International broke his commitment to appear before J Street students because there were other speakers on other panels with whom he disagreed. There was speculation that perhaps donor pressure had caused Fingerhut to withdraw.[45]

The students attending the J Street conference were outraged. They saw Fingerhut's decision, like Hillel's guidelines, as reflecting opposition to open discussion of Israel-related issues. Some 250 student members of J Street staged a protest march to Hillel headquarters that was covered by the *Washington Post*. The students left letters for Fingerhut asking for a meeting with him and criticizing him for giving in to "more conservative donors instead of engaging with the full range of student voices— including those on the more liberal end."[46] Fingerhut's written response was conciliatory, indicating that there was

work to do in the Jewish community at large to be one people that respects, honors and celebrates its diversity rather than fearing it. This incident taught me just how deep the divide is. I don't yet have all the answers to how we will bridge this divide, but as Hillel's president, I am committed to working with you to find them and I have no doubt we will be successful.[47]

In the three years since this confrontation Hillel International has softened its stance toward J Street U. I suspect Hillel's leaders concluded that it was in Hillel's interest to allow an outlet for progressive Jewish students who are critical of the Israeli government but supportive of the idea of a Jewish state. Although Hillel International has not changed its guidelines, neither has it expelled any local Hillel chapters. In recent years the conflicts between J Street and Hillel have related to specific programs and speakers.[48]

I have emphasized the role of J Street on campus because I think Jewish college students should be exposed to a nuanced position between Hillel International's current hard-line conservatism ("Israel right or wrong") and BDS. I am persuaded that a majority of Jewish students—including vast numbers who are not yet involved—want Israel to remain both Jewish and democratic; they favor a two-state resolution and are critical of some Israeli government policies. But too many have been unwilling to become involved.

The good news is that J Street has carved out a place for itself on campus. J Street U is being tolerated by Hillel and is providing support for liberal Jewish students who want to find a voice. But much work remains to be done on campus to engage what I see as a largely silent and ambivalent majority.

CONFLICT OVER RELIGION

The second divisive issue for American Jews is the growing power of the Orthodox rabbinate in Israel and its apparent disdain for the religious practices of most American Jews. Orthodox rabbis, many of whom are ultra-Orthodox, essentially control Israel's religious institutions and wield tremendous financial and political power. They not only determine personal status issues such as marriage, divorce, and burial, but they are also backed by political parties that constantly seek to expand the influence of halacha into other areas of government. The Orthodox rabbinate also considers itself *the* authority on Judaism worldwide, and it seeks to spread the view that authentic Judaism requires a commitment to halacha.

One consequence is that members of the Israeli government regularly make stunningly insulting comments that outrage many American Jews. One conspicuous example occurred in 2015 when the minister of Religious Services suggested that Reform Jews were not really Jews at all. "The moment a Reform Jew stops following the religion of Israel, let's say there's a problem," the minister, David Azoulay, said in a radio interview. "I cannot allow myself to call such a person a Jew."[49]

This was not an isolated example. Israel Eichler, a member of the Knesset affiliated with an ultra-Orthodox party, compared Reform Jews to mentally ill patients. Moshe Gafni, head of the Knesset's Finance Committee, said that "Reform Jews are a group of clowns who stab the Holy Torah," adding that "there will never, ever be recognition for this group of clowns, not at the [Western] Wall or anywhere else." Rabbi David Yosef claimed that Reform Jews are "idolaters—simply and literally."[50]

Such appalling comments invariably provoke condemnation from American Jews.[51] This is one subject on which the American Jewish establishment doesn't hesitate to speak out. Jonathan Greenblatt, CEO of the Anti-Defamation League, condemned the comments as akin to hate speech and warned that such reckless talk "risks...long-term damage" to the relationship between American Jews and Israel.[52] Some Israelis also denounced the comments, and Prime Minister Benjamin Netanyahu called Azoulay's remarks "hurtful" and not reflective of government policy.[53] But the offenders have suffered no real consequences: Netanyahu did not expel Minister Azoulay from his cabinet.[54]

The ultra-Orthodox establishment further enrages and insults many American Jews by pushing for government policies that marginalize the non-Orthodox. The latest uproar was provoked in June 2017 when Netanyahu reneged on an agreement to build a new "egalitarian" space at the Western Wall, one of Judaism's holiest sites. Because the Wall is controlled by the Chief Rabbinate, worshippers there must follow the same rules that prevail in an ultra-Orthodox synagogue. The egalitarian space would have been an area where mixed-gender worship was permitted and where women could chant prayers, read the Torah, and even celebrate a bat mitzvah—none of which is allowed in Orthodox synagogues.[55] When the Netanyahu government agreed in 2016 to build this space, it capped years of negotiations between the Israeli government and liberal Israeli and American Jewish groups, including the Reform and Conservative movements. But the ultra-Orthodox managed to kill the project—or, technically, "suspend" it—before it could be implemented. Moreover, on the same day that Netanyahu bowed to pressure on that deal, his government pushed through the Knesset a law providing that the Israeli Chief Rabbinate has the sole power to determine whether a conversion to Judaism is valid.

These two actions sparked vehement protests by prominent members of the American Jewish establishment—again to no avail. Isaac Fisher, an American real estate tycoon and a member of the board of AIPAC, said he would make no further financial contributions to Israel until the government reversed the decisions.[56] The president of the Union for Reform Judaism denounced the actions as striking "at the very heart of some core commitments of Jewish life."[57] In Israel the Board of Governors of the Jewish Agency, which included a number of Americans, canceled a dinner with Netanyahu in protest.[58] An article in *Foreign Policy* contended, "An unprecedented rift between Israel and American Jewry threatens to erupt into a permanent schism."[59]

This situation raises a number of tantalizing questions. Given the importance to Israel of American support and money, why do ultra-Orthodox Israeli officials feel compelled to demonize Reform Jews? Don't they care about maintaining the relationship? I suspect the ultra-Orthodox do not care about a relationship with American Jews who are not, in their eyes, religiously observant. But surely other Israelis do care. So the core question is: Why does the Orthodox rabbinate in Israel have the political power to push the Israeli government around?

The political power of the ultra-Orthodox is partly due to the structure of Israel's government. Israel has a parliamentary democracy, where no single party ever has a majority in the Knesset. To form a government, the prime minister must cobble together a coalition and maintain it. The withdrawal of a single party can mean the loss of a parliamentary majority and the need for new elections. Thus, the ultra-Orthodox religious parties, either alone or in combination, can wield substantial influence, especially with respect to government policies touching on religious affairs.

In 2017 Netanyahu's government held a razor-thin majority: a 61-seat coalition in a Knesset with 120 members. As one commentator wrote, "Netanyahu knows that in order to hold on to power, he needs the cooperation of ultra-Orthodox parties Shas and United Torah Judaism, and nowhere has this reality played out more dramatically than at the Western Wall."[60]

But the structure of the Israeli government isn't the whole story. After all, the ultra-Orthodox are a minority even within Israel; secular Israelis outnumber them four to one. Why don't these secular Israeli Jews defend Reform and Conservative Judaism more vigorously? When Israeli officials demonize Reform Jews as idolaters, don't secular Israeli Jews feel equally attacked?

The answer to this puzzle lies in three profound differences between the American and Israeli Jewish communities, despite the fact that both feature a broad spectrum of religious observance, ranging from nonobservant to ultra-Orthodox.

In America, Judaism is organized by denomination. Most American Jews—70 percent—identify with a denomination, and a majority of those are Reform or Conservative. Only 10 percent are Orthodox. In Israel, by contrast, virtually all religious Jews are what Americans would consider Orthodox. Reform and Conservative Judaism hardly exist there.[61]

The second difference is the proportion of Jews who observe traditional Jewish law. Ten percent of Israel's Jewish population are ultra-Orthodox, or *haredi*, and live apart from the rest of Israeli society. (Their birth rates are very high, and they are a growing sector.)[62] Another 10 percent of Israelis are quite strictly observant but integrated into Israeli society. And some 40 percent describe themselves as "traditional"—they may not strictly observe the Sabbath or the daily prayer rules imposed by halacha, but they generally follow kosher dietary rules and attend services for the major holidays in synagogues that segregate men and women. (In other words, some 60 percent of Israeli Jews sometimes attend religious services in synagogues that Americans would consider Orthodox.)

The third difference relates to Jews who don't observe traditional Jewish law. Some 40 percent of Israeli Jews describe themselves as "secular" (*hiloni*). But they are more traditionally Jewish than most American Jews. For example, compared to many of America's Reform Jews (35 percent) and "Jews of no religion" (22 percent), the hilonim are far more knowledgeable about Judaism. Hebrew is their native language. They take Bible courses in their secular Israeli schools. Jewish holidays are *national* holidays. Many hilonim light Shabbat candles on Friday nights and refrain from eating pork. They live in a culture suffused with Jewish cultural and religious symbols, where Jews are a majority and dominate political life. Their "religious" commitment is to Zionism: loyalty to the Jewish state and the Jewish people.

Most secular Israelis have had little exposure to Reform or Conservative Judaism and don't see these branches as relevant to their lives. I suspect that's why they don't feel attacked when the Orthodox rabbinate has harsh words for these denominations. My hunch is that most secular Israelis would agree with the Orthodox rabbinate that the only real form of Judaism is Orthodox, not Reform or Conservative. However, they don't hesitate to speak up when the Orthodox rabbinate tries to extend the reach of halacha into areas where it *will* affect them. For example, they oppose further Sabbath restrictions on public life and call for the reduction of subsidies for the ultra-Orthodox, who have traditionally been exempt from military service.

All this suggests to me that American Judaism and Israeli Judaism are not likely to converge anytime soon. The liberal American denominations don't currently have a powerful presence in Israel, and I doubt that Reform or Conservative rabbis will soon receive the recognition they crave from Israel. I hope I am wrong. The good news is that the American Jewish establishment has found its voice and is willing to criticize Israeli government policies that undercut the legitimacy of Reform and Conservative Judaism as deeply inconsistent with our American Jewish values of religious pluralism. Whether our outspokenness will have any effect is not so clear.

THE UNITED STATES AND Israel are the two most important Jewish communities in the world, each with a Jewish population of about six million. The primary challenge each community faces is very different. Israel's primary challenge is how to manage being both Jewish and democratic in the face of serious security concerns. In America the primary challenge is passing on a meaningful Jewish identity to the next generation in a community where intermarriage is common.

These two challenges are interconnected and somewhat in conflict. How Israel manages its challenge is affecting its relationship with liberal American Jews, especially young ones. If the next generation of American Jews feels emotionally disconnected from Israel, they will lack a source of Jewish identity that their elders have found inspiring. To the extent they are ashamed of Israeli policies, this may undermine their Jewish identity further.

What can American Jews do to prevent this loss? That's the challenge I've tried to highlight in this chapter. It's a challenge that encompasses two sets of relationships: the relationship between liberal American Jews and Israel, and the dynamic *among* American Jews with relation to Israel.

With regard to the first relationship, liberal American Jews know Israel has an interest in maintaining its relationship with us, especially with our teenagers and young adults. Israel won't soon outgrow its need for our support or that of the US government in meeting its security needs. However, political issues in Israel currently seem to be dwarfing the importance of that relationship. For Israel's own good and the good of the Jewish people as a whole, liberal American Jews will need to be vocal and persistent.

On the religious issues, Reform and Conservative Jews must continue to insist that Israel not allow its Orthodox rabbinate to become the sole arbiters of authentic Judaism. They must insist that Israeli government policies reflect greater respect for religious pluralism. When Israeli officials speak contemptuously about Reform Jews, it corrodes the relationship between American Jews and Israel. When the Israeli government abrogates a long-negotiated agreement at the Western Wall that was specifically designed to recognize Reform and Conservative Jews as part of the Jewish people, it poisons the relationship further.

On the Israeli-Palestinian issue, American Jews who are politically liberal on domestic issues are centrists, and they're torn between loyalty to Israel and dismay over its policies. The challenge here is to overcome the temptation to be silent. Too many American Jews are sitting this one out. If a two-state resolution of the conflict is to remain viable and if Israel is to remain both Jewish and democratic, these "ambivalent centrists" must find their voice and use a megaphone. To save Israel from its own worst tendencies, we must support those elements in Israel that still favor a two-state solution but don't have enough political power to implement it.

In order for American Jewish centrists to develop such a strong voice, they will need to confront the second relationship I spoke of earlier: the unhealthy dynamic among American Jews. They must refuse to be cowed into silence by the large number of conservative or center-right Jews who believe in "Israel right or wrong." The ambivalent centrists must stop being afraid that healthy dialogue and criticism will harm Israel. If anything, silence will harm it more.

For those American Jews more inclined to be in the AIPAC camp—who are uncomfortable when other American Jews express criticism of Israeli policies—I would note that in Israel itself a substantial number of Israeli Jews voice their opposition to the continued expansion of West Bank settlements. The recent Israeli documentary *The Gatekeepers* featured five former leaders of the Shin Bet—the Israeli internal security force responsible for counter-terrorism—expressing the destructive impact of continued occupation. Why should American Jews with similar viewpoints be silenced? There is more than one way to support Israel. Open debate among American Jews can help us all develop a deeper understanding of Israel's challenges, and tolerance of opposing views is essential for preserving Jewish identity here in America.

10

THE CHALLENGE OF INTERMARRIAGE

THE SURVEY DATA are stunning: for American Jews today, intermarriage is now more the rule than the exception.[1] Among Jews who have married since 2005, about 58 percent have chosen a non-Jewish spouse.[2] A century ago, by contrast, the intermarriage rate among American Jews is thought to have been less than 5 percent.[3] This remarkable change reflects the fact that endogamy—the notion that Jews should only marry other Jews—is no longer the controlling norm.

My own family's experience reflects these trends. My maternal grandparents, both born in America in the 1880s, had three children, each of whom married a Jew. Those three couples had a combined total of six children, including me. The four oldest of the six—of which I was one—married Jews, but the two youngest married "out." My generation produced a total of fifteen children. Of the eleven who married, *nine* have married non-Jews, including my younger daughter, Allison. Like me, many in my generation of Americans have grandchildren with a non-Jewish parent. The question some of us ask is: Will our grandchildren grow up to think of themselves as Jewish?

Traditional Jewish law has long dictated that a Jew must marry another Jew.[4] Traditionally observant Jews still see endogamy as a religious obligation. Until fairly recently most American Jews followed this custom even if they did not feel bound by halacha.[5] Today, however, social attitudes toward intermarriage have changed. Many Jews and non-Jews alike accept intermarriage. This change has sparked alarm in the Jewish community and an intense debate over how Jewish institutions should respond to the increasing intermarriage rates among American Jews.

Two basic schools of thought have emerged. One view is that the primary institutional response to intermarriage should be to discourage it because without endogamy the Jewish community will disappear. This bleak outlook rests on the belief that once a Jew intermarries, he or she is "lost to Judaism" and, perhaps even more importantly, is unlikely to raise Jewish children. I don't quarrel with the right of Jewish parents to urge their children to marry only a Jew. Sharing that preference with one's children, when coupled with a substantial religious upbringing, may well influence the decisions of some young people. But at an institutional level, I don't think trying to promote endogamy is likely to have much impact on young Jews who were not raised in highly observant homes.

The second view is that interfaith couples are far from "lost" and that the best response to intermarriage is to embrace them and encourage them to raise their children as Jews. I stand firmly in this camp. I think trying to discourage intermarriage is a fool's errand. It's unlikely to work, given current social trends. Far from promoting the survival and distinctiveness of the Jewish people, it risks alienating many young Jews and, for those who intermarry, their children as well.

Why Intermarriage Is Increasing and What It Means

As long as Jews were persecuted and lived in insular communities -- and as long as Christians were reluctant or forbidden to marry them -- it was not difficult for the Jewish community to enforce endogamy. Throughout the Diaspora the rabbinic prohibition against intermarriage was clear, and Jewish social norms reinforced it. Jewish leaders, believing that endogamy was necessary to preserve group distinctiveness, marginalized those who married out.[6] Jewish families exerted tremendous pressure on young people to marry within the tribe.

Compared to their counterparts in Europe, American Jews were typically more socially integrated with gentiles, but most American Jews continued to embrace endogamy. For most of the twentieth century all three major Jewish denominations (including Reform) enforced the prohibition against intermarriage by refusing to allow rabbis to officiate at interfaith weddings.[7] Family pressure reinforced the norm: in extreme cases traditionally observant Jewish parents sat *shiva*—that is, recited the prayers for the dead—for a child who married out, and they then cut off all relations. I was told that my Orthodox paternal great-grandparents sat shiva for their daughter, Dorothy, when she married an Italian Catholic.

Until the mid-twentieth century the rate of marriage between Jews and non-Jews remained very low. I found no systematic national surveys on the subject, but scholars estimate that the rate was less than 5 percent until about 1940[8] and only 6 percent in the decade after World War II.[9]

The American intermarriage rate began its rapid climb in the 1960s, rising to about a third by 1970 and 58 percent by 2000. (See table below.) If one excludes the Orthodox, the current rate is even higher: among the non-Orthodox who have married since 2000, the intermarriage rate is 72 percent.[10]

INTERMARRIAGE, BY YEAR OF MARRIAGE
(percentage of Jewish respondents with a non-Jewish spouse)

Married in	
2005–2013	58
'00–'04	58
'95–'99	55
'90–'94	46
'85–'89	41
'80–'84	42
'75–'79	36
'70–'74	35
Before 1970	17
Overall	44

Source: "2013 Survey of U.S. Jews," Pew Research Center.

Why did this change occur? Because of a cluster of social developments that have reinforced one another:

The Decline of Traditional Jewish Law as a Dominant Factor in the Lives of Most Jews

The vast majority of American Jews no longer believe that obeying Jewish law is central to being Jewish.[11] A majority of American Jews are either Reform, or affiliated with no denomination and not religious at all.[12] A religious law prohibition against intermarriage per se is unlikely to have much influence on either of these groups.

Contemporary evidence shows that the further away a Jew moves from traditional Judaism, the more likely he or she is to intermarry. (See table below.)[13] Whatever the causal relationship, the data suggests a strong connection between secular Jews and religious intermarriage.[14]

INTERMARRIAGE BY RELIGIOUS DENOMINATION
(among married Jews, percentage whose spouse is . . .)

Denomination	% Jewish	% Not Jewish
NET Jewish	56	44
Orthodox	98	2
Conservative	73	27
Reform	50	50
No denomination	31	69

Source: "2013 Survey of U.S. Jews, February 20–June 13, 2013," Pew Research Center. Figures may not add to 100 percent due to rounding.

The Decline in Anti-Semitism and the Increased Social Integration of American Jews

As we've discussed, Jews are now welcome to live, study, and work virtually anywhere in the United States. They have also become one of the wealthiest and most educated groups in the country,[15] which has eroded class barriers between Christians and Jews. Increased social integration increases the chances that young Jews will meet and fall in love with non-Jews, with whom they have much in common. Far more than in any previous time in American history, young Jews come into frequent contact with potential mates who have similar values and educational background but are not Jewish. People are more likely to marry those they see often and those they see as similar. Jews, after all, make up only 2 percent of the American population.

The Increasing Acceptance of Intermarriage by Jews and Non-Jews Alike

In the past, intermarriage across religious lines was unusual in America, not just for Jews but for Catholics and Protestants as well.[16] In the 1950s sociologist Will Herberg argued that religion served as a social sorting mechanism: Catholicism, Protestantism, and Judaism were the three main divisions. *Within* each group ethnic intermixing through marriage was acceptable. For example, Italian Catholics could marry Irish Catholics; Protestants of diverse ethnic backgrounds could marry one another, and Jews of German heritage might marry Jews whose ancestors came from Eastern Europe.[17] But intermarriage *across* religious lines was somewhat taboo.

That's no longer the case. "Both the norms governing religious intermarriage and actual marriage patterns [have] moved toward greater interfaith openness and integration, as religiously insular generations were succeeded by their more open-minded children," political scientist Robert Putnam observes.[18] Today 50 percent of married Americans have a spouse who originally came from a different religious tradition, and 30 percent are in interfaith unions.[19]

As a result, many Christian families now welcome the idea of a child marrying a Jew. As Sylvia Barack Fishman notes in her book *Double or Nothing?: Jewish Families and Mixed Marriage*, "No social phenomenon expresses the extraordinary new status of American Jews more than their attractiveness as romantic and marital partners for mainstream Christian Americans."[20]

Many Jews have become equally accepting of intermarriage. Among Jewish parents, fewer than half express a strong preference that their children marry Jews.[21] According to a study published in 2000, only 39 percent of American Jews agreed with the statement "It would pain me if my child married a gentile." Even among Jews who said Jewishness was "very important" in their lives, only about half (54 percent) said they would be upset if their child intermarried.[22]

The Rise of Marriage as an Individual Choice, Not One Constrained by Family and Group Ties

The modern understanding is that "marriage is primarily a romantic partnership rather than, as has historically been the case, a pragmatic contractual arrangement sanctioned by a larger community," Rebecca Mead noted in the *New Yorker*. Some commentators view this shift as a triumph of American individualism. The choice of mate is now seen as essentially personal: a love story, not a statement of ethno-religious identity and certainly not an abandonment of it.

For Jews, a Radical Change in the Meaning of Intermarriage

In the past most Jews viewed intermarriage as a deliberate choice to abandon one's religion, family, and community.[23] For some of those marrying out, their motivation might well have included a desire to escape the burdens of being Jewish; intermarriage might have advanced their prospects in Christian society. But whatever their intentions, those who intermarried did so with the understanding that they would be marginalized, if not exiled, from the Jewish community.

Today only the Orthodox still view intermarriage as an abandonment of Judaism. The larger Jewish community sees it differently. Most Jews who intermarry don't want to escape their heritage. Many are proud to be Jewish and want to pass that identity on to their children. The larger community seems to understand and support this view of intermarriage.

All five of these powerful forces have contributed to the high rate of intermarriage, and none of them seems likely to reverse course in the foreseeable future. Absent some dramatic change in these underlying forces—for example, a sharp and lasting spike in anti-Semitism or a widespread return to Orthodoxy by Jews who are not Orthodox now—it's hard to see how Jewish parents or institutions can make a significant dent in the intermarriage trend.

WHAT'S THE PROBLEM WITH INTERMARRIAGE?

The policy alarm over intermarriage stemmed partly from a 1990 Jewish population survey suggesting that interfaith parents were much less likely than in-married parents to raise their children in the Jewish faith.[24] (Scholars have coined the term *in-married* to indicate that both spouses are Jewish.) A later survey suggested that the children of intermarriage were much more likely to marry non-Jews themselves, compounding the potential losses over multiple generations.[25] This led many Jews, not irrationally, to assume that intermarriage was a disaster that would decimate the Jewish community because a huge portion of the children were being lost.

In 2013, when the Pew Research Center released the first comprehensive study on American Jews in more than a decade, it seemed to confirm the depressing news.

Among Jews with a Jewish spouse, a much higher percentage of respondents reported they were raising their children "Jewish by religion" than among intermarried couples.[26]

Further, the study confirmed that children of intermarriage were more than twice as likely to intermarry themselves.[27] Thus, the study seemed to reinforce the pessimistic view that intermarriage meant the inevitable loss of future generations to Judaism.

But in reporting its findings, the Pew study did not focus on two issues relevant to intermarriage: how the adult children of intermarriage were turning out and whether their rate of Jewish identification differed by age cohort. Prompted by several scholars, Pew researchers dug deep into their data and found a dramatic trend that contradicted all previous assumptions: over time a *rising* share of adult children of intermarriage were choosing to identify as Jews. The generational differences were astonishing. Among the oldest cohort of children of intermarriage—age sixty-five and older (also called the Silent Generation)—only 25 percent identified as Jews. Among the youngest cohort, those between ages eighteen and twenty-nine (millennials), 59 percent identified as Jews.[28] Moreover, the younger the respondent, the more likely he or she was to identify as Jewish *by religion*.[29]

This increased retention rate was big news in the Jewish world. As Brandeis professor Leonard Saxe, a leading social psychologist, noted, "We may be at a moment in time when intermarriage, while a challenge, is actually promoting the expansion and renewal of American Jewry."[30]

What was going on with the children of intermarriage? Why were so many millennials (those born after 1980)[31] identifying as Jews, compared to those born earlier? According to Saxe, the answer lay in how they had been raised. Compared to their older counterparts, millennial children of intermarriage were more likely to have been raised Jewish by religion, to have received some Jewish education, and to have celebrated a bar or bat mitzvah. This, in turn, was likely due to two developments. One was that as the intermarriage rate increased, "Jewish partners in interfaith marriages increasingly came from the ranks of the more highly affiliated and connected segments of the population," Saxe wrote. In other words, the Jewish partners were more often securely rooted in their Jewish identities and eager to pass their Jewish identity on to their children.

The second factor was a massive push by Jewish institutions to reach out to interfaith families.[32] As Saxe and other scholars explain it, the millennial generation benefited from the panic that had hit the Jewish community a generation before. When the 1990 National Jewish Population Survey (NJPS) reported that among recently married Jews, more than half (52 percent) had married out, Jewish leaders feared a tipping point had been reached, meaning that the Jewish community would begin to lose future generations rapidly.[33] This sparked major investment in Jewish education—preschools, day schools, Hebrew schools, summer camps, youth and teen programs, campus Hillels—and vigorous efforts to welcome interfaith families.

The millennials were the first cohort to experience these changes, and the Pew study was the first major study to include data on "how the adult children of intermarriage actually turned out," Theodore Sasson, a professor of Jewish studies at Middlebury College, explained. "The grim predictions made in the 1990s may have proved wrong because Jewish organizations, federations, and private foundations did what they needed to do to turn the tide."[34]

Brandeis scholars were aware of the turning tide even before the Pew study. In 2008 their own research had enabled them to mount a direct attack on the prevailing narrative that intermarriage was the "greatest threat to American Jewish life."[35] In their study, Fern Chertok, Benjamin Phillips, and Leonard Saxe asked: What motivates people to identify as Jews and raise Jewish children? To what extent does intermarriage make a difference?[36]

They found that the most significant predictor of Jewish identity was not whether one had intermarried parents but instead how one was raised. Their key finding was that children who received similar levels of Jewish upbringing showed similar levels of Jewish engagement as adults, regardless of whether they had one Jewish parent or two. The conclusion: "Jewish socialization in the form of Jewish education, experience of home ritual, and social networks plays a far more important role than having intermarried parents. . . . It is engagement and not intermarriage that presents both the greatest challenge and the most promising arena for intervention."[37]

RABBINICAL RESPONSES TO INTERMARRIAGE

As intermarriage rates have soared, each of the Jewish religious denominations has been forced to decide whether and how much to adapt. The strikingly different responses of the three major American denominations reflect a continuum between two poles: accommodation and resistance.

The Reform movement in the United States has made huge efforts to accommodate intermarriage.[38] The movement started reaching out to intermarried couples in the late 1970s, and in 1983 it recognized the legitimacy of patrilineal descent for children who are being raised as Jews.[39] Today the movement fully accepts children of interfaith families into its congregations, Hebrew schools, and youth groups. It welcomes non-Jewish spouses as active participants in the congregation and puts no pressure on them to convert.

The Reform movement makes a point of expressing *gratitude* to non-Jewish spouses for helping to raise Jewish children. This appreciation is often expressed during services in Reform temples. As the Reform movement's "Premarital Counseling Guide for Clergy" notes, "The Jewish community has been blessed to have had so many individuals from other faith backgrounds give the gift of raising Jewish children. Tremendous appreciation needs to be expressed by the partner, the partner's family, and the Jewish community for giving this gift to Judaism."[40]

Still, sensitive issues remain within the Reform movement. One such issue is whether rabbis should preside at interfaith weddings. Officially, the Reform rabbis' organization, the Central Conference of American Rabbis, discourages officiating unless both members of the couple are Jewish, but it leaves it up to each rabbi to decide whether he or she will do so.[41] Forty years ago very few Reform rabbis would officiate at such weddings, but today about half do.[42]

Some Reform rabbis who do not officiate admit to anguish about having to say no. Senior Rabbi Howard Jaffe of Temple Isaiah in Lexington, Massachusetts, says, "I am aware of the impact of my saying, 'I love you, I want to welcome you into the Jewish community, but I am not able to officiate.' I know that, in most cases, the words 'I am not able' are heard as 'I am rejecting you,' even though that is not the message I am intending."[43] Jaffe says he assures interfaith couples that he will be happy to work with them before and after the wedding and to welcome them into the community. Other rabbis will agree to officiate only if the couple meets certain conditions, such as joining a synagogue or committing to raise their future children in the Jewish faith. I think the movement has come a long way since 1999, when a Reform rabbi refused to marry my daughter Allison because she flunked the "Christmas Tree test." Today I suspect rabbis are handling such conversations with a lot more sensitivity.

At the opposite end of the spectrum are the Orthodox, who make no concessions to intermarriage. They make up about 10 percent of American Jewry. Orthodox rabbis will not officiate at or attend the wedding of any "mixed" couple unless the non-Jewish spouse first converts. Such conversions are very rigorous and time consuming. Moreover, the rabbi must believe the spouse is genuinely committed to leading an observant Jewish life by Orthodox standards; converting only in order to marry is not seen as a valid reason for conversion. If the couple marries without an Orthodox conversion, the non-Jewish spouse cannot participate in Orthodox congregational life. The children of a non-Jewish mother, absent conversion, are not treated as Jewish.

The Orthodox think they have "the answer" to intermarriage for all Jews: Be strict and stick to your guns. Provide children with a thorough religious education, including attendance at a Jewish day school. Make it clear that intermarriage will not be tolerated.

It's an answer that works for them. Only 2 percent of Orthodox Jews marry out, and those who remain tend to have large families, leading to predictions that this segment of the Jewish population will grow. However, the overwhelming majority of American Jews are not about to become Orthodox and raise their children in that tradition.

The Conservative movement is caught between the Reform and Orthodox poles and is struggling to decide how to respond to intermarriage. Constituting 18 percent of America's Jews, the denomination is shrinking. The Conservative movement's stated position on intermarriage, tightly enforced by the Rabbinical Assembly, is identical to that of the Orthodox: intermarriage is barred, gentile spouses must convert before there can be a Jewish marriage, rabbis are forbidden to officiate at or even attend interfaith weddings, and the children of a non-Jewish mother, absent conversion, are not considered Jewish.

But that stance has hardly insulated the movement from the forces of social change affecting intermarriage. Unlike many Orthodox, Conservative Jews are fully integrated into American society, and among the recently married more than a quarter have married out.[44] The movement is under intense pressure from its congregants to allow Conservative rabbis to participate in mixed-marriage ceremonies.

This has placed the Conservative movement in a difficult spot. Despite its ban on intermarriage, it shares the Reform goal of engaging intermarried couples and retaining the next generation. In 2017 the movement took an important step: it voted to admit non-Jewish spouses as members of Conservative congregations.[45] The movement has also made it easy for parents to arrange the conversion of children of non-Jewish mothers; the ceremony is simple and joyous. But to many congregants, especially those whose children are intermarrying, these accommodations aren't enough.

The movement struggles with the inescapable tension—critics call it "perceived hypocrisy"—between claiming to prohibit intermarriage on the one hand and, then later, after the couple has married, accepting them (and their temple dues) on the other.[46] Many ask why the movement cannot adapt on intermarriage when it has been flexible in other areas. In 1950 the movement accommodated suburban life by allowing Jews to drive to synagogues on Shabbat. Later it approved mixed-gender seating at services, eating fish in non-kosher restaurants, the ordination of women and homosexuals, and same-sex marriage. These adaptations have made it harder for Conservative leaders to justify holding the line on intermarriage. After all, a Conservative Jew who is marrying a gentile and wants to have a Jewish ceremony can easily find a Reform rabbi to officiate—and may never return to Conservatism.

Conservative leaders are determined to resolve this tension without doing too much violence to the traditional ban on intermarriage. In a recent opinion piece four movement leaders explained that the survival of Jewish tradition depends on "changing as little as possible as late as possible, modifying it only when necessary and when there isn't already a solution within the system of halachah." Thus, they said, the wedding ceremony should remain reserved for marriage between two Jews, but in every other way the movement welcomes non-Jewish spouses "with open arms." The leaders promised to support interfaith couples "by being present as pastors before the wedding, as rabbinic guides and companions after the wedding and as loving friends during the wedding period."[47]

Such pronouncements, however, haven't relieved the pressure many Conservative rabbis feel. Some are quietly bending the rules and others are in open revolt. According to a recent—albeit disputed—survey of Conservative rabbis, 40 percent have violated the ban on attending interfaith weddings, and the same percentage would officiate at such weddings if allowed to do so.[48] Seymour Rosenbloom, a retired rabbi from Philadelphia, was expelled from the Rabbinical Assembly in 2016 after officiating at his stepdaughter's interfaith wedding and writing an editorial about it.[49] B'nai Jeshurun, a large nondenominational Manhattan synagogue with roots in the Conservative movement, announced its intention to start officiating at interfaith weddings in 2017.[50] Adina Lewittes, after twenty-seven years as a Conservative rabbi, resigned from the movement because the ban on intermarriage "increasingly chafed against my calling to engage Jews with their heritage." She now performs interfaith ceremonies, selectively, for Jews who care about "being Jewish and participating in Jewish life."[51]

I predict that the Conservative movement will soon allow individual rabbis to attend and participate in interfaith weddings, even if they are not permitted to officiate.

My personal view is that the movement should acknowledge children with a Jewish father as Jews, but I think this is unlikely any time soon.

THE LONG-TERM IMPACT OF high intermarriage rates on the American Jewish community remains to be seen. Although some doubt that the community can survive successive generations of intermarriage, I remain optimistic. There are promising signs. The most recent research suggests that a majority of millennials who are children of intermarriage are choosing to identify themselves as Jewish.

One challenge for the American Jewish community is to sustain this momentum. To those institutions embracing intermarried couples and their children, I say, Bravo! We need this work to maintain a diverse and vibrant community.

But I must emphasize that I do *not* think intermarriage in and of itself is the greatest threat to Jewish continuity. Contemporary research suggests a much more nuanced picture. Studies have shown that although intermarriage is certainly a challenge, the increasing "thinness" of Jewish engagement generally, even among people who have two Jewish parents, is a more pressing concern.

The larger challenge, as I see it, is how to increase the quality of Jewish engagement in a world where intermarriage is not likely to decline. What's the primary message we should be imparting to today's Jewish children? I have two grandchildren who are children of intermarriage and two grandchildren who have two Jewish parents. I would give all four of them the same message: "The issue is not whether you marry 'in' or 'out.' The issue is: Do you make the Jewish tradition a meaningful part of your life, and do you pass that tradition on to your future children?"

11

Raising a Jewish Child

SUPPOSE YOU WANT to give your child—or grandchild—every reason to choose to be part of the American Jewish community as an adult. How should you proceed?

There is no way to guarantee this outcome, but there are certainly ways to lay a foundation. Evidence suggests that certain strategies can increase the *likelihood* that children will grow up to identify as Jewish. In this chapter we'll examine the most promising strategies for parents, grandparents, and other family members.

This chapter is not meant for those parents who are deeply committed to Judaism and whose lives involve regular religious observance. If this describes your family home, you don't need my advice. Your children are being steeped in Jewish religion and culture, and as adults they will almost certainly identify as Jews.

Instead, this chapter is meant for those who face a more challenging task: raising Jewish children when one or both parents are not religiously inclined. You might be an intermarried couple or you might both be Jewish. The key is: at least one of you does not identify with being Jewish in a religious sense, and yet as a couple you want to instill a Jewish identity in your children. This chapter is for you.

Be Willing to Negotiate with Your Spouse or Partner Early and Often

If you're part of a couple, the process of building your child's Jewish foundation starts with that relationship. If you're intermarried, you and your spouse are bringing different ethnic and religious traditions to the marriage. Even if you and your spouse are both Jewish, you might have very different ideas about *how* to be Jewish. You may have been raised to follow different Jewish practices, or one of you may be much more religiously observant than the other. You may have very different attitudes toward Israel. There are many ways to be Jewish, and as a couple you will have to make some decisions. What level of religious observance will be followed in your home? What values does each of you want to pass on to your children?

The answers to these questions won't be static; they will evolve over time. You and your spouse are bound to have differences of opinion at various stages in your child's life. Things will come up that you can't anticipate. The process of raising Jewish children may even intensify your own religious identity, which in turn may influence how you feel about certain issues.

For example, how will you and your spouse celebrate holidays in the home? Which Jewish holidays will you observe, and how involved will each of you be in those celebrations? Will you join a temple, and if so, which one?

For some couples the Christmas tree is a fraught issue. Although in the 1940s and 1950s it wasn't unusual for Reform Jews to have Christmas trees in the home, the Reform movement has increasingly discouraged the practice. Today most Jewish couples don't have Christmas trees,[1] but many interfaith couples do.[2] For some Jews the absence of a tree is considered a statement of principle: "We are not Christians." If you grew up in such a home, you may find yourself married to someone, Jewish or not, who grew up with a living room festooned with Christmas ornaments and for whom a tree evokes warm memories of childhood. You may end up negotiating the tree issue from several angles: symbolic, religious, and emotional.

For intermarried couples who want to raise Jewish children, there is even more to negotiate. To what extent, if at all, will you honor the religious background of the non-Jewish spouse? Is any observance of the other religion in the home acceptable to both of you? Will you celebrate Christmas and Easter as secular holidays? How will you help your children understand the significance to them of Hanukah versus that of Christmas?

Most intermarried couples have some relationship with Christian festivities.[3] According to a recent study of millennial children of inter-marriage, 86 percent celebrated Christmas "with a special meal or by dec-orating their home," and about half said they "attended Christian religious services at least a few times a year."[4] But intermarried parents who are consciously raising their children *as Jews* are more likely to struggle with such decisions, and they tend to resolve any apparent conflict by treating Christmas as a secular American holiday, much like Thanksgiving.[5] Many visit their Christian relatives on Christmas and allow their children to receive Christmas presents, but they explain to their children that this is Grandma and Grandpa's holiday, not theirs. I don't think there's any-thing wrong with this practice. To me that doesn't constitute raising kids as "both."[6] If celebration of some Christian holidays as cultural events is what it takes to persuade a non-Jewish spouse to join a temple and partic-ipate in raising Jewish children, it may be a very worthwhile compromise.

The purpose of this discussion, however, is not to identify all the pos-sible issues that may arise for negotiation; rather, it is to emphasize the importance of engaging in negotiation itself. As a teacher of negotiation, I would give the same advice on the subject of raising Jewish children as I give on all other subjects. In a nutshell, it consists of four principles.

Don't avoid. Conflict is normal and inevitable. You may be tempted to avoid it, but resist that temptation. As Paul Cowan points out in his book *Mixed Blessings: Overcoming the Stumbling Blocks in an Interfaith Marriage*, many couples try to preserve harmony by suppressing their reli-gious differences and hoping everything will work out. He calls these dif-ferences "time bombs" destined to explode. They typically go off at times of stress: during the December holidays, when a child is born, when a child begins asking questions about religious identity, or when a loved one dies.[7] These are not ideal moments to be dealing with unresolved con-flicts about how you and your spouse are raising your children religiously. Instead of avoiding your differences or making concessions you aren't comfortable with, negotiate until a solution becomes clear.

Understand what makes such negotiations hard. As a teacher of negotiation, I view such discussions as "difficult conversations" because they trigger strong feelings and identity issues on both sides. My colleagues Doug Stone, Sheila Heen, and Bruce Patton have written a marvelous book, appropriately titled *Difficult Conversations: How to Discuss What Matters Most*, about how to approach such negotiations productively.[8] They conceptualize these as having three different dimensions, which are useful to think about separately. The first dimension—the "what happened" conversation—typically becomes an argument: What happened or should happen? Who's right and who's wrong? This dynamic often leads to deadlock instead of problem solving. The second dimension is about the emotions, such as guilt, anger, and self-doubt, that each person is experiencing but often not directly expressing. The third dimension is about the identity-related questions that lie beneath the emotions: What do I fear this situation says about me? The key to having a productive conversation is to shift the focus of the spoken conversation from "Who's right?" to "How do we each interpret the situation?" It also turns on each person's ability to identify—and perhaps express—the emotions and identity issues that the conversation is triggering for them.

When you and your spouse experience conflict over your children's religious upbringing, each of you may experience strong emotions, especially if aspects of your identity are under pressure. Consciously or subconsciously, each of you may be wondering: What does this conflict say about me as a spouse? What does it say about me as a parent? What does it say about me as a son/daughter/Jew/Christian? That's a lot to handle in one negotiation. Understanding the complexity of such negotiations can make them easier to manage. But making that shift requires a lot of practice and self-awareness, especially for individuals who grew up in families that handled conflict poorly, either by suppressing it, meeting it with explosive behavior, or a combination of both.

Take a problem-solving approach to exploring differences. Good communication requires using two fundamental skills at the same time: listening and talking. I don't mean *selective* listening and *argumentative* talking; I mean listening to understand the other person's point of view and talking in a way that helps the other person understand what's important to you. When you're under stress, it's hard to do either of these things well. In my negotiation classes I refer to these skills as empathy and assertiveness. A good negotiator needs to demonstrate a lot of both.

Empathy means listening nonjudgmentally to the other person's perspective, drawing them out with genuine curiosity, and demonstrating that you understand what they said—without necessarily agreeing. This technique, often called "active listening," can be extremely challenging to use when you're in conflict; indeed, you may worry that if you truly understand your spouse's point of view, you have to agree with it. That's why it is important, on occasion, to make it clear that you are not agreeing, just eager to understand. The reason to engage in empathetic listening is that it can pave the way for problem solving. For most people, it's more important to be understood than to be agreed with. Once your spouse feels heard, he or she will typically be more willing to listen.

Assertiveness means expressing what's important to you in language the other person can understand. It means being persistent in articulating your interests and calmly standing up for them without attacking the other person. In order to do this skillfully, you may first need to take some time to figure out what's important to you and why. Until *you* fully understand the *why*, you won't be able to explain it to your spouse.

Ask for help. You and your spouse are not the only couple facing these issues. There are many resources available for couples trying to raise Jewish children. These include rabbis, organizations, and professionals who specialize in counseling interfaith couples.[9] Some offer workshops and other events. Don't hesitate to seek help from any of these varied resources.[10]

HOW PARENTS CAN BUILD A CHILD'S JEWISH IDENTITY

Various studies have shown that four elements of Jewish life have the greatest impact in making children feel connected to Judaism: Jewish activities in the home, a Jewish education, Jewish social networks, and exposure to Israel.[11]

If your childhood was not filled with Jewish experiences or Jewish learning, you can build up that storehouse now. Non-Jewish spouses might be interested in learning too. This is not as hard a task as it may seem. There are Jewish study courses at every synagogue and Jewish community center. There is a wealth of information online, including detailed instructions on how to observe each holiday, complete with videos on how to recite blessings and prepare traditional foods.[12] Judaism classes and Torah study classes are also available online. But one of the best ways to educate yourself is to become affiliated with a synagogue before your children are born; this will also provide you with a community that includes other couples like you.

Jewish Holidays and Rituals in the Home

When Jewish adults are interviewed about what most shaped their Jewish identity, many report that it was not going to synagogue but rather what they did at home. Home is where children absorb basic Jewish values and enjoy the sensory pleasures of Jewish rituals, songs, and food.

Shabbat is an especially significant and beautiful ritual; indeed, many believe it's the "core experience for transmitting Judaism" to children.[13] I regret that Dale and I never celebrated Shabbat at home. The beauty and importance of Shabbat was powerfully impressed on me last year when one of my seminar students, an ultra-Orthodox Jew, invited everyone from the seminar to his home for Shabbat dinner. He had two young children, a son and a daughter, and a very pregnant wife who, despite the demands of work and home, cooked us an extraordinary dinner. Before the meal she lit the candles and recited the customary blessing. Her husband said prayers over the wine and challah (sweet braided bread). He had both children on his knee as he recited the traditional Hebrew blessing over each child, covering their bowed heads with his hands. Dale and I were quite moved by this, and it was easy to see how making Shabbat a weekly family ritual can foster strong connections to Judaism.

Reform rabbis now encourage young families to observe Shabbat with a Friday night dinner at home. I'm glad my daughters sometimes do so in their homes. The ritual is quite short, and a Friday night dinner is something busy couples can usually manage. If you didn't celebrate Shabbat as a child and want to learn how it's done, many synagogues and Jewish organizations have websites explaining the process step by step, including videos on how to say the prayers in both Hebrew and English.[14] It's a lovely way to create a tradition that children will enjoy and remember. It is a Shabbat tradition to set aside money for charity in a little blue *tzedakah* box. Children can be tasked with generating a list of worthy causes.

When I was growing up, almost every Friday night my parents, my brother Jimmy, and I would go across town to my paternal grandparents' apartment for dinner. These meals were so free of ritual that I didn't associate them with anything Jewish. Only years later, when I was about forty, did I realize that we had in a sense been observing Shabbat.

I grew up in the last days of Classical Reform Judaism, in the 1950s. In those days the denomination was very light on Hebrew and ritual, and the emphasis was on demonstrating one's religious commitments through ethical action and progressive ideals.[15] Neither of my parents was religiously observant. My mother's family had been Reform for several generations, and she had little patience for religious ritual. My father had been raised in a traditional household that kept kosher. My grandfather had been president of Kansas City's Orthodox synagogue, but my father had become a Reform Jew in college.[16]

It's hard to believe how clueless I was about the religious tradition that lay behind these family Friday night meals with my grandparents. When I think back to my grandparents' dining room on those evenings, I realize there were candles flickering on the sideboard. But I recall no prayers. I suspect my grandmother lit the candles and recited the Hebrew prayer before we arrived, perhaps in consideration of my mother's discomfort with ritual. That was the way religion was negotiated in the Mnookin family: so subtly that the children missed the point. Even so, I have wonderful memories of those Friday night dinners, and I was very close to my grandparents, both paternal and maternal.

Annual holidays are also essential in creating Jewish memories and building Jewish connectedness, and many are celebrated primarily at home. Passover can make a significant impression on children because of the elaborate meal, singing, and stories that recount the Jewish exodus from Egypt. When they're old enough to read, children often enjoy their special role in the Seder: the youngest child (or children) launches the telling of the Passover story by asking the traditional Four Questions, which attempt to explain how Passover is "different from all other nights."[17] Many children also have fond memories of eagerly awaiting the hunt for the *afikomen*, a piece of matzo that has been hidden somewhere in the house; the finder(s) often receive a prize.

Hanukah, a relatively minor holiday with regard to religious significance, can be truly magical for children because it brings eight days of lighting and blessing candles, exchanging gifts, and playing the gambling game called *dreidel*.[18] The Jewish calendar is filled with other holidays, such as Purim and Sukkot, to explore. For Purim, the spring festival, there are carnivals and costume parties that children typically love. For Sukkot, the seven-day autumn harvest festival, families can build a *sukkah*—a temporary outdoor hut meant for dining and sleeping—in the backyard, and kids can spend a night or two sleeping outside under it. (Building this structure has become easier in recent years as sukkah kits have become available online.)

Religious holidays aside, there are many ways within the home to transmit Jewish culture to children, such as food, books, activities, and your own storytelling. Each holiday has its own special foods: apples and honey cake for Rosh Hashanah, latkes (potato pancakes) for Hanukah, *hamantaschen* (triangular pastries filled with poppy seeds or fruit preserves) for Purim, challah for Shabbat. You can find child-friendly recipes online and invite your children to help with the preparations. Of course, Jewish foods can be eaten any time of year, and the cuisine is extremely varied, with influences from North Africa, the Middle East, and Europe.

Reading to children can also help spark their interest in Judaism. If your children are six months to eleven years old, PJ Library, through its website, will send you Jewish-themed books for free. Older children can join the program on their own. It's a fantastic way for you to learn along with your children. As the website explains, "We know that something magical happens when parents sit down together to read with their children. PJ Library shares Jewish stories that can help your family talk together about values and traditions that are important to you."[19] Many of the books have won awards, and they cover everything from Jewish holidays to Jewish values such as tzedakah (helping those in need), visiting the sick, and *teshuvah* (atonement). The site offers complementary videos and activities for teaching Jewish values.[20] Other organizations, such as the Jewish Book Council, can help you find Jewish-themed books for teens and young adults.[21]

Don't forget to tell your children stories about their own family history. Encourage your parents and other relatives to do so as well.

Jewish Education and Religious Observance Outside the Home

You and your spouse don't have to do everything yourselves. Judaism is meant to be practiced in community, and that means joining a synagogue, even if you aren't religious. As odd as it may sound, given my lack of enthusiasm for religious observance and the fact that for much of my adult life I have not been affiliated, I've come to the conclusion that it's very hard to transmit a Jewish identity to children without the help of a temple or synagogue. Affiliation provides children with at least three important ways to experience being Jewish: religious services, religious school (also available for adults), and a sense of belonging to a Jewish community.

Many children enjoy Shabbat services, which feature live music, singing, dancing, and the theatrical moment when the Torah is removed from the ark and paraded around the sanctuary. Many synagogues offer children's Shabbat services for different age groups, which can be attended with or without parents. This is also true on High Holy Days, when services are also often filled with music.

Religious school is a social setting where young children can meet other Jewish kids while learning about the holidays, Torah stories, and Hebrew alphabet. It can begin as early as kindergarten. As children get older, they learn traditional blessings, explore tzedakah and other ethical concepts, study a bit of Jewish history, and learn about Israel in Hebrew school.

Around age eleven they may start preparing for their bar/bat mitzvah, the coming-of-age ceremony that will take place when they are twelve or thirteen. Even if you don't belong to a temple, your child can have a bar/bat mitzvah. There are independent (unaffiliated) Hebrew schools that offer religious education through the bar/bat mitzvah and beyond. There are also freelance tutors who will tailor the ceremony to your child.[22]

A bar or bat mitzvah involves hard work. A child must learn to read and chant in Hebrew, read from the Torah and typically lead the congregation in prayer, and deliver a speech they have written. The ceremony itself initiates the child into the adult Jewish community as a person responsible for his or her own actions—traditionally, as a person responsible for observing the commandments of Jewish law. Completing this process often gives children a real sense of accomplishment and can be a potent way to strengthen Jewish identity.

A young person's religious education should extend past the bar/bat mitzvah. This can be a hard sell; many teens quit religious school right after their bar/bat mitzvahs. But those who continue their Jewish education, either at the temple or elsewhere, find the teen programs stimulating and fun. Both of my granddaughters attended Sunday school through their confirmation at age sixteen, and they enjoyed it.

The most powerful way to give a child a solid Jewish education is to send them to a Jewish day school. Some of my Harvard Law School students have gone to Jewish day schools, and their depth of knowledge and commitment to their identity as Jews has impressed me. Jewish day schools are a comparatively recent phenomenon, and most are located in major cities. When I was growing up there were none in Kansas City; now there is one. Nationally, as of 2008–2009, there were more than eight hundred. But these schools don't appeal to all Jewish parents. They tend to be expensive and much more traditionally religious than most American Jewish families are. The overwhelming majority are Orthodox. Among the schools counted in 2008–2009, only seventeen were affiliated with the Reform movement and about fifty with the Conservative movement. About one hundred were designated "Community"—that is, interdenominational—schools.[23] Many Jewish parents also feel that a parochial school creates too much religious segregation for a child.

Jewish Social Networks

Helping your child build friendships with other Jewish children is another way to build Jewish identity. Youth groups for preteens and teenagers offer social opportunities outside of a religious setting and can create strong friendships.

My granddaughters participated in temple youth groups and appreciated the groups for different reasons. My granddaughter Hailey really enjoyed meeting Jewish kids of different ages. She especially valued her friends from youth group because she found them to be less socially competitive than her peers at school. Hailey also looked forward to the activities: overnights, leadership training, and events with kids from other temples. My granddaughter Sophia was in a youth group that turned out to be mostly girls. It was led by an excellent social worker who encouraged them to talk about the challenges they were facing at age thirteen and fourteen. For Sophia it was meaningful to share a supportive environment with both a sensitive adult who was not a parent and with other engaged and curious Jewish teens.

B'nai B'rith Youth Organization (BBYO), the nondenominational organization for Jewish teens, operates worldwide and offers programs that combine fun, education, and community service.[24] One of its primary goals is simply to "keep Jewish social circles together at this age," executive Matt Grossman has said.[25]

Jewish summer camps, especially sleep-away camps, offer bonding experiences that can lead to Jewish friendships and strengthen Jewish identity. I went to Camp Thunderbird, an eight-week sleep-away camp in northern Minnesota on Lake Plantagenet. In the 1950s upper-middle-class kids—at least in the Midwest—were typically sent off to Jewish summer camps for eight weeks. Thunderbird was Jewish only in the sense that all the campers were Jewish; I recall no religious services or Jewish-themed activities. Its sole reason for existence was that gentile summer camps in the Midwest didn't take Jewish kids. Nonetheless, it did reinforce my Jewish identity. I made friends there that I've kept ever since.

Most Jewish camps today more self-confidently and deliberately expose campers to Jewish rituals and values, and there is evidence that a Jewish summer camp can contribute to a child's Jewish identity.[26]

The college years are another prime time for building these ties.[27] Although you will have far less control over your children's choices at this stage, you can still encourage them to take advantage of Jewish offerings on campus.[28] Jewish studies courses have seen dramatic growth on college campuses since 2000. Predominantly Jewish fraternities and sororities still flourish on some campuses.[29] At many colleges a campus Hillel provides a way for Jewish students to make friends and participate in activities connected with Jewish religion and culture. A recent Brandeis University study found that Hillel activities can be influential and meaningful in building Jewish identity, especially for children of intermarriage. The study noted that when children of intermarriage enter college, their levels of Jewish knowledge and engagement tend to lag behind those of children with two Jewish parents. But when children of intermarriage participate in Hillel or Chabad (an Orthodox campus group), take Jewish-related courses, and/or make a Birthright Israel trip, they are significantly more likely to identify as Jews, celebrate Jewish holidays, and believe it is important to raise Jewish children.[30] The study found that the impact on students who experience both a campus program and Birthright is "profound."[31]

Exposure to Israel

A trip to Israel can be transformative for young people, especially those whose Jewish identity is undeveloped or uncertain. It connects them to the Jewish people in an extraordinary way. Many parents take their children to Israel as part of a family holiday or a group tour organized by their synagogue. Some synagogues organize group tours for high school students as well.

More than five hundred thousand young people have made a trip to Israel with Birthright Israel on free ten-day group tours around the country. To qualify, a young person must be of "Jewish descent with at least one Jewish parent" or have converted. The organization's mission is to fortify Jewish identity by connecting young Diaspora Jews with Israelis of the same generation. Philanthropists Charles Bronfman and Michael Steinhardt first endorsed this idea, and the State of Israel, the Jewish Federation system, and many private donors now support it as well.[32]

Birthright alumni sometimes say the trip changed their lives. A Jewish student attending Loyola Marymount University, a Catholic university in Los Angeles, wrote a powerful blog post making this point. The student, Caroline Burt, wrote that before her Birthright trip "I felt like a fake Jew. Although I grew up in a spiritual household, I never went to synagogue, I never went to Hebrew school and I never had a bat mitzvah. In fact, even calling myself a Jew felt like a lie. I'm attending a Catholic school. I'm actually the worst Jew ever."[33] While in Israel she celebrated her bat mitzvah, an opportunity provided on some Birthright trips. "In just 10 days, I found a part of myself that, subconsciously, I knew was missing. A whole community of Jews opened its arms and took me in. In addition, simply being with other American Jews and comparing stories made me feel at home. I hadn't previously realized that for a large part of my life I had been an outcast, but being a Jew in a largely Christian society had a profound impact on me. In Israel, I finally found people who had the same identity struggles as me."[34]

HOW GRANDPARENTS AND EXTENDED FAMILY CAN HELP RAISE JEWISH CHILDREN

As a grandparent (or aunt, uncle, or cousin), you may care a great deal that younger generations in your family identify as Jewish, even if, like me, your own Jewish identity wasn't very strong when you were younger. The good news is that you can be an influential role model for these children. Especially if you provide them with Jewish experiences that complement those they are getting at home.[35]

My sister-in-law, Wendy Mnookin, whose Jewish journey became serious only in midlife, is a testament to the fact that it's never too late to further one's Jewish education and share it with children and grandchildren. Like my brother and me, Wendy was raised Reform with a very thin Jewish education. As their three children were growing up, Wendy and Jimmy joined and then left a Conservative synagogue in Newton, Massachusetts. Unfamiliar with the Jewish prayers, they felt disconnected at services, and when their children objected to Hebrew school three times a week, they caved. The family attended High Holy Day services at Brandeis University, and the children went to Sunday school there. With tutoring, the children were later able to celebrate their bar and bat mitzvahs at the Brandeis Chapel.

It wasn't until all three children had left home that Wendy and Jimmy felt the lack of a synagogue anchor. "We wanted a place where we could observe life passages, celebrate with community, and deepen our Jewish commitment," Wendy says, explaining their decision to join the nearby Conservative synagogue—the same one they had left years earlier. This time, though, in order to feel more comfortable at services, Wendy took classes. After several years of studying Jewish history and practice, Wendy asked the rabbi what was next. "Your adult bat mitzvah," the rabbi answered. To her surprise, when she brought up the idea with Jimmy, he was enthusiastic and wanted to participate as well, so they enrolled in a two-year program at their synagogue for adults who hadn't had a bar or bat mitzvah when they were young and now wanted to fill in that gap. They were immensely proud, Wendy relates, when they stood up before the congregation and celebrated their *b'nai mitzvah* (as the ceremony is called when two or more people celebrate the ritual together). Their children gave a family party, complete with a poster-size photo for guests to sign—just as the children had had at their own parties years before.

While Wendy and Jimmy were increasing their involvement in Judaism, all three of their children married non-Jews. None of the children was married by a rabbi, although each included elements of the Jewish marriage ceremony in the service.

"Our own Jewish journeys," Wendy says, "made us more accepting of our children's choices. Look at me—my family had a tree at Christmas, and here I am, an active member of a Conservative congregation and a committed Jew. Who knows what our children's journeys will hold?"

And what about the grandchildren? Wendy and Jimmy have four young grandchildren, all of whom are being raised as Jews. "This would be impossible," Wendy says, "without buy-in from our daughters-in-law. We are extremely lucky that they were open to creating Jewish families."[36]

On Wendy's seventieth birthday the children gave Wendy and Jimmy a surprise gift: a conversion ceremony for all four grandchildren at a nearby *mikvah* (ritual bath). The ceremony was held at Mayyim Hayyim, a beautiful light-filled space for conversion, attended by rabbis from two synagogues (one from Wendy and Jimmy's, the other from son Seth and daughter-in-law Sara's). "We didn't call it conversion, though," Wendy says, "since the grandchildren already considered themselves Jewish." This ceremony means that the Conservative movement will recognize as Jews the three grandchildren whose mothers are not Jewish. "I'm not sure the actual conversion will be important to any of the grandchildren, since their most likely affiliation is Reform, but it was important to us. And it was especially meaningful because it showed our children's acknowledgment of how important Judaism is to us and a commitment on their part to continue identifying as Jews."

Wendy is the first to say that her experience is somewhat unique. Embarking on a path to develop Jewish learning does not guarantee that one's grandchildren will undergo conversion. And that wasn't her goal, after all. I look at Wendy and Jimmy's experience not as a blueprint for Jewish grandparents but rather to suggest ways grandparents can support and inspire the Jewish development of grandchildren.

Start by Communicating Your Values to Your Adult Children

If, like Wendy and Jimmy, you were not very invested in your Jewish identity when your children were growing up but are more committed now, talk to them about your Jewish journey. "It's more likely for the grandchildren to be Jewish if the parents participate in a meaningful way," Wendy says. "So we try to share with the parents our ongoing experience. [They] didn't see much active involvement in the Jewish community [from us] when they were growing up, so it's something we have to communicate now."

She accomplishes this by discussing with her children what she's learning as well as her questions and concerns about Judaism. She makes it clear that she is not trying to tell her children what they should do but rather including them in the conversation.

Encourage Family Celebrations of Jewish Holidays

If you live near your children, you can encourage them to celebrate Shabbat—sometimes in your home, sometimes in theirs. Wendy has made needlepoint challah covers for all three children, and Jimmy brings challah over to the Brookline team every Friday morning. "We're trying to encourage the spirit of Shabbat that we celebrated when they were growing up," Wendy says.

Welcoming your children and grandchildren to special holiday celebrations in your home may strengthen their connection to Jewish tradition. Taking charge of a holiday or two has the added benefit of giving your busy children, caught up in the pressures of parenthood and career, a reprieve from the responsibility of organizing a religious event. For example, organizing a Seder can be daunting, so your children may appreciate not having to figure out the meal and the service themselves. Wendy hosts the family Passover Seder both for her grandchildren's benefit and for the pleasure of telling her children, "We'll take care of it."

"I used to go to Passover Seder at my grandfather's, who was Orthodox," she recalls. "He did the whole Seder in Hebrew. My cousins and I would go under the table and play, and in the background we would hear my grandfather droning on in Hebrew. One of the reasons I really wanted to learn Hebrew [later] was because my grandfather's words have stayed with me. It didn't matter that we were playing under the table; we were soaking it in."

You can also introduce your grandchildren to other Jewish holidays. For some years now Wendy and Jimmy have been celebrating Sukkot, the harvest festival. They enlist the help of their son Seth and his family, who live nearby, to construct and decorate the sukkah next to the house and then eat a festive meal inside. "The grandchildren love it," Wendy says. "It's practically camping out."

Bring Your Grandchildren to Services

If you belong to a temple, bring your grandchildren to Shabbat services. As noted, many temples offer children's Shabbat services tailored to short attention spans, but the adult service can also be festive. "Shabbat Alive, on Friday nights, is a big treat," Wendy says. "There's music, and sometimes the grandchildren dance in the aisles." When preparing for a weekend visit to Wendy and Jimmy, their five-year-old granddaughter now says, "I'm packing my temple clothes," meaning she hopes to go to temple and intends to wear something nice.

When bringing the grandchildren to adult services, Wendy lets them bring books to read. "I want it be fun," she says, "and there are some long sections of Hebrew that they can't understand." She believes they will absorb the memory of the service—the prayers, the chanting, the music—even if they are not paying strict attention.

Find Ways of Conveying What Your Jewish Heritage Means to You

As the various holidays approach, send your grandchildren books about the holiday. Read or discuss the books together so the grandchildren better understand what they are celebrating. You can do this by video conference if the grandchildren don't live nearby. If they know they will be celebrating a particular holiday with you, reading a book ahead of time will stoke their anticipation. Wendy started her collection of such books on PJ Library.

Talk with your grandchildren about what they are doing in religious school and let them know you support those activities. Share your family stories and memories—the Haggadah the family created together or the Seder with the cousins playing under the table.

Most importantly, have fun with them. "I think that some of their decisions on Judaism will reflect good times they've had with us, whether those occasions had anything to do with Judaism or not," Wendy says. "Having fun together blends into their awareness that we are Jewish and it's important to us, and it becomes a piece of the whole."

Conclusion

"WHEN ARE WE GOING TO BECOME JEWISH?"

My daughter Jennifer's challenge, posed more than thirty-five years ago, implicitly raised the question: What does it mean to be Jewish?

"Become Jewish?" I responded. "We *are* Jewish. We're just not very religious."

My defensive answer reflected an assumption shared by most Jews and embedded in traditional Jewish law: ancestry alone makes us Jewish, so there's no need to *do* anything and no need to choose. To her credit, Jennifer disagreed.

In this book you have accompanied me as I've explored the nature of American Jewish identity and described aspects of my own Jewish journey. When I was in my thirties I thought being Jewish had little to do with my life. Today, although I remain nonobservant, being Jewish is a much more conscious and salient part of my identity because of choices I have made. An important choice was writing this book, which required me to educate myself on issues that Jewish scholars have debated for centuries, then to wrestle with those issues and come up with my own answers. This process made me feel more Jewish than ever. It required the kind of intellectual struggle that Jewish tradition encourages. It also removed any trace of discomfort I felt about proclaiming my Jewishness to the world. Once I had battled my way through Jewish history and the issues unique to American Jewish identity, I understood my earlier ambivalence toward being Jewish as the product of a particular time and place. I understood why so many Jews in the 1950s were taught to downplay their Jewishness; why now, sixty years later, such caution is no longer necessary; and why I am proud to be Jewish.

The paradox of the book's title reflects how much has changed for American Jews over the course of my lifetime. Jews have never had it so good in terms of public acceptance, and yet many of us worry that, for our descendants, Jewish identity is at risk. In my youth Jewish identity was supported by five traditional sources: descent, religious affiliation, endogamy, anti-Semitism, and support for Israel. Today fewer of us find those sources meaningful or inspiring. For Jews like me, who find no comfort in religion, what is our Jewish identity based on? This is one of the implicit questions I've been exploring in these pages.

I began the book with Erik Erikson, not because of his fame as one of the world's most influential theorists on identity but because his personal story was filled with conflicts about identity, especially Jewish identity.

Was Erik Erikson Jewish? To an outside observer the answer would depend on whether one gives more weight to descent or choice. His mother was a Danish Jew, so he was halachically Jewish. He was raised in a German Jewish home and celebrated a bar mitzvah. But as an adult, he made significant choices that distanced him from that identity. He abandoned Judaism as a religion. He married a non-Jewish woman, and they raised their children as Protestants. He dropped his Jewish name, Homburger, in favor of an assumed Scandinavian name, Erikson. Toward the end of his life he occasionally attended church services with his wife. Did he stop being a Jew? According to my standard, yes. He no longer wished publicly to identify himself as Jewish and part of the American Jewish community.

I used Erikson's story to introduce my own theory of identity. I am not an identity essentialist. I don't believe people are or are not a single thing; instead, our personal identities are composed of many strands, of which being Jewish may be one. Among American Jews the salience of the Jewish strand varies enormously from person to person. Moreover, that salience isn't fixed; it may vary considerably over a person's lifetime, as it has for me. In Erikson's case, after he came to America he chose to avoid public identification as a Jew. I think he had every right to do that. But Marshall Berman, whose book review emphasized Erikson's family background, stated flatly that Erikson was a Jew and accused him of being less than authentic. As I've noted, Jewish identity has a collective dimension: others view you as a member of a group. I have no doubt that many Jews—and probably some gentiles—agreed with Berman: the matrilineal standard meant Erikson was a Jew.

As you know, I reject the matrilineal standard as a way of defining who is a Jew in America today. Its religious pedigree isn't as ancient as most people think; it was created by rabbis after the biblical period for reasons that aren't clear. More important, it leaves no room for choice. It doesn't allow a person like Erikson to opt out of being Jewish, and it subjects him to attack by Jews who suspect him of trying to make a secret escape. It rejects exemplary Jews like Reform rabbi Angela Buchdahl because she doesn't have a Jewish mother, and it ropes in people like Madeleine Albright, whose parents never told her about her Jewish ancestry. I believe that everyone, whether Jewish by birth or not, should be allowed to choose for themselves whether and how to be Jewish.

One unusual aspect of the matrilineal standard is that it qualifies a person as Jewish even if she has no commitment to the Jewish religion. And as we've seen, many American Jews *don't* have much commitment to Judaism as a religion. If being Jewish depended on belief in a personal God or going to synagogue, a substantial proportion of Americans who proudly identify themselves as Jewish would flunk the test. This poses a major challenge to maintaining Jewish identity in America. For those of us who are not committed to Judaism as a religion, what is it that makes us Jewish? Is it *just* descent—or something more?

It's not "Jewish blood." The Nazis relied on such racial notions to justify murdering millions of Jews, and the notion of a Jewish race is abhorrent today. I reject the notion that Jews can be defined by heritable physical or biological characteristics that are unique to Jews. There is no Jewish gene, and blood tests based on DNA would be both under- and overinclusive.

I was intrigued when I started to think about peoplehood. Jews are raised to believe that they are part of a distinct "people," "tribe," or "nation" with religious and ethnic dimensions and a shared history. No one is born thinking they are part of a people. These ideas must be taught.

I was raised to feel a connection with other Jews, and I count myself as part of the Jewish people. But the idea of Jewish peoplehood doesn't help us define who is a Jew. It contains no membership requirements. How do you become part of the people? If it's only through maternal descent or conversion, we're back to square one: the matrilineal principle. I like the idea of a Jewish people, but only if the tribe is inclusive enough to embrace those of mixed ethnicity and those who marry into the tribe.

Examining Israel's struggles with Jewish identity didn't provide me with an answer to this problem. But it did reinforce my feeling that self-identification, rather than proof of descent, can play a role in defining who is Jewish and that the definition can vary according to context.

In trying to find a single standard that satisfied me, by far the most difficult question was the role of descent. Ultimately I gave up looking for a single standard and proposed a two-part test. For the American Jewish community as a whole—the Big Tent—the standard should simply be public self-identification. For each group or organization under the Big Tent, more stringent requirements for membership and participation may be set, but only for that subgroup.

I acknowledge that the first part of this approach is rather radical. Admission to the Big Tent requires *no Jewish ancestry*. Nor does it require religious conversion to Judaism. I eliminated the religious requirement for non-Jews because none exists for Jews by birth. If it were possible to implement some form of secular or humanistic conversion for non-Jews—one that required learning the basics of Jewish religion, history, and culture—I would support it. But in the meantime self-identification is good enough.

But self-identification doesn't solve the problem—it's just a start. What challenges does the Jewish community have to confront in order to draw young people into the Tent and keep them there? The waning of anti-Semitism is great news, of course, in that the cost of proudly asserting our Jewishness is close to nil. But it also removes a powerful force that used to encourage many young Jews to seek shelter inside the Tent. What are the forces that remain?

For some of us, caring about Israel and its survival is still a compelling draw. But for others it's an exhausting dilemma. Many Jews, despite their commitment to Israel's survival, are dismayed by the Israeli government's policies relating to the Israeli-Palestinian conflict and the political power of the Orthodox rabbinate. These policies fuel conflicts among American Jews between the Orthodox and the rest of us. They also risk alienating young Jews, whom we most need to entice into the Tent.

Many Jews believe the greatest threat to American Jewish identity is intermarriage. I disagree. Surveys show that many children of mixed religious heritage grow up to have a strong Jewish identity—*if* they are raised as Jews and feel actively embraced by the community.

Rather than intermarriage, I think the greatest challenge is disengagement. Many Americans proudly think of themselves as Jewish, but they can't necessarily answer the question I asked above: Why is being Jewish meaningful to you?

Those who are religiously committed to Judaism have a clear answer. Religion is perhaps the most powerful force drawing people into the Tent. I wish I *were* religious. I wish I found the experience of ritual emotionally gratifying. I envy those who find deep meaning, comfort, and strength in their religious faith. And I envy them for having such a straightforward way—or so it seems to me—to articulate what they hope to pass on.

For the nonreligious, what makes being Jewish meaningful? If my grandchildren asked me this question, what would I tell them? After much reflection I've come to the conclusion that what I love most about being Jewish are three things: what I call the Jewish head, the Jewish heart, and the Jewish heritage. All three have roots in the religion.

By the Jewish head, I mean our people's commitment to education and the life of the mind. We are the "people of the book." Judaism is a text-based religion that "makes literacy a primary duty," Rabbi Jonathan Sacks has noted. "The Talmud goes so far as to rank study as higher even than prayer as a religious act."[1] Our religious texts, starting with the Torah, are basically books of law. The tradition encourages not just questioning and debate but also analysis and interpretation. It's no coincidence that so many

Jews have chosen intellectual professions. In a different age I might have been a rabbi. I love to engage with texts and law. I like to think through complicated problems. Although writing this book has been maddening at times, what I've loved most about the process has been learning.

By the Jewish heart, I mean our commitment to *tikkun olam*, a Hebrew phrase that means "repairing the world." This key tenet of Judaism dates back to the Mishnah, the body of rabbinic teachings codified around 200 CE.[2] As many Jews define the concept today, it expresses our obligation to pursue social justice and help make the world a better place through acts of kindness and compassion, particularly for the less privileged. When I was growing up I absorbed this idea from my parents, grandparents, and religious schooling: that I had an obligation to engage in social action to help heal the world. When I went into the field of conflict resolution I didn't think of it as expressing tikkun olam, and my motivation certainly wasn't religious, but I don't think the choice was an accident: I feel the connection to Jewish values.

In fact, I've come to the conclusion that many of us who are not religious are in effect practicing the religion through our social commitments. If you are a lawyer who donates pro bono services to needy individuals and organizations, you could choose to think of it as an expression of tikkun olam. If you support the ACLU, the Environmental Defense Fund, or any number of liberal organizations, you might be engaging in tikkun olam. Dale and I belong to a marvelous organization called Facing History and Ourselves, which trains educators to teach history with an understanding of racism, prejudice, and anti-Semitism. The organization doesn't label itself Jewish, but it was founded by a Jewish educator and its members are disproportionately Jewish. Its goal is to "Help Create a More Compassionate and Ethical World"[3]—a clear reference to tikkun olam.

By Jewish heritage, I mean the remarkable three-thousand-year story of the Jewish people, including our American Jewish story, which now extends back nearly four centuries. What a story! One of the great pleasures of working on this book was learning about American Jewish history, which I find quite moving. It's a story of survival that began long before my time, and I feel part of it. The heritage is very rich. What I would tell my grandchildren is: I hope someday you connect to this story. There are so many different ways you could see yourself as part of it.

The Jewish head, heart, and heritage are not unique to Judaism; the values underlying them transcend Jewish boundaries. But I am proud that they are so central to our religious and cultural tradition.

I have also decided that it's not enough simply to define *why* one identifies as a Jew; there's a second question I have challenged myself to answer: How does being Jewish affect how I'm living my life?

"Every reflective human being," says Lord Jonathan Sacks, the former chief rabbi of Great Britain, "will ask at some time in his or her life: Who am I? Why am I here? *How then shall I live?*"[4]

Choosing to self-identify as a Jew has little meaning if it has no effect on how one lives. What I'm suggesting is a conceptual shift in how we define being Jewish. Instead of a status, it should be a choice. Instead of something one *is*, which doesn't require any thought or effort, it should be something one actively *does*.

A former student of mine helped me find an answer. When I met her, she was engaged to a Jewish man and was in the process of converting to Judaism. To support this transition, her rabbi recommended that she engage in three sorts of activities each week. One involved *study*, a second involved *having a Jewish experience*, and the third involved *community engagement with other Jews*.

The rabbi made it clear that these categories included many options, both religious and nonreligious. Jewish study could involve learning about Jewish history and culture as well as religion. *Having a Jewish experience* might involve watching the movie *Fiddler on the Roof*, visiting a Jewish museum or memorial, cooking a traditional Jewish meal, dining at a kosher restaurant, lighting candles on Shabbat, or reciting a Jewish prayer. *Community engagement with other Jews* might involve going to synagogue, of course, but it could also involve participating in an activity related to Israel or doing volunteer work in a Jewish organization where, as a Jew along with other Jews, she was seeking to help others.

My aspiration for the Jewish New Year is every week to engage in some form of Jewish study, have a Jewish experience, and engage in some sort of community activity with other Jews. The study part is easy for me because of my fascination with the history. I count as a Jewish experience watching films that qualify for Jewish film festivals. In terms of community work with other Jews, I am involved in several Israeli NGOs, serve on the Harvard Hillel board, and am active in Jewish nonprofits both here and in Israel. I may not hit the mark every week for all three categories.

Thank you for joining me on this journey. You now know how I think about the challenges facing the American Jewish community and why our community should be inclusive. I have also shared why I am choosing to be Jewish, why being a part of our diverse tribe is meaningful for me, and how being Jewish does make a difference in how I am living my life.

I'm not trying to sell you my answers. But I hope I have persuaded you that the questions driving this project are important ones. For the American Jewish community as a whole: Is it not time that we become more inclusive and view being Jewish as a choice, not an ascribed status? And for those who choose to be Jewish: Why is being Jewish important to you, and how does being Jewish affect the way you live your life?

Acknowledgments

WRITING BOOKS HAS NEVER BEEN EASY, at least for me. But writing this one was especially challenging—intellectually and emotionally. It is with profound gratitude that I now acknowledge those who helped me meet these dual challenges and complete this book.

The intellectual challenge is easy to describe. This book's subject matter is largely far afield from my expertise. Jewish studies is not my specialty. Doing the necessary research to write an informed book about Jewish identity and the challenges facing the American community was a daunting and time-consuming task. Along the way I was constantly reminded about how little I knew, how much relevant scholarship there was, and how few obvious answers there were to many difficult problems. Nevertheless, because I enjoy research, facing the intellectual challenges turned out to be very stimulating and even fun.

But facing the emotional challenges of writing this book was not fun. The second and more fundamental reason writing this book was difficult relates to its personal nature. It required me to explore some tough questions: Why did I care whether my grandchildren thought of themselves as Jewish? Could I explain what being Jewish meant in terms of how I was living my life? Midway into the project I complained over lunch to my colleague Dr. Alan Stone, a psychiatrist on the Harvard Law School faculty who also happens to be Jewish, that writing this book was the hardest project I had ever undertaken. He wryly replied, "Of course it's hard. You are working out your own *mishigas* [the Yiddish word for 'craziness'] about being Jewish." Disclosing my evolving and complicated feelings about my own Jewish identity did not come easily for me. I am not into confessionals.

Without the encouragement and support of Jim Levine, I would never have undertaken or completed this project. Jim is my agent, but more importantly, he is my dear friend. From the outset Jim believed in this book. Over the past four years he played a key role in helping me shape the book proposal and, later, the book itself. He carefully read many chapter drafts. His editorial suggestions were always valuable. More importantly, when I became discouraged, Jim bucked me up and expressed confidence in me and the importance of the project.

In a sense this book had a long incubation period, going back many decades to my youth in Kansas City. But the idea that I should write a book relating to Jewish identity was triggered much more recently. About seven years ago I had conversations with my faculty colleague Randall Kennedy about his book *Sellout: The Politics of Racial Betrayal*. This brave book concerns racial identity and explores, among other issues, the question of who counts as black in America. Randy makes a radical argument: that Americans of black ancestry should have the freedom to shape their own racial identity, even if that involves choosing to "pass" as white. But he acknowledges that "the specter of the 'sellout' haunts the African-American imagination. A long-oppressed minority situated in the midst of a dominant white majority, blacks fear that whites will favor and corrupt acquiescent Negroes who, from positions of privilege, will neglect the struggle for group elevation." The challenges facing Jewish Americans and African Americans are hardly the same. But Randy's book led me to pose a radical question: Suppose being Jewish in America were thought of as a matter of personal choice rather than as an ascribed characteristic. Doesn't the specter of assimilation and intermarriage similarly haunt the American Jewish imagination?

Many people helped me formulate and develop my ideas. Along the way I had stimulating talks with many family members and friends. Early in the project I remember especially helpful conversations with Ben Heineman, Richard Shweder, and Rachel Cowan. During visits to Israel I had particularly thought-provoking discussions with Moshe Halbertal, Donniel Hartman, and Gilead Sher. I also wish to thank Noah Feldman, who heads a new HLS Program on Jewish and Israeli law.

Several people helped me with specific chapters of the book. My daughter Jennifer made valuable suggestions about how best to organize the introduction and the chapter on Erikson. Alan Stone read an early version of the Erikson chapter, as did Professor Gordon Fellman. The chapter on the matrilineal principle relies heavily on the scholarship of Professor Shaye Cohen, who graciously reviewed that chapter. Aviva Meyer, Yochai Benkler, and Gabby Blum read the chapters relating to Israel. Fern Chertok generously gave me comments on the intermarriage chapter. Wendy Mnookin's contribution to the chapter on raising a Jewish child is conspicuous.

As I was writing chapters I received helpful editorial advice from Josh Burek, Temma Ehrenfeld, and Katie Shonk. Eugene Kogan, Jim Dale, and Robert Pozen later read and offered useful comments on a number of chapters, as did Sanford Levinson and Maya Steinitz.

During the entire period I was writing this book Harvard Law School was my professional home, and for most of that time Martha Minow was its dean. I am grateful to Martha for personal encouragement and indispensable institutional support for my research. Funds from the Harvard Law School and the Harvard Negotiation Research Project allowed me to hire gifted student research assistants over the years. They tracked down sources, wrote background memoranda, and, later, checked citations. I am grateful to Hannah Belitz, Aaron Blacksberg, Ariana Bloom, Alicia Brudney, Sophie Daroff, Isaac Gelbfish, Kelsey Jost-Creegan, Lea Malewitz, Orlea Miller, Maria Naimark, Corey Omer, James Pollack, Zalman Rothschild, David Salant, David Seidler, Shelly Simana, Ilan Stein, and Benjamin Weintraub as well as students in my fall 2017 Seminar on Jewish Identity. My faculty assistant Caryn Shelton-May patiently prepared the final manuscript. The law school's library staff—especially the FRIDA team headed by George Taoultsides—did an astounding job of finding often obscure books and periodicals and later helping me cite several chapters.

With Jim Levine's help, I was lucky enough to land a contract with PublicAffairs. Peter Osnos—this imprint's founding editor—took a personal interest in this book and acted as its champion after PublicAffairs became a part of Hachette Book Group. Peter connected me with Lisa

Kaufman, who offered marvelous editorial advice when the book was in process. I also wish to thank Hachette's Michelle Welsh-Horst and Melissa Raymond, who later shepherded the book through the publication process.

My greatest editorial debt is once again owed to Kathy Holub, who also worked with me when I wrote *Bargaining with the Devil*. During the last eighteen months Kathy was not simply an editor but also my writing coach. She was my sparring partner who helped me sharpen my thoughts. Over this period I sent Kathy portions and drafts of both finished and unfinished chapters. Kathy went through my prose word by word, line by line, and improved my writing. She pushed me to clarify and simplify my language and, most importantly, to be more vulnerable by saying what I really thought. Together we went through an iterative editorial process that involved more writing and rewriting than I suspect either of us anticipated or would care to remember. Lastly, Kathy kept me on schedule to deliver the manuscript by December 31, 2017, the date specified in my contract with PublicAffairs.

Family matters. And how blessed I am in that regard. This book is dedicated to the memory of my grandfathers, Jacob Mnookin and George M. Sittenfeld. Many decades after their deaths I still find inspiration in their love, generosity, and pride in being Jews in America. I take pride today in being part of the extended Mnookin and Sittenfeld clans. It is my deepest hope that my daughters, Jennifer and Allison; their husbands, Joshua Dienstag and Cory Olcott; and perhaps most importantly, my four marvelous grandchildren—Sophia, Hailey, Isaac, and Eli—will enjoy learning more about my thinking on an important and challenging set of issues. Finally, I must thank my wife, Dale, the love of my life, for her patience and support. She steadfastly expressed confidence that I would complete this project.

Robert H. Mnookin
Cambridge, Massachusetts
May 2018

NOTES

INTRODUCTION

1. Reform Jews prefer the word *temple* to *synagogue*.

2. Will Herberg's classic study captured my own experience growing up in the Middle West of the 1950s. Membership was socially obligatory, quite apart from one's religious beliefs. Herberg claimed that American social life was divided into three separate parts, one Protestant, one Catholic, one Jewish: a "triple melting pot." Will Herberg, *Protestant-Catholic-Jew: An Essay in American Religious Sociology* (Chicago: University of Chicago Press, 1955).

3. I've since learned that the Hebrew words are "Nitzotz Ha Yehudi."

4. "A Portrait of Jewish Americans," Pew Research Center, October 1, 2013, http://assets.pewresearch.org/wp-content/uploads/sites/11/2013/10/jewish-american-full-report-for-web.pdf.

5. "America's Changing Religious Landscape," Pew Research Center, May 12, 2015, www.pewforum.org/2015/05/12/americas-changing-religious-landscape.

6. "A Portrait of Jewish Americans."

7. "America's Changing Religious Landscape."

8. Zach Pontz, "Richard Dawkins Perplexed by High Number of Jewish Nobel Prize Winners," *Algemeiner*, October 29, 2013, www.algemeiner.com/2013/10/29/richard-dawkins-perplexed-by-high-number-of-jewish-nobel-prize-winners.

9. Thomas B. Morgan, "The Vanishing American Jew," *Look*, May 5, 1964, 42–46.

10. Alan M. Dershowitz, *The Vanishing American Jew: In Search of Jewish Identity for the Next Century* (New York: Little Brown and Company, 1997).

11. Leonard Saxe, "The Sky Is Falling! The Sky Is Falling!" *Tablet Magazine*, December 3, 2014, www.tabletmag.com/jewish-news-and-politics/187165/pew-american-jewry-revisited.

CHAPTER 1: THE PUZZLING NATURE OF JEWISH IDENTITY

1. Marshall Berman, "Erik Erikson, the Man Who Invented Himself," *New York Times* (Sunday Book Review), March 30, 1975, www.nytimes.com/books/99/08/22/specials/erikson-history.html.

2. Lawrence J. Friedman, *Identity's Architect: A Biography of Erik H. Erikson* (New York: Scribner, 1999), 432.

3. Robert Coles, *Erik H. Erikson: The Growth of His Work* (Canada: Little, Brown & Company, 1970), 181.

4. Erik Erikson, *Life History and the Historical Moment* (New York: W. W. Norton & Company, 1975), 142.

5. Friedman, *Identity's Architect*.

6. Ibid., 29.

7. *New York Times*, May 13, 1994, obituary.

8. Friedman, *Identity's Architect*, 29–30.

9. Ibid., 30. Several years later, shortly after Erik's birth, Karla would learn from a Salomonsen relative that her husband Valdemar had died in October 1902.

10. Ibid., 30.

11. Theodor formally adopted Erik in 1911, when Erik was nine. Ibid., 34.

12. Ibid., 39.

13. Ibid., 298.

14. Ibid.

15. Ibid., 433.

16. Ibid., 39.

17. Ibid., 433.

18. Ibid., 30. Friedman told me he tracked down two Danish photographers named Erik who were alive at the right time, but neither was a court photographer, and Friedman thought the evidence was too thin to assert that either man was Erikson's father.

19. Ibid., 433.

20. Ibid., 38.

21. Ibid., 41.

22. Ibid., 38, 42.

23. Ibid., 83.

24. Ibid.

25. Robert S. Wallerstein, "Erik Erikson and His Problematic Identity," *Journal of the American Psychoanalytic Association* 62, no. 4 (August 2014): 662.

26. Ibid.

27. Friedman, *Identity's Architect*, 83.

28. Ibid., 315.

29. Wallerstein, "Erik Erikson and His Problematic Identity," 665.

30. Friedman, *Identity's Architect*, 439. Robert and Judy Wallerstein, who were Jewish, apparently told Erikson's biographer that they felt uneasy about Erik's interest late in life in Saint Stephen's Church and its young rector. Ibid., 440.

31. Wallerstein, "Erik Erikson and His Problematic Identity," 666.

32. Friedman, *Identity's Architect*, 439.

33. The letter is quoted at length in Wallerstein, "Erik Erikson and His Problematic Identity," 669–671. It was published after Erikson's death in E. H. Erikson, "Erikson on His Own Identity," *DoubleTake*, Fall 2000, 32–34.

34. Wallerstein, "Erik Erikson and His Problematic Identity," 669.

35. Friedman, *Identity's Architect*, 34.

36. Ibid., 37.

37. Ibid., 105.

38. Ibid., 108.

39. Ibid., 244–245. Berkeley offered him a professorship in psychology with a lectureship in psychiatry. In 1950 Erikson refused to sign a loyalty oath required by the University of California and resigned his Berkeley professorial appointment. Ibid., 249.

40. Ibid., 304–309.

41. Seth J. Schwartz, Koen Luyckx, and Vivian Vignoles, eds., *Handbook of Identity Theory and Research* (New York: Springer, 2011), back cover.

CHAPTER 2: THE MATRILINEAL PRINCIPLE

1. See the discussion of the Brother Daniel case in Chapter 6, 104–110.

2. See Shaye J. D. Cohen, "The Origins of the Matrilineal Principle in Rabbinic Law," *Association for Jewish Studies* 10, no. 1 (Spring 1985): 19–53: 52. See generally Shaye J. D. Cohen, "The Matrilineal Principle in Historical Perspective," *Judaism: A Journal of Jewish Life and Thought* 34, no. 1 (Winter 1985), 5–13; Shaye J. D. Cohen, *From the Maccabees to the Mishnah* (Philadelphia: Westminster Press, 1987); Shaye J. D. Cohen, *The Beginnings of Jewishness: Boundaries, Varieties, Uncertainties* (Berkeley: University of California Press, 1999).

3. Cohen, "Origins of the Matrilineal Principle," 21.

4. Ibid., 21.

5. Ibid., 22.

6. Ibid., 7. For women, "the act of marriage was functionally equivalent to the later idea of conversion." Ibid., 21.

7. Cohen, *From the Maccabees to the Mishnah*, 42.

8. See Cohen, "Origins of the Matrilineal Principle," 30.

9. These earlier laws, known as the "Oral Law," were meant to clarify the commandments of the written Torah and explain how to carry them out. Beginning with Moses, they were presumably handed down orally from generation to generation until first recorded in the Mishnah in the second century. The legal principles found in the Mishnah would be developed further in the Talmud over the next two centuries. See, for example, "Judaism: The Oral Law—Talmud & Mishna," Jewish Virtual Library, www.jewishvirtuallibrary.org/the-oral-law-talmud-and-mishna.

10. Cohen, "Origins of the Matrilineal Principle," 52.

11. Shaye J. D. Cohen, "From the Bible to the Talmud: The Prohibition of Intermarriage," Jewish Theological Seminary, New York, 23. See also Cohen, *From the Maccabees to the Mishnah*, 41–42.

12. Cohen, "From the Bible to the Talmud," 23; Cohen, *From the Maccabees to the Mishnah*, 41–46.

13. Cohen, "From the Bible to the Talmud," 23.

14. Ibid., 36.

15. Cohen, "Origins of the Matrilineal Principle," 30. This is Cohen's translation, and he added the materials in brackets.

16. Ibid., 30.

17. The word *mamzer* is often translated into English as "bastard" or "illegitimate child." Traditionally it was thought that an ordinary Jew was prohibited from marrying a mamzer and that the taint of this status would be passed down through many generations. In actual contemporary practice the legal status of a mamzer under Jewish law has evolved. Today even rabbis who accept traditional Jewish law adopt various legal and interpretive strategies to avoid imposing the taint of mamzer status. See Rabbi Elie Kaplan Spitz, "Mamzerut," EH 4.2000a, www .rabbinicalassembly.org/sites/default/files/public/halakhah/teshuvot/19912000 /spitz_mamzerut.pdf; Rabbi Louis Jacobs, "What Is a Mamzer? Jewish Children Born from Forbidden Sexual Relations Pose Ethical and Communal Challenges," My Jewish Learning, www.myjewishlearning.com/article/the-mamzer-problem.

18. Cohen, "Origins of the Matrilineal Principle," 49.

19. Ibid., 42–50.

20. Ibid., 52.

21. Cohen, "The Matrilineal Principle in Historical Perspective," 11.

22. Ibid., 22. See also Annette M. Boeckler, "Matrilineality in Judaism" (English translation of "Das Mutterprinzip," an article that appeared in the German Jewish weekly *Juedische Allgemeine Wochenzeitung*, May 3, 2013, www.juedische-allgemeine .de/article/view/id/15829).

23. Cohen, *The Beginnings of Jewishness*, 306.

24. Cohen, "Origins of the Matrilineal Principle," 49.

25. See note 17 of this chapter.

26. Cohen, *The Beginnings of Jewishness*, 290 fn88.

27. Cohen rejects this rationale for a second reason: rabbis made exceptions to the matrilineal rule in certain cases, such as rape, and determined the child's status by a different method. He gives two examples of such exceptions. First, if an unmarried pregnant woman identifies the father as a Jewish priest, some rabbis say she is to be believed and the child inherits the father's status. Second, in cases of rape the offspring is "presumed to have the same status as the majority of the people where the rape occurred." In neither case does the matrilineal rule apply. See Cohen, "Origins of the Matrilineal Principle," 41. I am not persuaded that such exceptions are significant enough to warrant rejecting the "mater certa" rationale.

28. Note that if one of the spouses had been born a gentile but had converted before marriage, the marriage was valid and the child was a Jew.

29. See Cohen, "Origins of the Matrilineal Principle," 40–41. "If a woman is married, the law presumes that her husband is the father of her child."

30. There are other possibilities, but I suspect they were much less common. For example, the mixed couple might stay together without marrying. I doubt such

a couple would have been long tolerated in a Jewish community. If the couple chose to live with the foreign tribe and perhaps marry there, I doubt the rabbis were much concerned with the Jewish status of the child.

31. The passages are Deuteronomy 7:3–4, Leviticus 24:10, and Ezra 10:2–3. Cohen, "The Matrilineal Principle in Historical Perspective," 8; Cohen, "The Origins of the Matrilineal Principle," 24–25, 36–37.

32. Tzvi Freeman, "Was Jewishness Always Matrilineal?" Chabad.org, https://web.archive.org/web/20170809002813/http://www.chabad.org:80/library/article_cdo/aid/945298/jewish/Was-Jewishness-Always-Matrilineal.htm.

33. Ibid.

34. See "Children of intermarriages," Reform Judaism.org, https://reformjudaism.org/ask-rabbi-topic/children-intermarriages. The Reconstructionist denomination made the same change fifteen years earlier in 1968. See "Reconstructionists Will Recognize Children of Mixed Marriages as Jewish," *Jewish Telegraphic Agency*, May 8, 1968, www.jta.org/1968/05/08/archive/reconstructionists-will-recognize-children-of-mixed-marriages-as-jewish.

35. Debra Nussbaum Cohen, "What's Unnerving About Angela Buchdahl? She Talks About God," *Forward*, January 19, 2014.

36. Rahel Musleah, "Profile: Angela Buchdahl," *Hadassah Magazine*, June/July 2013, www.hadassahmagazine.org/2013/06/26/profile-angela-buchdahl.

37. Angela Warnick Buchdahl, "Kimchee on the Seder Plate," *Sh'ma Journal: A Journal of Jewish Ideas* (2003), http://shma.com/2003/06/kimchee-on-the-seder-plate.

38. See generally Michael Dobbs, *Madeleine Albright: A Twentieth-Century Odyssey* (New York: Henry Holt & Company, 2000).

39. Michael Dobbs, "Albright's Family Tragedy Comes to Light," *Washington Post*, February 4, 1997, www.washingtonpost.com/wp-srv/politics/govt/admin/stories/albright020497.htm; Barry James and *International Herald Tribune*, "Conversion of Albright's Jewish Family Followed a Well-Trod Path," *New York Times*, February 8, 1997, www.nytimes.com/1997/02/08/news/conversion-of-albrights-jewish-family-followed-a-welltrod-path.html.

40. Caitlin Yoshiko Kandil, "The Madeleine Effect," *Moment* magazine, November 1, 2012, www.momentmag.com/the-madeleine-effect; Franklin Foer, "Did She Know?" *Slate*, February 16, 1997, www.slate.com/articles/news_and_politics/the_gist/1997/02/did_she_know.html.

41. Dobbs, "Albright's Family Tragedy Comes to Light."

42. Ibid.

43. Kandil, "The Madeleine Effect."

44. Steven Lee Myers, "Albright Learns That She Lost 3 Ancestors in the Holocaust," *New York Times*, February 4, 1997, www.nytimes.com/1997/02/04/world/albright-learns-that-she-lost-3-ancestors-in-the-holocaust.html.

45. Dobbs, "Albright's Family Tragedy Comes to Light."

46. Ibid.

47. Foer, "Did She Know?"

48. Frank Rich, "The Albright Question," *New York Times*, February 19, 1997, www.nytimes.com/1997/02/19/opinion/the-albright-question.html.

49. Lally Weymouth and *Newsweek* Staff, "As I Find Out More, I'm Very Proud," *Newsweek*, February 23, 1997, www.newsweek.com/i-find-out-more-im-very-proud -174798.

50. Ibid.

51. Dobbs, *Madeleine Albright*, 10.

52. Orthodox rabbinic authority holds that if you have a Jewish mother, even if you are unaware of your Jewish heritage, you are still a Jew. You would not need to go through a formal conversion to join the Jewish community because you would never have lost your Jewish status. See, for example, Menachem Posner, "How Do I Know If I Am a Jew?" Chabad.org, www.chabad.org/library/article_cdo/aid/3408865 /jewish/How-Do-I-Know-If-I-Am-a-Jew.htm.

53. Jaweed Kaleem, "Madeleine Albright Discusses Her Jewish Background and Her New Book, 'Prague Winter,'" *Huffington Post*, April 27, 2012, www.huffingtonpost .com/2012/04/27/madeleine-albright-prague-winter_n_1460500.html.

54. Rich, "The Albright Question."

55. Kandil, "The Madeleine Effect."

56. Manuel Roig-Franzia, "In New Book, Madeleine Albright Describes Holocaust's Great Cost to Her Family," *Washington Post*, April 25, 2012, www .washingtonpost.com/lifestyle/style/in-new-book-madeleine-albright-describes -holocausts-great-cost-to-her-family/2012/04/25/gIQA3bxkhT_story.html ?utm_term=.4216dec33f05.

57. Kaleem, "Madeleine Albright Discusses Her Jewish Background."

58. Kandil, "The Madeleine Effect."

59. Kaleem, "Madeleine Albright Discusses Her Jewish Background."

CHAPTER 3: MUST A JEW PRACTICE JUDAISM?

1. There are two different dimensions to religious commitment: beliefs and observance. Beliefs are internal and subjective. Acts of observance relate to behavior, such as reciting prayers or attending religious services.

2. Renee Montagne, *Morning Edition* interview, November 4, 2011, www.npr .org/2011/11/04/142010920/daily-show-producers-book-blasphemy-or-hilarity.

3. See, for example, "Catechism of the Catholic Church," www.vatican.va /archive/ENG0015/_INDEX.HTM; Anglican Church in North America, "To Be a Christian: An Anglican Catechism," http://anglicanchurch.net/?/main/catechism; "Evangelical Lutheran Worship: Small Catechism of Martin Luther," http://ctkelc .org/wp-content/uploads/2012/01/Martin-Luthers-Small-Catechism.pdf.

4. See The Religion of Islam, "How to Convert to Islam and Become a Muslim," www.islamreligion.com/articles/204/how-to-convert-to-islam-and-become-muslim.

5. MJL Staff, "Dogma & Doctrine," My Jewish Learning, www.myjewish learning.com/article/doctrine-dogma.

6. "The Thirteen Principles of Jewish Faith," Chabad.org, www.chabad.org /library/article_cdo/aid/332555/jewish/Maimonides-13-Principles-of-Faith.htm.

7. Medieval sourcebook, "Maimonides: The 13 Principles and the Resurrection of the Dead," Fordham University, https://sourcebooks.fordham.edu/source /rambam13.asp.

8. I subsequently discovered that Rabbi Hayim Halevy Donin, a very thoughtful Orthodox rabbi, has come up with the same list. See Hayim Donin, *To Be a Jew: A Guide to Jewish Observance in Contemporary Life* (New York: Basic Books, 1972), 12–27.

9. "The Thirteen Principles of Jewish Faith"; Moshe Halbertal, *Maimonides: Life and Thought*, trans. Joel Linsider (Princeton, NJ: Princeton University Press, 2014), 136, originally citing Moses Maimonides, Introduction to *Pereq Heleq*.

10. See, for example, Marc Shapiro, "Maimonides' Thirteen Principles: The Last Word in Jewish Theology?" *Torah U-Madda Journal* 4 (1993): 194–213.

11. Daniel Septimus, "Must a Jew Believe in God?" My Jewish Learning, www .myjewishlearning.com/beliefs/Theology/God/About_God/Must_I_Believe.shtml.

12. See Genesis 32:22–31. See also MJL Staff, "Who Was Jacob?" My Jewish Learning, www.myjewishlearning.com/article/jacob. Like most things in the Bible, the etymology of the word *Israel* (which is a composite of two root Hebrew words) can be interpreted in different ways. It might mean he who "prevails with God" or he who "strives with God." Others suggest it means "God is straight" or "God rules." See, for example, Jane E. Lythgoe, "The Meaning of ISHaRaAL (Israel) in Ancient Hebrew—AL (God) [Is] Straight," Yehweh Not Yahweh, August 4, 2010, http:// yehweh.org/profiles/blogs/the-meaning-of-isharaal-israel; Elon Gilad, "Why Is Israel Called Israel?" *Haaretz*, April 20, 2015, www.haaretz.com/.premium-why-is-israel -called-israel-1.5353207; Stephen A. Geller, "The Struggle at the Jabbok: The Uses of Enigma in a Biblical Narrative," 53, https://web.archive.org/web/20140814005141 /http://jtsa.edu/Documents/pagedocs/JANES/1982%2014/Geller14.pdf.

13. Menachem Kellner, *Must a Jew Believe Anything?* (Portland, OR: Littman Library of Jewish Civilization, 1999), 8.

14. Ibid., 18. According to Kellner, the biblical meaning of the Hebrew word *emunah*, typically translated as "belief" or "faith," is "trust in" rather than "believe that." "The basic, root meaning of *emunah* is trust and reliance, not intellectual acquiescence in the truth of certain propositions." Ibid., 15.

15. Rabbi Harold M. Schulweis, "From God to Godliness: Proposal for a Predicate Theology," February 1975, 7, http://hmsi.info/wp-content/uploads/2017/01 /from-god-to-godliness-proposal-for-predicate-theology.pdf.

16. Eugene Borowitz, *Liberal Judaism* (New York: Union of American Hebrew Congregations, 1984), 129–131.

17. Ibid., 130. Writing about Borowitz's vision of Judaism, Dana Evan Kaplan states, "From a theological point of view, the acceptance of such a broad spectrum of beliefs makes it impossible to present a clear and compelling religious vision that could motivate followers to sacrifice for the sake of God. There are simply too many images of God for the group to agree on any one. On the other hand, this theological diversity allows the Reform movement to reach out to a broad spectrum of people who differ not only in their lifestyles, but also in their religious convictions." Dana Evan Kaplan, *American Reform Judaism: An Introduction* (New Brunswick, NJ: Rutgers University Press, 2003), 62–63.

18. See Mordecai Kaplan, *The Meaning of God in Modern Jewish Religion* (New York: Behrman's Jewish Book House, 1937). Other writers have also wrestled with this issue. See, for example, Richard Rubenstein, *After Auschwitz: Radical Theology and Contemporary Judaism* (Indianapolis: Bobbs-Merrill, 1966); Harold M. Schulweis, *Evil and the Morality of God* (Cincinnati: Hebrew Union College Press, 1984); Rabbi Rachel Sabath Beit-Halachmi, "Radical Theology: Confronting the Crises of Modernity," My Jewish Learning, www.myjewishlearning.com /article/radical-theology-confronting-the-crises-of-modernity.

19. Such basic prayers as the Shema and Kaddish are not recited.

20. Founded in 1963 by Sherwin T. Wine, a rabbi trained in Reform Judaism, the Society for Humanistic Judaism now has ten thousand members in about twenty-five congregations in various American cities. Rabbi Barry Cohen, "Humanistic Judaism," My Jewish Learning, www.myjewishlearning.com/article /humanistic-judaism; "Focus on Issues: Secular Humanistic Jews Seeks to Attract Unaffiliated," November 13, 1995, *Jewish Telegraphic Agency*, www.jta.org/1995 /11/13/archive/focus-on-issues-secular-humanistic-jews-seeks-to-attract -unaffiliated. Congregations are listed at www.shj.org/communities/find-a-community. The society's website says, "Humanistic Judaism embraces a human-centered philosophy that combines rational thinking with a deep connection to the Jewish people and Jewish culture. Humanistic Judaism integrates the celebration of Jewish identity with the belief in using human reason and human power as the best vehicle for improving the world." Society for Humanistic Judaism, "Humanistic Judaism," www.shj.org/humanistic-judaism.

21. See David Gonzalez, "Temple with No Place for God Seeks a Place," *New York Times*, June 11, 1994, www.nytimes.com/1994/06/11/nyregion/temple -with-no-place-for-god-seeks-a-place.html.

22. "Reform Jews Reject a Temple Without God," *New York Times*, June 13, 1994, www.nytimes.com/1994/06/13/us/reform-jews-reject-a-temple-without-god.html.

23. Kimberly Winston, "Atheist Jews: Judaism Without God? Yes, Say American Atheists," *Huffington Post*, September 26, 2011, www.huffingtonpost .com/2011/09/23/atheist-jews-judaism-without-god_n_978418.html, citing Robert Putnam and David Campbell, *American Grace: How Religion Divides and Unites* (New York: Simon and Schuster, 2010).

24. "A Portrait of Jewish Americans," Pew Research Center, October 1, 2013, 74.

25. Ibid. As earlier noted, the 2013 Pew Survey estimated that 22 percent of self-identified American Jews were what Pew called "Jews of no religion." These were people who, when asked about their religion, did not select Judaism but instead indicated they were atheists (6 percent), agnostic (4 percent), or responded "nothing in particular" (12 percent). Nonetheless, "aside from religion, they consider themselves Jewish or partially Jewish." See Ibid., 18, 32. The 22 percent estimate roughly corresponds to the 23 percent who, in a separate question, indicated they did not believe in God.

26. Ibid., 74.

27. Ibid., 74.

28. Winston, "Atheist Jews."

29. Babylonian Talmud: Tractate Shabbat 31a, www.sefaria.org/Shabbat.31a?lang =bi. See also Adam Kirsch, "Standing on One Foot," *Tablet*, November 6, 2012, www.tabletmag.com/jewish-life-and-religion/115743/standing-on-one-foot.

30. See Barry W. Holtz, *Rabbi Akiva: Sage of the Talmud* (New Haven, CT: Yale University Press, 2017), 174.

31. *Mitzvot* is the plural of *mitzvah*. A secondary meaning of *mitzvah* is "good deed."

32. The Orthodox community can be divided between the Modern Orthodox and the Haredim. The term *Haredim* refers to members of different groups and sects, such as Chabad-Lubavitch and Satmar. The Haredim, sometimes referred to as "ultra-Orthodox," typically live in segregated communities and often wear distinctive dress; the Modern Orthodox are more integrated into contemporary American society.

33. See, for example, "Jewish Dietary Laws (Kashrut): Overview of Laws & Regulations," Jewish Virtual Library, www.jewishvirtuallibrary.org/overview-of-jewish -dietary-laws-and-regulations.

34. See, for example, Rabbi Edward Feld, "What We Eat: Looking at Kashrut Through a Conservative Lens," www.cjvoices.org/article/what-we-eat-looking-at -kashrut-through-a-conservative-lens. Feld writes, "Food laws in the Talmud are a way of constructing a barrier between Jews and the larger society. Roman and Persian cultures were perceived as threatening. Restricting diet minimized the contact between Jews and non-Jews."

35. See, for example, "The Shabbat Laws," Chabad.org, www.chabad.org/library /article_cdo/aid/95907/jewish/The-Shabbat-Laws.htm.

36. Elizabeth A. Harris, "For Jewish Sabbath, Elevators Do All the Work," *New York Times*, March 5, 2012, www.nytimes.com/2012/03/06/nyregion/on-jewish -sabbath-elevators-that-do-all-the-work.html.

37. The ultra-Orthodox interpret halacha as generally prohibiting men and women from even touching each other unless they are immediate family members. Exceptions, of course, are made for activities where touch is required, especially for doctors and anyone intervening to save a person's life.

38. "Issues in Jewish Ethics: 'Kosher' Sex," Jewish Virtual Library, www.jewish virtuallibrary.org/quot-kosher-quot-sex.

39. Rabbi Alana Suskin, "Menstruation and 'Family Purity' (Taharat Ha-Mishpacha)," My Jewish Learning, www.myjewishlearning.com/article/menstruation -and-family-purity-taharat-ha-mishpach; "Issues in Jewish Ethics: 'Kosher' Sex."

40. Like the other denominations, the Reform celebrate the Sabbath from sunset on Friday until sunset on Saturday. During the high-water mark of the Classical Reform movement, some congregations moved the Sabbath services to Sunday. See Tobias Brinkmann, *Sundays at Sinai: A Jewish Congregation in Chicago* (University of Chicago Press, 2012), 96, 142.

41. "U.S. Public Becoming Less Religious," Pew Research Center, November 3, 2015, 13, http://assets.pewresearch.org/wp-content/uploads/sites/11/2015 /11/201.11.03_RLS_II_full_report.pdf.

42. "A Portrait of Jewish Americans," 60. About half had belonged to a synagogue or temple at some point during their lives. Many Jewish families join to send their children to religious school but later drop out after the children have celebrated their bar or bat mitzvah.

43. Ibid., 75–76.

44. Ibid., 75.

45. Ibid., 77.

46. Ibid., 77.

47. On the first and second nights of Passover families gather to hold Seders. During Passover Jews who follow tradition do not eat any food that has been leavened.

48. "A Portrait of Jewish Americans," 77.

CHAPTER 4: THE PUZZLE OF "JEWISH BLOOD"

1. The more liberal Reform standard, which includes patrilineal Jews, is equally based on descent.

2. Flavius Josephus, *The Jewish War* (New York: Penguin, 1981), 27.

3. For a discussion of Disraeli's theory of the "Jewish race," see Isaiah Berlin, "Benjamin Disraeli, Karl Marx and the Search for Identity," in *Against the Current: Essays in the History of Ideas*, ed. Henry Hardy (London: Random House, 1979), 273–275.

4. George Eliot, *Daniel Deronda* (Mineola, NY: Dover Publications, 2017).

5. Eric L. Goldstein, "Different Blood Flows in Our Veins: Race and Jewish Self-Definition in Late Nineteenth Century America," *American Jewish History* 85, no. 1 (March 1997): 33.

6. Ibid., 33.

7. Ibid., 29.

8. Ibid., 33–34, noting that Jewish fears of social integration during this period most often "focused on marriages between Jews and gentiles, which were occurring on a small but previously unheard of scale."

9. Ibid., 39, quoting Leo N. Levi.

10. Ibid., 47–53.

11. Ibid., 41. See also Goldstein, *The Price of Whiteness: Jews, Race, and American Identity* (Princeton, NJ: Princeton University Press, 2006), 98: "Few social phenomena expressed the commitment of acculturated Jews to a racial self-understanding during the early twentieth century as did their avoidance of intermarriage."

12. Goldstein, "Different Blood," 42.

13. Ibid., 38.

14. Ibid., 35.

15. Ibid., 38.

16. Goldstein, *The Price of Whiteness*, 86.

17. Goldstein, "Different Blood," 37.

18. Goldstein argues that the idea of Jewish race remained appealing to many Jews during the twentieth century, notwithstanding the rise of scientific racism and the Nazi party. *The Price of Whiteness*, 184–185.

19. James Carroll, "Pope Francis and the Renunciation of Jewish Conversion," *New Yorker*, December 16, 2015. See generally James Carroll, *Constantine's Sword: The Church and the Jews* (Boston: Houghton Mifflin, 2001).

20. Ibid.

21. William Nicholls, *Christian Anti-Semitism: A History of Hate* (Northvale, NJ: Rowman & Littlefield, 2004), 263.

22. María Elena Martínez, *Genealogical Fictions: Limpieza de Sangre, Religion, and Gender in Colonial Mexico* (Stanford, CA: Stanford University Press, 2008), 50, 52.

23. Carroll, "Pope Francis." This restriction against Jews was not formally appealed until 1946. Ibid.

24. It is claimed that "To some degree, the Nazi theories of racial hygiene borrow from and extend the racist views propounded in Spain during the Holy Inquisition." "Limpieza de Sangre," www.estherlederberg.com/Eugenics%20(Anecdotes)/Limpieza%20de%20Sangre.html; Martínez, *Genealogical Fictions*, 13.

25. Madison Grant, *The Passing of the Great Race* (New York: Charles Scribner's Sons, 1916), ch. 2.

26. Timothy W. Ryback, "A Disquieting Book from Hitler's Library," *New York Times*, December 7, 2011, www.nytimes.com/2011/12/08/opinion/a-disquieting-book-from-hitlers-library.html.

27. Ella Howard, "Immigration and Americanization, 1880–1930," Digital Public Library of America, https://dp.la/primary-source-sets/sets/immigration-and-americanization-1880-1930.

28. Ben Wattenberg, in conversation with Alan Kraut, "FMC Program Segments, 1900–1930: The New Immigrants, Head Shapes, and the Melting Pot: Franz Boas vs. Scientific Racism," www.pbs.org/fmc/segments/progseg2.htm.

29. Frederick Jackson Turner (1901), cited in Wattenberg, "FMC Program Segments, 1900–1930."

30. See Karen Brodkin, *How Jews Became White Folks and What That Says About Race in America* (New Brunswick, NJ: Rutgers University Press, 1998), 28; Wattenberg, "FMC Program Segments, 1900–1930." The myth that Jews were a distinct and inferior race persisted even in the face of empirical research challenging the basis for scientific racism. In the late nineteenth century the German Anthropological Society conducted a study to determine the physical differences between Jewish and Aryan children. The conclusion was that the children in the two groups were more alike than different. Phyllis Goldstein, *A Convenient Hatred: The History of Anti-Semitism* (Brookline, MA: Facing History and Ourselves, 2012), 204.

31. Carl M. Degler, *In Search of Human Nature: The Decline and Revival of Darwinism in American Social Thought* (New York: Oxford University Press, 1991), 61.

32. Ibid., 61. "Culture…in the twentieth century became…an alternative to a racial explanation."

33. Immigration Act of 1917 (Asiatic Barred Zone Act), H.R. 10384; Pub.L. 301; 39 Stat. 874. 64th Congress; February 5, 1917.

34. The 1924 law set country quotas based 2 percent each year on the population proportion of those who were already living in the United States as of the 1890 census. The Immigration Act of 1924 (The Johnson-Reed Act), Office of the History of the Department of State, https://history.state.gov/milestones/1921-1936/immigration-act.

35. The United States was the first country to undertake compulsory sterilization programs for the purpose of eugenics. The eugenics movement contributed to the passage of state laws allowing coercive sterilization. Though Pennsylvania was the first to enact sterilization legislation in 1907, it was followed by a number of states. Edwin Black, "The Horrifying American Roots of Nazi Eugenics," History News Network, September 2003, http://historynewsnetwork.org/article/1796; Lutz Kaebler, "Eugenics: Compulsory Sterilization in 50 American States," presentation at Social Science Historical Association, www.uvm.edu/~lkaelber/eugenics/PA/PA.html.

36. For an English translation of the laws, see Facing History and Ourselves, "The Nuremberg Laws," www.facinghistory.org/holocaust-and-human-behavior /chapter-6/nuremberg-laws.

37. A religiously observant Jew could not be a *Mischling*; he was a Jew. Walter Lacquer and Judith Baumel, eds., *The Holocaust Encyclopedia* (New Haven, CT: Yale University Press, 2001), 453.

38. A Mischling of the first degree, or half-Jew, was a person with two Jewish grandparents who (1) did not practice Judaism and (2) was not married to a Jew as of September 15, 1935. (If either factor applied, you were a Jew, not a Mischling.) "A Mischling of the second degree, or quarter-Jew, was someone with one Jewish grandparent or an Aryan married to a Jew. In 1939, 72,000 first-degree Mischlinge and 39,000 second-degree Mischlinge were still living in Germany." Shoah Resource Center, "Mischlinge," www.yadvashem.org/odot_pdf/Microsoft%20Word%20-%206504.pdf. The racial Jewishness of the grandparents was determined by their affiliation with the Jewish religious community. See also Lacquer and Baumel, *The Holocaust Encyclopedia*, 453.

39. John M. Steiner and Jobst Freiherr von Cornberg, "Willkür in der Willkür: Befreiungen von den antisemitischen Nürnberger Gesetzen," *Vierteljahrshefte für Zeitgeschichte* 46, no. 2 (April 1998): 143, 182. Categorization was often complicated by intermarriage and successful assimilation. During the Nazi period persons with Jewish heritage often concealed it and used a variety of methods to avoid detrimental characterization.

40. M. F. Ashley Montagu, *Man's Most Dangerous Myth: The Fallacy of Race* (New York: Harper, 1942), 353. Because he believed that so many people had false ideas about race, Montagu urged that the term be abandoned and that the term *ethnic group* be used instead.

41. Jon Entine, *Abraham's Children: Race, Identity, and the DNA of the Chosen People* (New York: Grand Central Publishing, 2007), 265–266; Jonathan Zimmerman, "Donald Trump, Jews and the Myth of Race: How Jews Gradually Became 'White,' and How That Changed America," *Salon*, April 9, 2017, www.salon.com /2017/04/09/donald-trump-jews-and-the-myth-of-race-how-jews-gradually -became-white-and-how-that-changed-america.

42. Quoted in Entine, *Abraham's Children*, 250–251. Full text at UNESCO, "Four Statements on the Race Question," http://unesdoc.unesco.org/images/0012 /001229/122962eo.pdf, 30.

43. See generally UNESCO, "Four Statements on the Race Question" (Paris, France: Oberthur-Rennes, 1969), 30–35, http://unesdoc.unesco.org/images/0012 /001229/122962eo.pdf. In 1950, 1951, 1964, and 1967 UNESCO issued four statements "to make known the scientific facts about race and to combat racial prejudice." See UNESCO, "Four Statements on the Race Question."

44. Ibid., 33.

45. Ibid., 35.

46. Ibid., 36–38.

47. Ibid., 37.

48. Ibid., 38.

49. See US Census Bureau, "About," www.census.gov/topics/population/race /about.html. Since 2000, surveys have offered the option to check more than one box for race. But because of continuing popular confusion over the difference between "race" and "origin," the agency is considering eliminating both terms and using the word "category" instead. See, for example, D'vera Cohn, "Census Considers New Approach to Asking About Race—by Not Using the Term at All," *Fact Tank*, Pew Research Center, June 18, 2015, www.pewresearch.org/fact-tank /2015/06/18/census-considers-new-approach-to-asking-about-race-by-not-using -the-term-at-all.

50. Stephen Molnar, *Human Variation: Races, Types, and Ethnic Groups* (Englewood Cliffs, NJ: Prentice-Hall, 1983), 16. In the nineteenth century one "scientific" survey suggested there were twenty-nine races, while another listed only four. See Dictionary of Races or Peoples, S. Doc., No. 662, 61st Cong. 3d Sess. 3 (1911), quoted in

Gary A. Greenfield and Don B. Kates Jr., "Mexican Americans, Racial Discrimination, and the Civil Rights Act of 1866," *California Law Review* 63, no. 3 (1975): 676.

51. Molnar, *Human Variation*, 17.

52. See David M. Chalmers, *Hooded Americanism: The History of the Ku Klux Klan* (Durham, NC: Duke University Press, 1987), 352; Naomi Cohen, "'Shaare Tefila Congregation V. Cobb': A New Departure in American Jewish Defense?" *Jewish History* 3, no.1 (Spring 1988), 96–97.

53. *The New Order*, March 1979, 3 (emphasis in original).

54. *Shaare Tefila Congregation v. Cobb*, 606 F. Supp. 1505, 1508 (1985).

55. *Shaare Tefila Congregation v. Cobb*, 481 U.S. 615, 617 (1987).

56. Ibid., 615, 617–618.

57. Entine, *Abraham's Children*, 266.

58. 23andMe uses thirty-one population groups to report its analysis. 23andMe, "Reference Populations," https://customercare.23andme.com/hc/en-us/articles/212169298#European.

These are created by looking for clusters of DNA markers. For "Ashkenazi," the sample size of the comparison set of people who self-identified as Ashkenazi Jews in my report was 1,305 people.

59. These percentages applied for its "standard" view, with a "confidence" level of 75 percent. I take this to mean that 23andMe thinks the odds are three to one that at least 96 percent of my markers match those of the Ashkenazi reference set. 23andMe reports ancestry percentages at two other confidence levels: "speculative" at 51 percent, and "conservative" at 90 percent. Under the conservative view I am 87.9 percent Ashkenazi. For the speculative, or 51 percent confidence level, the Ashkenazi figure was a whopping 98.4 percent.

60. M. F. Hammer, J. J. Redd, E. T. Wood et al., "Jewish and Middle Eastern Non-Jewish Populations Share a Common Pool of Y-Chromosome Biallelic Haplotypes," *Proceedings of the National Academy of Sciences* 97, no. 12 (June 6, 2000): 6769.

61. See Harry Ostrer, *Legacy: A Genetic History of the Jewish People* (New York: Oxford University Press, 2012), 92–93, 114; Nicholas Wade, "Genes Suggest European Women at Root of Ashkenazi Family Tree," *New York Times*, October 8, 2013, www.nytimes.com/2013/10/09/science/ashkenazi-origins-may-be-with-european-women-study-finds.html (indicating that many Jewish men found mates from European and other communities where they migrated after the Diaspora).

62. Wade, "Genes Suggest European Women at Root of Ashkenazi Family Tree."

63. Entine, *Abraham's Children*, 218, referring to the 2002 Center for Genetic Anthropology study.

64. Ibid., 12–13.

65. Ostrer, *Legacy*, 88–89; Nicholas Wade, "Studies Show Jews' Genetic Similarity," *New York Times*, June 9, 2010, www.nytimes.com/2010/06/10/science/10jews.html.

66. Wade, "Studies Show Jews' Genetic Similarity."

67. Entine, *Abraham's Children*, 78–79.

68. Ibid., 80.

69. Ibid., 87.

70. Ibid., 87.

71. Ibid., 89.

72. Avshalom Zoossmann-Diskin, "Are Today's Jewish Priests Descended from the Old Ones?" *HOMO Journal of Comparative Human Biology, Zeitchrift für vergleichende Biologie des Menschen*, 51, no. 2 (2001): 156–162.

73. Entine, *Abraham's Children*, 89.

74. Ibid., 91, originally quoting Neil Bradman and Mark Thomas, "Genetics, the Pursuit of Jewish History by Other Names," *Judaism Today*, Autumn 1998, 6.

75. Wade is said to have made this comment in 2010 at a conference at Cold Harbor Laboratory. David Reich, *Who We Are and How We Got There: Ancient DNA and the New Science of the Human Past* (New York: Pantheon Books, 2018), 253.

76. Ibid.

77. Although the incidence of the disease is very rare in the general population, the genetic mutations responsible for the disease are also somewhat more common among the Old Order Amish in Pennsylvania, the Cajun population of Louisiana, and French-Canadians. Cleveland Clinic, "Tay-Sachs Disease," https://my.clevelandclinic.org /health/diseases/14348-tay-sachs-disease.

78. Dor Yeshorim, "FAQ," https://doryeshorim.org/faq.

79. Gina Kolata, "Using Genetic Tests, Ashkenazi Jews Vanquish a Disease," *New York Times*, February 18, 2003, www.nytimes.com/2003/02/18/science/using -genetic-tests-ashkenazi-jews-vanquish-a-disease.html. According to geneticist Michael Kaback, an architect of the screening, the incidence of Tay-Sachs plummeted by 90 percent between 1970 and 2000 in North America. Michael M. Kaback, "Population-Based Genetic Screening for Reproductive Counseling: The Tay-Sachs Disease Model," *European Journal of Pediatrics* 159, no. 3 (December 2000): 193. In Israel only one child had the disease in 2003, with none reported in 2004. Tamara Traubman, "Tay-Sachs, the 'Jewish Disease,' Almost Eradicated," *Haaretz*, January 18, 2005, www.haaretz.com/1.4706480.

80. Norton and Elaine Sarnoff Center for Jewish Genetics, "Carrier Screening," www.juf.org/cjg/Get-Screened.aspx. An appendix in Jon Entine's book contains long lists of "Jewish Diseases."

81. On average, women have less than a 0.1 percent chance of having one of these genes. Subsequent studies found that about one in eight hundred women and men in the general population carries one of the three mutations. In contrast, approximately one in forty Jews (2.5 percent) is a carrier, extraordinary for a cancer-producing gene. These mutations can increase the lifetime risk of developing breast cancer to as high as 85 percent and the risk of developing ovarian cancer to up to 50 percent. Entine, *Abraham's Children*, 273.

82. Ibid., 282–285.

83. Ibid., 288–289.

84. Ibid., 289.

85. As we have seen, the Spanish, the Jesuits, and the Nazi government each had somewhat different ancestry-based tests for whether a person was a member of the Jewish race. The matrilineal rule is ancestral, and to an extent the new Reform test is too. In the United States a variety of racial tests were applied to determine whether a person was an African American for purposes of enforcing anti-miscegenation and segregation laws. I believe there were three primary approaches: (1) ancestry tests that looked back some number of generations for black antecedents; (2) proportion or percentage tests that determined what fraction of a person's ancestors were black; and (3) appearance tests that determined race by a visual appraisal of a person's physical characteristics. See generally Angela M. Guidetta, "Who Is Batson Black?: Deconstructing the Myth of Racial Identity and Stereotyping," *Rutgers Race and Law Review* 8, no. 2 (2007): 321–347.

Today various Native American tribes apply ancestry tests to determine whether a person qualifies for tribal membership. These tests require showing that some percentage of a person's ancestors were members. US Department of the Interior, "A Guide to Tracing American Indian & Alaska Native Ancestry," www.bia.gov /sites/bia_prod.opengov.ibmcloud.com/files/assets/public/pdf/Guide_to_Tracing _AI_and_AN_Ancestry.pdf; Association on American Indian Affairs, "Frequently Asked Questions," www.indian-affairs.org/general-faq.html.

86. Robert Pollack, "The Fallacy of Biological Judaism," *Forward*, March 7, 2003. See also Robert Pollack, *The Missing Moment: How the Unconscious Shapes Modern Science* (Boston: Houghton Mifflin, 1999), 194.

87. Pollack, "The Fallacy of Biological Judaism."

CHAPTER 5: PEOPLEHOOD

1. Michael Walzer, "The Anomalies of Jewish Political Identity," in *Judaism and the Challenges of Modern Life*, ed. Moshe Halbertal and Donniel Hartman (New York: Continuum, 2007), 134. Nathan Glazer made a similar point when he wrote, "Judaism is tied up organically with a specific people, indeed, a nation. The tie is so intimate that the word 'Jew' in common usage refers ambiguously both to an adherent of the religion of Judaism and to a member of the Jewish people." Nathan Glazer, *American Judaism* (Chicago: University of Chicago Press, 1972), 3. Isaiah Berlin wrote that "Jews were a unique combination of religion, race and people . . . they could not be classified in normal terms." Isaiah Berlin, *The Power of Ideas*, ed. Henry Hardy (Princeton, NJ: Princeton University Press, 2013), 174–175. "Philosophers as well as sociologists have long understood being Jewish as entailing elements of both religion and ethnicity." Chaim Waxman, *Jewish Baby Boomers: A Communal Perspective* (Albany: State University of New York Press, 2001), 8. Martin Buber wrote, "Israel is a people like no other, for it is the only people in the world which, from its earliest beginning, has been both a nation and a religious community." Quoted in Steven Cohen and Jack Wertheimer, "Whatever Happened to the Jewish People," *Commentary*, June 2006, 33.

2. Cohen and Wertheimer, "Whatever Happened to the Jewish People," 33.

3. "A Portrait of Jewish Americans," 47. Pew found that 75 percent of American Jews report having a "strong sense of belonging to the Jewish people." Ibid., 52. Six in ten say that "being Jewish is mainly a matter of culture or ancestry, compared with 15% who say it is mainly a matter of religion." Ibid., 47, 53. See also Noam Pianko, *Jewish Peoplehood: An American Innovation* (New Brunswick, NJ: Rutgers University Press, 2015), 2.

4. See Exodus 19:5 (Complete Jewish Bible): "My own treasure from among all the peoples." See also Deuteronomy 14:2: "Because you are a people set apart as holy for ADONAI your God. ADONAI your God has chosen you to be his own unique treasure out of all the peoples on the face of the earth."

5. Donniel Hartman, *The Boundaries of Judaism* (New York: Continuum, 2007), 1.

6. In 1791 France was the first European nation to grant citizenship to Jews. Britain did so in 1856. Different German states granted Jews citizenship at various times during the nineteenth century. Citizenship throughout Germany came with unification in 1871. In Russia emancipation did not come until the revolution in 1917. See generally "Encyclopedia Judaica: Emancipation," Jewish Virtual Library, www.jewishvirtuallibrary.org/emancipation.

7. This "Jewish Enlightenment" is sometimes called the *Haskalah movement*. See Marie Schumacher-Brunhes, "Enlightenment Jewish Style: The Haskalah Movement in Europe" (original in German, published in English), April 19, 2012, http://ieg-ego .eu/en/threads/european-networks/jewish-networks/marie-schumacher-brunhes -enlightenment-jewish-style-the-haskalah-movement-in-europe. Schumacher-Brunhes notes that although the Jewish Enlightenment took different forms in different parts of Europe, "everywhere the goals of the proponents of the Haskalah were the same: to lead the Jews out of the religious ghetto, to integrate the Jewish world into the non-Jewish world and to bring separation to an end in favour of non-Jewish tendencies, customs and knowledge. The prerequisites for such integration were modernization and ending the centuries-old blending of religious and social life."

8. See, for example, Schumacher-Brunhes, "Enlightenment Jewish Style."

9. See, for example, Rabbi Louis Jacobs, "Haskalah, the Jewish Enlightenment," My Jewish Learning, www.myjewishlearning.com/article/haskalah (reprinted with permission from Louis Jacobs, *The Jewish Religion: A Companion* [New York: Oxford University Press, 2005]). As Jacobs notes, "An associate of Mendelssohn, Naftali Herz Wesseley (1725–1805), published his *Divrei Shalom Ve'emet* (Words of Peace and Truth), often described as the manifesto of the Haskalah, in which he made a typical Haskalah distinction between 'the law of man' and the 'law of God'; the former denoted Western patterns of life and secular learning, the latter, the traditional Jewish way of religious life and study." Jacobs further observes, "The [traditional] Rabbis saw clearly that the Haskalah was engaged in a transformation of Judaism, a shifting of its centre from the religious ideal of Torah study 'for its own sake,' with

secular learning at the most an adjunct, to secular learning 'for its own sake' with the study of the Torah as an adjunct."

10. Leora Batnitzky, *How Judaism Became a Religion: An Introduction to Modern Jewish Thought* (Princeton, NJ: Princeton University Press, 2011), 13. Mendelssohn "invent[ed] the modern idea that Judaism is a religion," Batnitzky writes. She goes on to suggest that, Mendelssohn notwithstanding, "Judaism does not quite fit" into this pattern.

11. Ibid., 16–19. See generally Moses Mendelssohn, *Jerusalem: Or on Religious Power and Judaism*, trans. Allan Arkush (Waltham, MA: Brandeis University Press, 1983).

12. See, for example, Rachel Seelig, "East European Jews in the German-Jewish Imagination," Ludwig Rosenberger Library of Judaica, www.lib.uchicago.edu/collex /exhibits/exeej. "The long and difficult path toward emancipation during the nineteenth century led German Jews to reject traditional notions of Jewish nationhood and to refashion themselves as 'German citizens of the Mosaic faith.'" See also "Ancient Jewish History: Assimilation," Jewish Virtual Library, www.jewishvirtuallibrary.org /assimilation, noting that although assimilating European Jews in the nineteenth century rejected any desire to return to Palestine and instead declared their allegiance to the nation-state in which they lived, "Jewish identity would be preserved in a redefinition as 'Germans of Mosaic faith' or 'Frenchmen of Mosaic faith,' and so on."

13. See, for example, David Philipson, Kaufmann Kohler, and H. Pereira Mendes, "Conferences, Rabbinical," *Jewish Encyclopedia*, www.jewishencyclopedia .com/articles/4592-conferences-rabbinical, detailing the resolutions made at the Frankfort-on-the-Main Conference of Rabbis on July 15–28, 1845.

14. Kahal Kadosh Beth Elohim, "History," www.kkbe.org/index.php?page= history. The congregation, founded in 1749, is one of the oldest in the United States.

15. The Philadelphia Conference of November 3–6, 1869, adopted the following among its principles: "The Messianic aim of Israel is not the restoration of the old Jewish state under a descendant of David, involving a second separation from the nations of the earth, but the union of all the children of God in the confession of the unity of God, so as to realize the unity of all rational creatures, and their call to moral sanctification." Quoted in Alan J. Avery-Peck, William Scott Green, and Jacob Neusner, eds., *Annual of Rabbinic Judaism: Volume 3: Ancient, Medieval, and Modern* (Boston, MA: Brill, 2000), 158.

16. The 1885 Conference was held in Pittsburgh, and the principles adopted became known as the Pittsburgh Platform. Article 5 of the Platform provided, "We consider ourselves no longer a nation, but a religious community, and therefore expect neither a return to Palestine, nor a sacrificial worship under the sons of Aaron, nor the restoration of any of the laws concerning the Jewish state." Until the Columbus Platform of 1937 the Pittsburgh Platform was the formal guideline of the Reform movement concerning the establishment of a Jewish homeland in Israel. "Reform Judaism: The Pittsburgh Platform," Jewish Virtual Library, www.jewishvirtuallibrary.org/the-pittsburgh-platform.

17. Theodor Herzl, *The Jewish State* (New York: Dover Publications, 1988), 76.

18. Ibid., 76.

19. See Jonathan D. Sarna, *American Judaism: A History* (New Haven, CT: Yale University Press, 2004), 151.

20. The estimate for the First Aliyah (1882–1903) is twenty-five thousand immigrants, for the Second Aliyah (1904–1914) it is thirty-five to forty thousand, and for the Third Aliyah (1919–1923) it is thirty-five thousand. Kerry M. Olitzky and Ronald H. Isaacs, *A Glossary of Jewish Life* (Northvale, NJ: Jason Aronson, 1992), 165–166; John Efron, Steven Weitzman, and Matthias Lehmann, *The Jews: A History* (New York, Routledge, 2016), 499.

21. On November 2, 1917, the British foreign secretary, Arthur James Balfour, wrote a letter to the British Zionist Federation, stating, "His Majesty's government view with favor the establishment in Palestine of a national home for the Jewish people." This letter became known as the Balfour Declaration.

22. The Council of the League of Nations, "The Palestine Mandate" (July 24, 1922), The Avalon Project, http://avalon.law.yale.edu/20th_century/palmanda.asp.

23. See Leonard Dinnerstein, *Antisemitism in America* (New York: Oxford University Press, 2004), 96, 246–247.

24. "Between 1924 and 1929, 82,000 Jews arrived, many as a result of anti-Semitism in Poland and Hungary.... Of these approximately 23,000 left the country.... Between 1929 and 1939, with the rise of Nazism in Germany, a new wave of 250,000 immigrants arrived." See "Aliyah," Jewish Virtual Library, www.jewishvirtuallibrary .org/aliyah.

25. See Melvin I. Urofsky, *American Zionism: From Herzl to the Holocaust* (Garden City, NY: Anchor Press/Doubleday, 1975), 81.

26. Jonathan Sarna, "Louis D. Brandeis: Zionist Leader," *Brandeis Review* (Winter 1992): 23.

27. See Urofsky, *American Zionism*, 247–248.

28. Ibid., 269.

29. Ibid., 279.

30. See ibid., 246–298.

31. Ibid., 305.

32. Reversing the 1885 Pittsburgh Platform, the Columbus Platform of 1937 stated, "In the rehabilitation of Palestine, the land hallowed by memories and hopes, we behold the promise of renewed life for many of our brethren. We affirm the obligation of all Jewry to aid in its upbuilding as a Jewish homeland by endeavoring to make it not only a haven of refuge for the oppressed but also a center of Jewish culture and spiritual life." Note that the platform did not call for the establishment of a Jewish state. "Reform Judaism: The Columbus Platform (1937)," Jewish Virtual Library, www.jewishvirtuallibrary.org/the-columbus-platform-1937. The Reform movement's ringing endorsement of the State of Israel was to come decades later.

The Statement of Principles for Reform Judaism, adopted at the 1999 Pittsburgh Convention, states, "We are committed to (Medinat Yisrael), the State of Israel, and rejoice in its accomplishments. We affirm the unique qualities of living in (Eretz Yisrael), the land of Israel, and encourage (Aliyah), immigration to Israel." "Statement of Principles for Reform Judaism," Mazor Guides, www.mazorguide.com/living /Denominations/ReformPrinciples.htm.

33. As I will show in the next chapter, for the Jewish people it is the peculiar coincidence of religion and ethnicity that has created special problems for Israel, problems that "militate against the project of 'becom[ing] a nation like every other nation.'" Christian Joppke, *Selecting by Origin: Ethnic Migration in the Liberal State* (Cambridge, MA: Harvard University Press, 2005), 165.

34. See Pianko, *Jewish Peoplehood*, 27–29. Kaplan had initially used the term *nationhood*. However, although he supported Zionism, after the State of Israel was founded he thought nationhood was too closely related to statehood and instead chose to use the term *peoplehood*. Ari Engelberg, "A Post-Modern Jewish Peoplehood for Israel," 4, www.jpeoplehood.org/wp-content/uploads/2013/03/6-Peoplehood_Papers _Postmodern_Ari_Engelberg-CONCEPT-and-ISRAEL.pdf, citing Ami Bouganim, "Jewish Sectarianism and Jewish Peoplehood," in *Building Jewish Peoplehood: Challenges and Possibilities*, ed. Ezra Kopelowitz and Menachem Revivi (Brighton, MA: Academic Studies, 2008), 87–108.

35. Pianko, *Jewish Peoplehood*, 1.

36. Ezra Kopelowitz and Ari Engelberg, "A Framework for Strategic Thinking About Jewish Peoplehood," *Jewish Philanthropy*, July 6, 2008, http://ejewishphilanthropy .com/a-framework-for-strategic-thinking-about-jewish-peoplehood.

37. See, for example, Shlomo Ravid and Varda Rafaeli, *Jewish Peoplehood Education: Framing the Field, The Global Task Force on Peoplehood Education* (Israel: Center for Jewish Peoplehood Education, 2011), online at www.jpeoplehood.org/wp-content /uploads/2012/10/TaskForceReport.pdf; Heilicher Jewish Day School, "Jewish Studies," www.hmjds.org/academics/jewish-studies.

38. Oranim, Academic College of Education Israel, "Jewish Peoplehood," http:// en.oranim.ac.il/node/223.

39. Erica Brown and Misha Galperin, *The Case for Jewish Peoplehood: Can We Be One?* (Woodstock, VT: Jewish Lights Publishing, 2009), 3.

40. Sylvia Barack Fishman, *The Way into the Varieties of Jewishness* (Woodstock, VT: Jewish Lights Publishing, 2007), 44.

41. Jay Michaelson, "Peoplehood: There's No There There," *The Forward*, April 16, 2008, https://forward.com/culture/13170/peoplehood-there-s-no-there-there-01678.

42. Ibid.

43. Shulamit Reinharz, "The 'Jewish Peoplehood' Concept: Complications and Suggestions," in *Reconsidering Israel-Diaspora Relations*, ed. Eliezer Ben-Rafael, Judit Bokser Liwerant, and Yosef Gorny (Boston, MA: Brill, 2014), 66. Reinharz attempted to describe what peoplehood did require of Jews not very committed to

the religion: "awareness of having a shared history with other Jews, possible participation in the celebration of a few holidays and customs, pride (or shame) in the accomplishments (or crimes) of other Jewish people and a sense of some responsibility to defend other Jews who are endangered."

44. Herzl, *The Jewish State*, 76 (emphasis added).

45. Pianko, *Jewish Peoplehood*, 2; Edward S. Shapiro, *We Are Many: Reflections on American Jewish History and Identity* (Syracuse, NY: Syracuse University Press, 2005), 28.

46. Pianko, *Jewish Peoplehood*, 2.

47. Brown and Galperin, *The Case for Jewish Peoplehood*, 41.

48. Rabbi Jonathan Sacks, *A Letter in the Scroll: Understanding Our Jewish Identity and Exploring the Legacy of the World's Oldest Religion* (New York: Simon and Schuster, 2000), 30.

49. Pianko, *Jewish Peoplehood*, 14–15, 56. George P. Shultz, who was President Reagan's Secretary of State, told me some years later that both he and President Reagan had been very impressed by the American Jewish community's solidarity with the plight of Jews in the Soviet Union.

50. Judy Maltz, "President Rivlin Meets High-Level Reform Mission, Says: We Are One Family," *Haaretz*, November 11, 2014, www.haaretz.com/misc /haaretzcomsmartphoneapp/high-level-reform-mission-meets-with-rivlin-1.5327449.

51. Benedict Anderson, *Imagined Communities: Reflections on the Origin and Spread of Nationalism* (New York: Verso, 2006), 6–7.

52. Ezra Kopelowitz and Ari Engelberg suggest that peoplehood requires that a Jew must experience a subjective "awareness of the underlying unity that makes an individual Jew a part of the Jewish people." Reinharz, "'Jewish Peoplehood,'" 76, originally citing "A Framework for Strategic Thinking about Jewish Peoplehood," position paper (Jerusalem: The Center for Jewish Peoplehood Education).

53. Chaim I. Waxman, *Jewish Baby Boomers: A Communal Perspective* (Albany: State University of New York Press, 2001), 153.

54. See Peter Singer, *The Most Good You Can Do* (New Haven, CT: Yale University Press, 2015), 117–118.

55. "A Portrait of Jewish Americans," 52.

56. Ibid., 52.

57. Brown and Galperin, *The Case for Jewish Peoplehood*, 2.

58. Herbert Gans, "Symbolic Ethnicity: The Future of Ethnic Groups and Cultures in America," *Ethnic and Racial Studies* 2, no. 1 (January 1979): 1.

59. Ibid., 9.

60. Ibid., 8–9.

61. Ibid., 9.

62. Ibid., 18.

63. Robert Wallerstein, "Erik Erikson and His Problematic Identity," *Journal of the American Psychoanalytic Association* 62, no. 4 (2014): 663.

64. David A. Hollinger, *After Cloven Tongues of Fire: Protestant Liberalism in Modern American History* (Princeton, NJ: Princeton University Press, 2013), 156.

65. Shaul Magid, "Be the Jew You Make: Jews, Judaism, and Jewishness in Post-Ethnic America," *Sh'ma Journal: A Journal of Jewish Ideas*, March 1, 2011, http://shma .com/2011/03/be-the-jew-you-make-jews-judaism-and-jewishness-in-post-ethnic -america.

66. Ibid.

67. Steven M. Cohen and Jack Wertheimer, "What Is So Great About 'Post-Ethnic Judaism?'" *Sh'ma Journal*, March 1, 2011, http://shma.com/2011/03 /what-is-so-great-about-post-ethnic-judaism.

CHAPTER 6: WHO IS A JEW IN ISRAEL?

1. The Law of Return, 5710-1950, 4 L.S.I. 114 (1949–1950); The Rabbinical Courts Jurisdiction (Marriage and Divorce) Law, 5713-1953, 7 L.S.I. 139 (1953–1954); The Population Registry Law, 5725-1965, 19 L.S.I. 288 (1964–1965); The Jewish Religious Services (Consolidated Version) Law, 5731-1971, 25 L.S.I. 175 (1971). See generally Moshe Samet, "Who Is a Jew (1958–1977)," *Jerusalem Quarterly* 36 (1985): 88–108.

2. The Establishment Clause and the Free Exercise Clause of the First Amendment of the US Constitution have been interpreted by the Supreme Court to guarantee both religious liberty and a "separation" principle between church and state.

3. Israel has no written constitution, but its May 14, 1948, Declaration of Independence reflects the aspiration that Israel would be a Jewish *and* democratic state that would respect the equal rights of all Israeli citizens. It provides, "THE STATE OF ISRAEL will be open for Jewish immigration and for the Ingathering of the Exiles; it will foster the development of the country for the benefit of all its inhabitants; it will be based on freedom, justice and peace as envisaged by the prophets of Israel; it will ensure complete equality of social and political rights to all its inhabitants irrespective of religion, race or sex; it will guarantee freedom of religion, conscience, language, education and culture; it will safeguard the Holy Places of all religions; and it will be faithful to the principles of the Charter of the United Nations." See Declaration of Establishment of State of Israel, May 14, 1948, www.mfa.gov.il/mfa/foreignpolicy/peace/guide/pages /declaration%20of%20establishment%20of%20state%20of%20israel.aspx.

4. The Rabbinical Courts Jurisdiction (Marriage and Divorce) Law. The law states that the rabbinical courts have the exclusive jurisdiction over "matters of marriage and divorce of *Jews* in Israel" (emphasis added).

5. The state recognizes marriages performed abroad between Israeli residents and citizens if they are deemed valid at the place where they were performed. This conclusion was reached by the Israeli Supreme Court in 2006. In HCJ 2232/03 *Plonit v. The Regional Rabbinical Court Tel Aviv*, P.D. 61(3) 496 (2006), the Israeli Supreme Court recognized the need for a process to dissolve marriages performed abroad. The Supreme Court stated that this result was required because of "the reality of life in Israel, [where] thousands of Jews who are citizens and residents of

Israel, wish to marry by means of a civil marriage that takes place outside Israel. This is a social phenomenon that the law should take into account" (ibid., President Emeritus A. Barak, para. 26). In addition, other alternatives to religious marriage and divorce have developed. Couples who cohabit and are "known to the public" as husband and wife have legal status. They are entitled to various rights and protections similar to those of married spouses, including tenant residence protection, social security benefits, benefits resulting from the death of a spouse as the result of a crime, and even protection against family violence. See CA 384/61 *State of Israel v. Pessler* [1962] Isr.S.C. 16(1) 102; Tenants' Protection Law (Consolidated Version), 5732-1972, 26 L.S.I. 204 (1971–1972); National Insurance Law (Consolidated Version), 5755-1995, S.H. 210 (1994–1995) (originally passed as National Insurance [Amendment No. 13] Law, 5733-1973, 27 L.S.I. 233 [1972–1973]); The Rights of Victims of Crime Law, 5761-2001, S.H. 1782 (2000–2001); The Prevention of Family Violence Law, 5751-1991, S.H. 1352 (1990–1991).

6. The Jewish Religious Services (Consolidated Version) Law.

7. Christian Joppke, *Selecting by Origin: Ethnic Migration in the Liberal State* (Cambridge, MA: Harvard University Press, 2005), 164. See chapter 5 at p. 84.

8. The status quo deal took the form of a letter Ben-Gurion sent on July 19, 1947, to the primary ultra-Orthodox political party (Agudat Yisrael). This party was historically non-Zionist in that they did not support the establishment of a Jewish state on religious grounds. They believed it was wrong to establish a Jewish state before the Jewish messiah arrived. To this day some ultra-Orthodox groups still refuse to recognize the legitimacy of Israel as a Jewish state. See Bernard Reich and David H. Goldberg, *Historical Dictionary of Israel* (Lanham, MD: The Scarecrow Press, 2008), 24.

9. The status quo agreement also contained other provisions in which Ben-Gurion promised that the new state would observe kosher dietary rules in all public facilities and observe the Jewish Sabbath by providing no public transportation and requiring most businesses to close. See Itamar Rabinovich and Jehuda Reinharz, eds., *Israel in the Middle East: Documents and Readings on Society, Politics, and Foreign Relations, Pre-1948 to the Present* (Waltham, NY: Brandeis University Press, 2008), 58–59; Daphne Barak-Erez, "Law and Religion Under the Status Quo Model: Between Past Compromises and Constant Change," *Cardozo Law Review* 30, no. 6 (2009): 2495–2507.

10. Micah Goodman, *Catch 67*, 127 (unpublished English translation). The fact that the Orthodox rabbinate has such broad authority in Israel has implications that create certain challenges for the non-Orthodox denominations in America. These issues are explored further in Chapter 9.

11. In 1965 the Registration of Inhabitants Ordinance was repealed and replaced by the Population Registry Law. Both the Ordinance and the Law stated that every inhabitant who has attained the age of sixteen years is entitled, after submitting an application, to obtain an identity card from the registration office and to use it as a means of identifying him or herself. Until 2002 the identity card included the category

of nationality. However, the category was eradicated after the Israeli Supreme Court ordered the minister of the Interior to register as Jews not only those who had undergone Orthodox conversions but also those who had undergone Reform or Conservative conversions. To minimize the impact of this ruling, Interior Minister Eli Yishai, a member of the ultra-Orthodox religious political party, issued an order to omit the nationality category from the identity cards. See Yair Auron, *Israeli Identities: Jews and Arabs Facing the Self and the Other* (New York: Berghahn Books, 2012), 85–86.

12. The Israeli Supreme Court has rejected a request to treat Israeli as a nationality. CA 8573/08 *Ornan v. The Minister of the Interior* (2013). The court said it feared that if the national identity of Jewish citizens of Israel were classified as "Israeli," it would imply that "Judaism is not a nationality... but is solely a religion," an idea antithetical to the founders' notions that Zionism was the national movement of the Jewish people and that this "national bond" united Jews in Israel with those of the Diaspora. See Yedidia Z. Stern and Jay Ruderman, "Op-Ed: Why 'Israeli' Is Not a Nationality," *JTA*, March 3, 2014, www.jta.org/2014/03/03/news-opinion/israel-middle-east /op-ed-why-israeli-is-not-a-nationality.

13. It is further assumed that if you claim Jewish nationality on the registration form, you will report your religion as Jewish, even if you are not observant.

14. Asher Cohen and Bernard Susser, "Jews and Others: Non-Jewish Jews in Israel," *Israel Affairs* 15, no. 1 (2009): 53.

15. Ruth Gavison, *The Law of Return at Sixty Years: History, Ideology, Justification* (Jerusalem: The Metzilah Center for Zionist, Jewish, Liberal and Humanist Thought, 2010), 62.

16. Joppke, *Selecting by Origin*, 178.

17. Gavison, *The Law of Return at Sixty Years*, 62 (emphasis added). The directive is dated March 10, 1958 (emphasis added).

18. Baruch Litvin and Sidney B. Hoenig, eds., *Jewish Identity: Who Is a Jew? Modern Responses and Opinions on the Registration of Children of Mixed Marriages* (Brooklyn: Ktav Publishing House, 2013), 13–15, 308–310.

19. Gavison, *The Law of Return at Sixty Years*, 63.

20. Joppke, *Selecting by Origin*, 178–179. This argument is a bit of a stretch. Inside Israel nothing in the directive required the rabbinate to accept an identity card designation of Jew. Before officiating at a wedding a rabbi could still require both parties to prove they had a Jewish mother.

21. Government Decision of July 20, 1958. See Gavison, *The Law of Return at Sixty Years*, 63.

22. Litvin and Hoenig, *Jewish Identity*, 11.

23. Ibid.

24. Ibid., 13–14.

25. Ibid., 14–15. See also Eliezer Ben-Rafael and Lior Ben-Chaim, *Jewish Identities in an Era of Multiple Modernities* (Tel-Aviv: Open University, 2006), 177–179 (in Hebrew).

26. Ibid., 213–215.

27. "'Who Is a Jew?'—Professor Isaiah Berlin's Memorandum to the Prime Minister of Israel, 23 January 1959," *Israel Studies* 13, no. 3 (2008): 170–177. See also Ben-Rafael and Ben-Chaim, *Jewish Identities in an Era of Multiple Modernities*, 175–189.

28. This was the view of Haim Cohn, later an Israeli Supreme Court justice (see Ben-Rafael and Ben-Chaim, *Jewish Identities in an Era of Multiple Modernities*, 247–261) and Hayim Hazaz, a Czech philosopher (ibid., 277–278).

29. Ibid., 232–235.

30. The new Interior minister was Haim Moshe Shapira, a member of the National Religious Party.

31. The meaning of the phrase "converted according to Halacha" is not entirely clear, in part because there is disagreement even among the Orthodox rabbinate about the requirements. See Steven Lipman, "Lost in Fierce Israel-Diaspora Debate: Standards Differ, Even Within Denominations," *New York Jewish Week*, July 19, 2017, http://jewishweek.timesofisrael.com/conversion-process-under-fresh-scrutiny. The purpose and effect of the phrase was to cast doubt on the validity of conversions to Judaism performed by Reform or Conservative rabbis. It should be noted that ten years later, in 1970, when the Law of Return and the Population Registry Law were amended to define a Jew as a person "born to a Jewish mother" or a convert, the phrase "converted according to Halacha" was *not* included. But for many years after 1970 some Orthodox groups continued to press unsuccessfully for amendments that would add the words "according to Halacha." See Samet, "Who Is a Jew," 109.

32. HC 72/62 *Oswald Rufeisen v. Minister of Interior*, Special Volume Selected Judgments Sup. Ct. Isr. 1 (1962).

33. Nechama Tec, *In the Lion's Den: The Life of Oswald Rufeisen* (New York: Oxford University Press, 1990), 3, 6, 8–9.

34. Ibid., 66–67.

35. Ibid., 134–138.

36. Ibid., 169.

37. Ibid., 218.

38. Ibid., 219.

39. Ibid., 218.

40. Shalom Goldman, *Jewish-Christian Difference and Modern Jewish Identity: Seven Twentieth-Century Converts* (Lanham, MD: Lexington Books, 2015), 137.

41. Tec, *In the Lion's Den*, 219.

42. Ibid., 220.

43. Ibid.

44. Ibid., 221.

45. *Oswald Rufeisen v. Minister of Interior*, 16.

46. Tec, *In the Lion's Den*, 226–227. Brother Daniel filed the lawsuit to assert a principle. He surmised that he eventually might have been able to become an Israeli

citizen through the naturalization process available to non-Jews, but he wanted to establish a legal precedent under the Law of Return.

47. *Oswald Rufeisen v. Minister of Interior*, 11–13, 19, 28–32.

48. Ibid., 2.

49. Ibid.

50. Ibid.

51. Ibid., 24–26.

52. Ibid., 27–28.

53. Although it was not strictly necessary to the court's ruling, the majority opinion included a long discussion of how apostates are treated under religious law. The attorney general, defending the government's decision to reject Brother Daniel's application, had argued that, under Jewish law, a Jew who converts to another faith is not considered "fully a Jew; he is only partly Jewish" (ibid., 7). The attorney general had cited several examples: an apostate may not inherit from his father and may not be counted as part of the ten-man quorum (*minyan*) required for public prayer services. A Jew should not charge interest when lending money to another Jew but may charge interest when lending to an apostate. Justice Silberg dismissed these examples, arguing that "according to the prevailing opinion in Jewish law…a Jew who is converted or becomes an apostate continues to be treated as a Jew for all purposes, save perhaps as to certain 'marginal' laws which have no real importance" (ibid., 3). Being Jewish, Silberg declared, is a permanent status that is "indivisible and absolute." In reaching this conclusion, Silberg attached great weight to precedents relating to marriage. Under Jewish law a marriage between a Jew and a non-Jew is invalid. But rabbinic precedents clearly indicate that if an apostate—including one who has converted to another religion—marries a Jewish woman, that marriage is legally valid and binding. Although not cited by the court, a second very important line of precedents in Israel treats apostates differently from gentiles; namely, an apostate who sees the error of his ways can return to the fold and become a Jew in good standing without going through the conversion process required of gentiles. See Isaac Gelbfish, October 19, 2015, Unpublished Memorandum, 2.

54. *Oswald Rufeisen v. Minister of Interior*, 11.

55. Ibid., 14.

56. Ibid., 32.

57. Ibid.

58. Ibid., 22.

59. Ibid., 23–24. Landau made it clear, however, that his attack on the "good faith" policy did not extend to Brother Daniel personally. Brother Daniel's "mood" was hardly ever-changing. He had consistently declared himself to be a Jew and a Zionist, and Landau appeared to recognize this. He wrote, "The good faith of the petitioner's declaration and his desire to assist in building up the State do him great honour and we are deeply indebted to him for his acts of bravery in the past. There remains, however, a manifest objective difficulty which prevents our acceding to his application" (ibid., 24). Justice Eliyahu Manny also ruled against Brother Daniel. He simply wrote, "I too

am of the opinion that the order nisi should be discharged for the reasons given in the judgments of my learned colleagues, Silberg J. and Landau J." (ibid., 24).

60. Ibid., 17.

61. Marc Galanter, "A Dissent on Brother Daniel," *Commentary* (July 1963): 10–17.

62. Justice Landau seemed to suggest it was the act of conversion—not Brother Daniel's beliefs—that disqualified him. He wrote, "The respondent was correct in the distinction he drew, for the purpose of the Law of Return, between a Jew and a non-Jew with regard to conversion from one religion to another. Our State is based on freedom of conscience and no Jew may therefore be compelled to declare himself an adherent of the doctrines of the Jewish faith when he is a non-believer. It follows, in my opinion, that a Jew who regards himself as non-religious discharges his duty to register his religion under the Registration of Inhabitants Ordinance, 1949, by so declaring to the registration officer. But a person who attaches so much importance to religious belief as to be converted of his own free will from one religion to another—and how much more so a person like the petitioner who has placed religion at the centre of his life—creates a complete contradiction which prevents his recognition as a Jew for the purposes of the Law of Return, although in point of origin he remains a Jew." *Oswald Rufeisen v. Minister of Interior*, 23.

63. Tec, *In the Lion's Den*, 231.

64. Ibid., 233.

65. "Their Legacies Remain . . . We Remember Oswald," Yad Vashem, The World Holocaust Remembrance Center. www.yadvashem.org/yv/en/exhibitions/communities/mir/rufeisen.asp. "From the moment he arrived in Israel he was adopted by the community of ex-Mir residents—especially the survivors—as one of their own."

66. Tec, *In the Lion's Den*, 247.

67. "Their Legacies Remain . . . We Remember Oswald."

68. There are other examples. The Cardinal of Paris, Jean-Marie Lustiger (1926–2007), and Marie-Théodor Ratisbonne (1802–1884) were both Jewish converts who became priests and remained very conscious of their Jewish roots and heritage. Ratisbonne, along with his brother who also converted, founded an order of nuns (the Sisters of our Lady of Zion) and schools for providing a Christian education to Jewish children.

69. HCJ 58/68 *Shalit v. Minister of the Interior*, 23(2) P.D. 477 (1970). These three justices—Zussman, Cohn, and Vitkon—relied on the 1965 Population Registry law, which they claimed still implicitly adhered to the open standard of self-declaration and gave parents the right to register children as they pleased. In light of this law, the justices wrote, and absent express legislative authorization, registration officials lacked the power to apply a religious law interpretation of the term *Jew* for purposes of nationality. In a separate opinion Justice Berenson wrote that the term *nationality* should be given its "ordinary meaning" and asserted that, among enlightened Israelis, Shalit's children would be thought of as having a Jewish nationality. The dissent, written by Justices Silberg and Kister, argued that "Jewish nationality" should be given an "objective" definition and should depend on the mother's religion.

Two other justices, Agranat and Landau, also dissented but offered no opinion on the merits of the case, saying it was improper for a court to rule against the position adopted by the government, which had been implicitly ratified by the Knesset.

70. See sources cited in note 5 of this chapter.

71. Cohen and Susser, "Jews and Others," 52–65.

CHAPTER 7: WHO IS A JEW IN AMERICA?

1. Moshe Halbertal, "On Modern Jewish Identities," in *Jewish Peoplehood: Change and Challenge*, ed. M. Revivi and E. Kopelowitz (Boston: Academic Studies Press 2008), 39.

2. Donniel Hartman, *The Boundaries of Judaism* (London: Continuum, 2008), 5 (emphasis added).

3. The use of the phrase *Big Tent* did not originate with me. The Jewish Outreach Institute, founded in 1998 by sociologist Egon Mayer, later changed its name to Big Tent Judaism and, among other things, sponsored a website under that name. Its stated goal was to provide an "independent, national, trans-denominational organization reaching out to unengaged and intermarried Jewish families, and helping the Jewish community better welcome them in." The website no longer exists, and in 2016 the organization laid off its staff because of financial difficulties. See Josh Nathan-Kazis, "Intermarriage Outreach Group 'Big Tent Judaism' Shrinks as Top Staff Leave," *The Forward*, August 18, 2016, https://forward.com /news/348019/intermarriage-outreach-group-shedding-staff. Later that year its executive director wrote an article suggesting that the organization no longer operates. See Rabbi Kerry Olitzky, "Success and Sunset," *Jewish Philanthropy*, December 23, 2016, ejewishphilanthropy.com/success-and-the-sunset.

4. H. L. A. Hart, "Positivism and the Separation of Law and Morals," *Harvard Law Review* 71, no. 4 (February 1958): 593, 607. "A legal rule forbids you to take a vehicle into the public park. Plainly this forbids an automobile, but what about bicycles, roller skates, toy automobiles? What about airplanes? Are these, as we say, to be called 'vehicles' for the purpose of the rule or not?"

5. Lon Fuller, "Positivism and Fidelity to Law: A Reply to Professor Hart," *Harvard Law Review* 71 (1958): 630, 663.

6. See "Vehicle," Merriam-Webster, www.merriam-webster.com/dictionary/vehicle.

7. See generally Pierre Schlag, "No Vehicles in the Park," *Seattle University Law Review* 23, no. 2 (1999), which suggests an approach to interpretation that focuses on the cultural context: whether there was a shared cultural understanding of the nature of a park and the functions it was meant to serve.

8. See Yaakov Ariel, "Unofficial Conversions: Non-Jewish Participants in Contemporary American Synagogues," in *Becoming Jewish: New Jews and Emerging Jewish Communities in a Globalized World*, ed. Tudor Parfitt and Netanel Fisher (Newcastle upon Tyne: Cambridge Scholars Publishing, 2016), 334–352; and Marx Dalia, "Participation of Non-Jewish Family Members in Bar/Bat-Mitzvah

Ceremonies in the American Reform Movement: Boundaries or Inclusion," in Parfitt and Fisher, *Becoming Jewish*, 353–368.

9. See discussion at page 199 in Chapter 10.

10. Doreen Carvajal, *The Forgetting River: A Modern Tale of Survival, Identity, and the Inquisition* (New York: Riverhead Books, 2012), 103.

11. Ibid., 7.

12. Ibid., 296–298.

13. Doreen Carvajal, interview with author, May 1, 2014.

14. John Tagliabue, "Jean-Marie Lustiger, French Cardinal, Dies at 80," *New York Times*, August 6, 2007.

15. Ibid.

16. *Jubu*, also spelled *Jewbu*, is a neologism popularized by Rodger Kamenetz's 1994 book, *The Jew in the Lotus: A Poet's Rediscovery of Jewish Identity in Buddhist India* (New York: HarperCollins, 1994). The term refers to a person of Jewish heritage who maintains Buddhist beliefs or practices. A "staggeringly high" percentage of American Buddhist leaders—more than half, by some estimates—are Jews by birth. Some Jubus practice Judaism combined with elements of Buddhist practice. "Jubu," The JC, www.thejc.com/judaism/jewish-words/jubu-1.8034.

17. Daniel J. Elazar, *Community and Polity: The Organizational Dynamics of American Jewry*, revised and updated ed. (Philadelphia and Jerusalem: The Jewish Publication Society, 1995), 20.

CHAPTER 8: CAN WE SURVIVE ACCEPTANCE?

1. AJC Survey of American Jewish Opinion 2017. Of those responding yes, 41 percent characterized it as a "very serious problem" and the remainder (43 percent) indicated that it was "somewhat of a problem." "AJC Survey of American Jewish Opinion 2017," AJC, September 13, 2017, www.ajc.org/news/ajc-survey-of -american-jewish-opinion-2017.

2. "Americans Express Increasingly Warm Feelings Toward Religious Groups," Pew Research Center, February 15, 2017, www.pewforum.org/2017/02/15/americans -express-increasingly-warm-feelings-toward-religious-groups. See text at note 136.

3. Leonard Dinnerstein, *Antisemitism in America* (New York: Oxford University Press, 2004), xiii.

4. Ibid., xix. For an outstanding in-depth treatment of this issue, see Carroll, *Constantine's Sword*.

5. Ibid., xiii.

6. See generally Mary C. Boys, *Redeeming Our Sacred Story: The Death of Jesus and Relations Between Jews and Christians* (New York: Paulist, 2013), 76–103.

7. Matthew 27:25 (English Standard Version).

8. Dinnerstein, *Antisemitism in America*, xx–xxi.

9. Jacob Katz, *From Prejudice to Destruction: Anti-Semitism, 1700–1933* (Cambridge, MA: Harvard University Press, 1980), 323.

10. Joshua Trachtenberg, *The Devil and the Jews: The Medieval Conception of the Jew and Its Relation to Modern Antisemitism* (Philadelphia: Jewish Publication Society, 1983), 23.

11. Alan Dundes, "A Study of Ethnic Slurs: The Jew and the Polack in the United States," *Journal of American Folklore* 84, no. 332 (April 1971): 186.

12. Walter Laqueur, *The Changing Face of Antisemitism: From Ancient Times to the Present Day* (New York: Oxford University Press, 2006), 56.

13. "Rabbi Brennglass and the Massena Blood Libel," in *Blessings of Freedom: Chapters in American Jewish History*, ed. Michael Feldberg (Hoboken, NJ: KTAV Publishing House, 2002), 132–133. See also Dinnerstein, *Antisemitism in America*, 101.

14. Maristella Botticini and Zvi Eckstein, *The Chosen Few: How Education Shaped Jewish History, 70–1492* (Princeton, NJ: Princeton University Press, 2012).

15. Dinnerstein, *Antisemitism in America*, 19.

16. William Shakespeare, *Merchant of Venice*, 3.1: "Hath not a Jew eyes? hath not a Jew hands, organs, dimensions, senses, affections, passions? fed with the same food, hurt with the same weapons, subject to the same diseases, healed by the same means, warmed and cooled by the same winter and summer, as a Christian is? If you prick us, do we not bleed? if you tickle us, do we not laugh? if you poison us, do we not die? and if you wrong us, shall we not revenge?"

17. For a particularly revealing analysis of the play and its relationship to anti-Semitism, see Stephen Greenblatt, "Shakespeare's Cure for Xenophobia: What the 'Merchant of Venice' Taught Me About Ethnic Hatred and the Literary Imagination," *New Yorker*, July 10 and 17, 2017.

18. Philip Graves, "The Truth About the Protocols: A Literary Forgery," *The Times*, London, August 16–18, 1921; "Proof That the 'Jewish Protocols' Were Forged," *New York Times*, September 4, 1921, 58.

19. Herman Bernstein documented the hoax in a book published in the United States. See generally Herman Bernstein, *The History of a Lie* (Memphis, TN: General Books, 2010 [1921]).

20. Max Wallace, *The American Axis* (New York: St. Martin's, 2005), 16.

21. Hamas Covenant 1988, Yale Law School, Lillian Goldman Law Library, http://avalon.law.yale.edu/20th_century/hamas.asp.

22. Nina Shea, "Major Publishers Protest Saudi Textbook Content," *National Review*, October 17, 2012, www.nationalreview.com/corner/330786. See Anti-Defamation League, "Islamic Antisemitism in Historical Perspective," in *The Theory and Practice of Islamic Terrorism: An Anthology*, ed. Marvin Perry and Howard E. Negrin (New York: Palgrave MacMillan, 2002), 207–218.

23. Peter Stuyvesant, "Manhattan, to the Amsterdam Chamber of Directors, September 22, 1654," in *The Jew in the American World: A Source Book*, ed. Jacob Rader Marcus (Detroit: Wayne State University Press, 1996), 29–30.

24. "Amsterdam Jewry's Successful Intercession for the Manhattan Immigrants, January 1655," in Marcus, *The Jew in the American World*, 30, 31.

25. Congregation Shearith Israel, www.shearithisrael.org.

26. Ira Rosenwaike, "An Estimate and Analysis of the Jewish Population of the United States in 1790," *Publications of the American Jewish Historical Society* 50, no. 1 (September 1960), 23, 34 (estimates between 1300 and 1500).

27. Kerry M. Olitzky, *The American Synagogue: A Historical Dictionary and Sourcebook* (Westport, CT: Greenwood Press, 1996), 3.

28. See "The Letter from Moses Seixas to George Washington," Facing History and Ourselves, www.facinghistory.org/nobigotry/the-letters/letter-moses-seixas-george -washington. See also "George Washington and His Letter to the Jews of Newport," Touro Synagogue, www.tourosynagogue.org/history-learning/gw-letter.

29. See, for example, Daniel Dreisbach, "These Letters Offer a Window into George Washington's Views on Religious Liberty," Institute for Faith, Work & Economics, February 16, 2015, https://tifwe.org/george-washingtons-view-on-religious -liberty. Washington wrote similar reassuring letters to Baptists, Quakers, and Catholics, who had also been persecuted as religious minorities in the American colonies. Ibid.

30. See Dreisbach, "These Letters Offer a Window into George Washington's Views on Religious Liberty." As Dreisbach notes, "This letter is notable for Washington's clear articulation of America's greatest contribution to, and innovation of, political society—the abandonment of a policy of religious *toleration* in favor of religious *liberty*" (emphasis in original). Ibid.

31. George Washington, "Letter to the Hebrew Congregation at Newport," Teaching American History, August 21, 1790, http://teachingamericanhistory .org/library/document/letter-to-the-hebrew-congregation-at-newport. As the scholar Daniel Dreisbach has noted, the last clause echoes an ancient Hebrew blessing from Micah 4:4. See Dreisbach, "These Letters Offer a Window into George Washington's Views on Religious Liberty." The Newport congregation remains intensely proud of this legacy; the Washington letter is read aloud every year in a public celebration. "History of Touro Synagogue Foundation," Touro Synagogue, www.tourosynagogue .org/history-learning/tsf-intro-menu/tsf-history-menu. US Supreme Court Justices Ruth Bader Ginsburg and Elena Kagan have given keynote speeches. "Touro Celebrates Its 250th Year," Touro Synagogue, www.tourosynagogue.org/index.php /upcoming-event-home/25-home-page/132-event-touro-celebrates-250th.

32. "Timeline in American Jewish History," Jacob Rader Marcus Center of the American Jewish Archives, http://americanjewisharchives.org/education/timeline.php.

33. Stanley F. Chyet, "The Political Rights of the Jews in the United States: 1776–1840," *American Jewish Archives* 10 (1958): 14, 22. As Chyet notes, "Not since the Edict of the Roman Emperor Caracalla, the *Constitutio Antoniniana* of 212 C.E., had a national government conferred citizenship on its Jewish subjects." Ibid.

34. Dinnerstein, *Antisemitism in America*, 14–16.

35. Chyet, "The Political Rights of the Jews in the United States," 67. The five holdouts were New Jersey, North Carolina, New Hampshire, Connecticut, and Rhode Island. New Hampshire, which had hardly any Jews, was the last of the

original thirteen states to confer full political equality on Jews, in 1877. Leon Hühner, "The Struggle for Religious Liberty in North Carolina, with Special Reference to the Jews," *American Jewish Historical Society* 15 (1906): 37.

36. Dinnerstein, *Antisemitism in America*, 11, 13; Leo Hershkowitz, "Some Aspects of the New York Jewish Merchant In Colonial Trade," in *Migration and Settlement: Papers on Anglo-American Jewish History*, ed. Aubrey L. Newman (London: Jewish Historical Society, 1971), 103–104; Michael Kammen, *Colonial New York: A History* (Oxford: Oxford University Press, 1996), 209, 240.

37. Dinnerstein, *Antisemitism in America*, 22–23.

38. Jonathan D. Sarna, "Anti-Semitism and American History," *Commentary*, March 1, 1981, 44.

39. Dinnerstein, *Antisemitism in America*, 17–18.

40. Ibid., 18–19, citing Elizabeth Peabody, *Sabbath Lessons* (1813), 49.

41. Ibid., 19, quoting Alfred Moritz Myers, *The Young Jew* (Philadelphia: American Sunday-School Union, 1848), 7.

42. Ibid., 22.

43. Ibid., 22–23; Jonathan Sarna, *American Judaism: A History* (New Haven, CT: Yale University Press, 2008), 69.

44. Sarna, *American Judaism*, 375, Appendix: American Jewish Population Estimates, 1660–2000. In 1840 there were about 15,000 American Jews; by 1860 the American Jewish population had increased to about 150,000. Ibid., 63.

45. Dinnerstein, *Antisemitism in America*, 30–31 (calling the Civil War "the worst period of antisemitism in the United States to that date").

46. Ibid., 31–33.

47. Ibid., 31, quoting an 1863 article in the *Detroit Commercial Advertiser*.

48. See "Anti-Semitism in the United States: General Grant's Infantry," Jewish Virtual Library, www.jewishvirtuallibrary.org/general-grant-s-infamy. The order stated, "The Jews, as a class violating every regulation of trade established by the Treasury Department and also department orders, are hereby expelled…within twenty-four hours from the receipt of this order."

49. Ibid.

50. Ibid.

51. Isaac Markens, *Lincoln and the Jews* (Baltimore, MD: American Jewish Historical Society, 1909), 12–13.

52. Ibid., 14.

53. See "Anti-Semitism in the United States: General Grant's Infantry." Kaskel's mission was supported by Jews across the country, who sent letters and telegrams to Washington. A delegation led by a rabbi followed to thank Lincoln for rescinding the order. Ibid. Lincoln reportedly assured the delegation of his support, saying, "To condemn a class is, to say the least, to wrong the good with the bad." Ibid. Lincoln further stated, "I do not like to see a class or nationality condemned on account of a few sinners." Markens, *Lincoln and the Jews*, 14.

54. Joakim Isaacs, "Candidate Grant and the Jews," *American Jewish Archives* 17, no. 1 (April 1965): 15.

55. H. W. Brands, *The Man Who Saved the Union: Ulysses Grant in War and Peace* (New York: Anchor Books, 2013), 422.

56. Ronald C. White, *American Ulysses: A Life of Ulysses S. Grant* (New York: Random House, 2016), 494–495. "In opening to Jews the possibility of government service, Grant continued his broader policy of reconciliation." Ibid., 495.

57. Jonathan Sarna, *When General Grant Expelled the Jews* (New York: Schocken, 2012), xii.

58. Ibid., 100–105.

59. Ibid., 135–136.

60. Ibid., xi–xiii.

61. Jonathan D. Sarna, "A Great Awakening: The Transformation That Shaped Twentieth-Century American Judaism," in *American Jewish Women's History: A Reader*, ed. Pamela S. Nadell (New York: New York University Press, 2003), 43, 47.

62. Markens, *Lincoln and the Jews*, 31; Ray Monk, *Robert Oppenheimer: A Life Inside the Center* (New York: Anchor Books/Random House, 2012), 12.

63. Benjamin Ginsberg, *The Fatal Embrace: Jews and the State* (Chicago: University of Chicago Press, 1993), 84.

64. Elliott Ashkenazi, "Joseph Seligman (1819–1880)," in *Immigrant Entrepreneurship: German-American Business Biographies, 1720 to the Present*, vol. 2, ed. William J. Hausman (Washington, DC: German Historical Institute, 2014), www .immigrantentrepreneurship.org/entry.php?rec=184es/13403-seligman.

65. Monk, *Robert Oppenheimer*, 12.

66. "A Sensation at Saratoga," *New York Times*, June 19, 1877.

67. Ibid.

68. Seligman also won vocal support from many non-Jews, including New York's gentile banking community and the clergyman Henry Ward Beecher, who delivered a sermon on the subject. Ibid.

69. Editorial Staff, "The Seligman Scandal, Antisemitism in Saratoga Springs," *Adirondack Almanack*, September 2, 2009, www.adirondackalmanack.com/2009 /09/the-seligman-scandal-antisemitism-in-saratoga-springs.html.

70. Robert C. Kennedy, "On This Day," HarpWeek, www.nytimes.com/learning /general/onthisday/harp/0728.html. The same year Corbin, Hilton, and others founded the American Society for the Suppression of the Jews.

71. John Higham, "Social Discrimination Against Jews in America, 1830– 1930," *Publications of the American Jewish Historical Society* 47 (September 1957): 12.

72. Richard E. Fraenkel, "'No Jews, Dogs, or Consumptives': Comparing Anti-Jewish Discrimination in Late-Nineteenth-Century Germany and the United States," Nineteenth-Century Anti-Semitism in International Perspective: Symposium at the German Historical Institute Paris, published May 12, 2016, http:// antisem19c.hypotheses.org/630#n12.

73. Ibid. See also Higham, "Social Discrimination Against Jews in America, 1830–1930."

74. Dinnerstein, *Antisemitism in America*, 58. Moreover, the Jewish presence became for the first time conspicuous. In 1877 there were only about 250,000 Jews in the United States. By 1914 there were about two million, most of them packed into urban slums. This was especially true in New York, where Jews made up nearly 28 percent of the city's total population by 1915. Sarna, *American Judaism*, 63, 151–153.

75. Michael C. LeMay, "An Overview of Immigration to the United States, 1865–1945," in *Transforming America: Perspectives on U.S. Immigration*, vol. 2, ed. Michael C. LeMay (Santa Barbara, CA: Praeger, 2012), 1, 5.

76. Dinnerstein, *Antisemitism in America*, 60.

77. Sarna, *American Judaism*, at 216.

78. Art Harris, "Leo Frank and the Winds of Hate," *Washington Post*, December 20, 1983, www.washingtonpost.com/archive/lifestyle/1983/12/20/leo-frank-and-the -winds-of-hate/cd999778-f44f-4f40-a483-8fbea9ec84c6/?utm_term=.d3f7ef09aada.

79. Wendell Rawls Jr., "After 69 Years of Silence, Lynching Victim Is Cleared," *New York Times*, March 8, 1982.

80. Elaine Marie Alphin, *An Unspeakable Crime: The Prosecution and Persecution of Leo Frank* (Minneapolis, MN: Lerner Publishing Group, 2010), 139. The Georgia Board of Pardons and Paroles issued a final statement pardoning Leo Frank. Ibid.

81. John Foster Fraser, *The Conquering Jew* (Forgotten Books, 2015 [1915]), 103–104, quoting Burton J. Hendrick, "The Jewish Invasion of America," *McClure's Magazine,* 1913, 136. Hendrick also wrote, "In the next hundred years, the Semitic influence is likely to be almost preponderating in the United States." Ibid., 165.

82. Leo P. Ribuffo, "Henry Ford and 'The International Jew,'" *American Jewish History* 69, no. 4 (June 1980): 442. See generally Victoria Saker Woeste, *Henry Ford's War on Jews and the Legal Battle Against Hate Speech* (Stanford, CA: Stanford University Press, 2012).

83. Adolf Hitler later applauded Ford's efforts. Ribuffo, "Henry Ford and 'The International Jew,'" 470. "The work is widely credited with influencing the writing of Adolf Hitler's *Mein Kampf.* Hitler kept a picture of Ford on the wall of his office in Munich, praised the automobile magnate in *Mein Kampf,* and later told a *Detroit News* reporter, 'I regard Henry Ford as my inspiration.'" Dinnerstein, *Antisemitism in America*, 83.

84. Dinnerstein, *Antisemitism in America*, 81.

85. Albin Krebs, "Charles Coughlin, 30's 'Radio Priest,'" *New York Times*, October 28, 1979, 44.

86. Ronald Modras, "Father Coughlin and Anti-Semitism: Fifty Years Later," *Journal of Church and State* 31 (1989): 231–232, citing David H. Bennett, *Demagogues in the Depression: American Radicals and the Union Party, 1932–1936* (New Brunswick, NJ: Rutgers University Press, 1969), 54.

87. Jerome Karabel, *The Chosen: The Hidden History of Admission and Exclusion at Harvard, Yale, and Princeton* (New York: Houghton Mifflin, 2006), 88–89.

88. A. Lawrence Lowell, letter to William Ernest Hocking, May 19, 1922, in Susanne Klingenstein, *Enlarging America: The Cultural Work of Jewish Literary Scholars, 1930–1990* (Syracuse, NY: Syracuse University Press, 1998), 43; Karabel, *The Chosen*, 86.

89. Karabel, *The Chosen*, 87.

90. Dinnerstein, *Antisemitism in America*, 85–86.

91. Karabel, *The Chosen*, 133, citing George W. Pierson, *A Yale Book of Numbers: Historical Statistics of the College and University 1701–1976* (New Haven, CT: Yale University, 1983), 118–120.

92. Sarna, *American Judaism*, at 219.

93. Leonard Dinnerstein, "Antisemitism in Crisis Times in the United States: The 1920s and 1930s," in *Anti-Semitism in Times of Crisis*, ed. Sander L. Gilman and Steven T. Katz (New York: New York University Press, 1991), 212, 217.

94. Jeffrey Gurock, "America's Challenge to Jewish Identity: A Historical Perspective on Voluntarism and Assimilation," in *A Portrait of the American Jewish Community*, ed. Norman Linzer, David J. Schnall, and Jerome A. Chanes (Westport, CT: Praeger, 1998), 20.

95. Woeste, *Henry Ford's War on Jews*, 267–272. Aaron Sapiro filed a libel suit against Ford that led to a mistrial. Before the retrial was to begin, Marshall persuaded Ford to settle the case and issue an apology. Ibid.

Marshall also played a role in resolving the blood libel incident in 1928, mentioned earlier in this chapter, when a four-year-old girl disappeared from her home two days before Yom Kippur, leading to public speculation that Jews had killed her and used her blood in a religious ritual. The girl was found unharmed a few hours later. Marshall demanded an investigation by the superintendent of the State Police into why a state trooper had interviewed the local rabbi about the alleged ritual. The investigation resulted in public apologies and suspension of the state trooper. Dinnerstein, *Antisemitism in America*, 101.

96. In the 1920s and 1930s the ADL conducted a successful campaign to ban Shakespeare's *The Merchant of Venice* from public schools on the grounds that the portrayal of Shylock promoted harmful stereotypes. By 1937 more than three hundred American cities had removed the play from their curricula. Dinnerstein, *Antisemitism in America*, 102.

97. Ibid., 102, 146.

98. Steven Windmueller, "Assessing the American Jewish Institutional Response to Global Anti-Semitism," *Jewish Political Studies Review* 17 (2005): 85.

99. Dinnerstein, *Antisemitism in America*, 148–149.

100. Edward S. Shapiro, "World War II and American Jewish Identity," *Modern Judaism* 10 (1990): 77.

101. Dinnerstein, *Antisemitism in America*, 151. The ADL, noting a substantial decrease in anti-Semitism in the 1948 political campaigns, attributed it to the "fact that there is economic prosperity and no national or international problems which are sharply and deeply dividing Americans." Ibid., 162.

102. Sarna, *American Judaism*, 276.

103. Public Papers of the Presidents of the United States, Harry S. Truman, 1949: Containing the Public Messages, Speeches, and Statements of the President, January 1 to December 31, 1949, 254. Truman stated, "I have called for legislation to protect the rights of all its citizens, to assure their equal participation in national life, and to reduce discrimination based upon prejudice." Ibid.

104. "Jews and the Civil Rights Movement," Religious Action Center of Reform Judaism, https://rac.org/jews-and-civil-rights-movement.

105. See Karabel, *The Chosen*, 330–331.

106. According to a 1964 ADL survey, 9.8 percent of American resort hotels still discriminated against Jews in 1963. "Anti-Jewish Discrimination in American Hotels Declines Sharply," Jewish Telegraphic Agency, January 31, 1964, www.jta.org/1964/01 /31/archive/anti-jewish-discrimination-in-american-hotels-declines-sharply.

107. Civil Rights Act of 1964, Pub. L. No. 88-352, 78 Stat. 241.

108. State Public Accommodation Laws, National Conference of State Legislatures, www.ncsl.org/research/civil-and-criminal-justice/state-public-accommodation-laws .aspx. The five states are Alabama, Georgia, Mississippi, North Carolina, and Texas.

109. In a sign of how widespread the use of restrictive covenants had become, three justices had to recuse themselves when they learned the deeds to their own homes contained such provisions. The other six justices produced a unanimous opinion in favor of the Shelleys. See Abigail Perkiss, "Shelley v. Kraemer: Legal Reform for America's Neighborhoods," Constitution Daily, May 9, 2014, https://constitutioncenter.org/blog /shelley-v-kraemer-legal-reform-for-americas-neighborhoods.

110. Federal Fair Housing Act of 1968, 42 U.S. Code, sec. 3604. See, for example, The Commonwealth of Massachusetts, Unlawful Discrimination Because of Race, Color, Religious Creed, National Origin, Ancestry or Sex, Mass. Gen. Laws ch.151B; New York Human Rights Law, N.Y. Exec. Law, sec. 290–301.

111. California passed the Unruh Civil Rights Act in 1959, making housing discrimination illegal. Cal. Civ. Code, sec. 51.

112. Will Carless, "A Specter from Our Past: Longtime Residents Will Always Remember the Stain Left on the Jewel by an Era of Housing Discrimination," La Jolla Light, April 7, 2005, www.lajollalight.com/sdljl-a-specter-from-our-past-longtime -residents-will-2005apr07-story.html.

113. Murray Friedman, *Philadelphia Jewish Life, 1940–2000* (Philadelphia: Temple University Press, 2003), xxxvi; Dinnerstein, *Antisemitism in America*, 237–238.

114. Lewis B. Ward, "The Ethnics of Executive Selection," *Harvard Business Review* 43 (1965).

115. Dinnerstein, *Antisemitism in America*, 237, citing John Coleman, a labor economist and former president of Haverford College who was then president of the Edna McConnell Clark Foundation.

116. Gerd Wilcke, "Shapiro: Du Pont Chief of a New Mold," *New York Times*, December 19, 1973, 65. The *New York Times* reported that Shapiro was the son of a

Lithuanian Jewish immigrant who owned a dry cleaning shop. "Very active in Jewish affairs and an acknowledged leader of the Jewish community in Wilmington, Del., Mr. Shapiro added that being a Jew had 'never been a handicap' during his more than 20 years with the company." Ibid.

117. Robert A. Bennett, "No Longer a Wasp Preserve," *New York Times*, June 29, 1986, www.nytimes.com/1986/06/29/business/no-longer-a-wasp-preserve.html ?pagewanted=all.

118. Jews in College and University Administration, American Jewish Committee, 1966 (reporting that "just under 0.8 per cent" of the presidents' posts in the 775 schools surveyed were held by Jews).

119. Dinnerstein, *Antisemitism in America*, 239.

120. Neil Rudenstine (Harvard 1991) is sometimes described as Harvard's first Jewish president, but this is not quite accurate: he was the son of an Italian Catholic mother and a Ukrainian Jewish father and considered himself an Episcopalian. In all events, his parentage might have posed an obstacle to appointment before the 1980s. See Ken Gewertz, "Rudenstine's Journey to Harvard Began at 14," *Harvard Gazette*, May 17, 2001, https://news.harvard.edu/gazette/story/2001/05/rudenstines-journey-to-harvard-began-at-14.

121. John Slawson and Lawrence Bloomgarden, *The Unequal Treatment of Equals: The Social Club, Discrimination in Retreat* (New York: Institute of Human Relations, American Jewish Committee, 1965), 7.

122. Ibid., 21–23.

123. In November 1990 the US Golf Association, which owns and operates the US Open, voted against staging future tournaments at clubs that discriminated against minority groups or women. Other major golf organizations quickly followed. As a result, many private clubs either changed their membership policies or admitted token members. See, for example, Jaime Diaz, "Shoal Creek Headed in Right Direction," ESPN, September 22, 2009, www.espn.com/golf/columns/story?columnist=diaz_jaime&id=4492157.

124. Jo-Ann Barnas and Mike Hendricks, "Watson Quits Club, Citing Bias in Denial of Bloch," *Kansas City Star*, November 30, 1990, www.kansascity.com/latest-news/article295410/Watson-quits-club-citing-bias-in-denial-of-Bloch.html.

125. Ibid. Before Bloch was admitted, L. Chandler Smith, the president of the club's board of directors, acknowledged that the club had no Jewish members, as far as he knew, or black members. Watson rejoined the club five years later. Ibid. See also "Watson Rejoins Country Club He Quit," *New York Times*, July 13, 1995, www.nytimes.com/1995/07/13/sports/sports-people-golf-watson-rejoins-country-club-he-quit.html.

126. See, for example, Dinnerstein, *Antisemitism in America*, 170: "Overt antisemitism went out of fashion, accompanied in many cases by a sense of bad conscience." See also Peter Novick, *The Holocaust in American Life* (New York: First Mariner Books, 2000), 113: "The fifteen or twenty years after the war saw the

repudiation of anti-Semitic discourse and its virtual disappearance from the public realm."

127. Sarna, *American Judaism*, 273, citing as examples Arthur Miller's *Focus* (1945), Saul Bellow's *The Victim* (1947), Laura Z. Hobson's *Gentleman's Agreement* (1947), Norman Mailer's *The Naked and the Dead* (1948), and Irwin Shaw's *The Young Lions* (1948).

128. Sarna, *American Judaism*, 273; Dinnerstein, *Antisemitism in America*, 152–153.

129. The producer, Darryl F. Zanuck of Twentieth Century Fox, was a Methodist from Nebraska, the only non-Jewish head of a major movie studio in the 1940s. At the time Jewish studio heads were still too timid to put Jewish issues on screen, fearful of triggering an anti-Semitic backlash. Indeed, a group of Jewish movie moguls pressured Zanuck not to make the movie. Zanuck, free of such fears, reportedly made the movie for two reasons: he wanted to make a breakthrough film, and he had once been the target of anti-Semitism similar to that portrayed in the novel. As a young man in Hollywood, he had been rejected from the exclusive Los Angeles Athletic Club because club officials incorrectly assumed he was Jewish. Although he eventually obtained membership in the club, "his initial rejection and the outrage he felt at the time were never forgotten." See Lynn Haney, *Gregory Peck: A Charmed Life* (New York: Da Capo Press, 2004), 148.

130. General Convention of the Episcopal Church (USA), A Resolution of the 1964 General Convention: "Deicide and the Jews," October 26, 1964, Council of Centers on Jewish-Christian Relations, www.ccjr.us/dialogika-resources/documents -and-statements/protestant-churches/na/episcopalian/685-ecusa64oct.

131. This document is known as *Nostra Aetate* (Latin for "In Our Time"). The official title in English is "Declaration on the Relation of the Church to Non-Christian Religions." According to one translation, the document reads, "Even though the Jewish authorities and those who followed their lead pressed for the death of Christ, neither all Jews indiscriminately at that time, nor Jews today, can be charged with the crimes committed during his passion." *Nostra Aetate*, Declaration on the Relation of the Church to Non-Christian Religions (October 28, 1965), www.nostreradici.it /enaetate.htm. For a full translation of the document, see Anti-Defamation League, "Nostra Aetate," www.adl.org/education/resources/glossary-terms/nostra-aetate.

132. Official statements made by the Baptist Church and the Evangelical Lutheran Church, although not explicitly rejecting the charge of deicide, also repudiated past anti-Semitic teachings and expressed deep regret. "In the long history of Christianity there exists no more tragic development than the treatment accorded the Jewish people on the part of Christian believers. . . . In the spirit of truth-telling, we who bear (Martin Luther's) name and heritage must with pain acknowledge also Luther's anti-Judaic diatribes and the violent recommendations of his later (16th-Century) writings against the Jews. . . . [W]e reject this violent invective, and yet more do we express our deep and abiding sorrow over its tragic effects on subsequent generations." Jewish Virtual Library, "Christian-Jewish Relations: Declaration of the Evangelical Lutheran Church in America to the Jewish Community,"

April 18, 1994, www.jewishvirtuallibrary.org/declaration-of-the-evangelical-lutheran -church-in-america-to-the-jewish-community.

In 1995 the Alliance of Baptist churches issued the following statement: "It is in recognition of a past and present among Baptists that is complicit in perpetuating negative stereotypes and myths concerning Jews, that we, the Alliance of Baptists meeting in convocation on March 4, 1995, at Vienna Baptist Church, Vienna, Virginia,

Confess our sin of complicity. Confess our sin of silence.

Confess our sin of interpreting our sacred writings in such a way that we have created enemies of the Jewish people.

Confess our sin of indifference and inaction to the horrors of the Holocaust.

Confess our sins against the Jewish people.

Offer this confession with humility and with hope for reconciliation between Christians and Jews."

http://www.sacredheart.edu/faithservice/centerforchristianandjewishunderstanding /documentsandstatements/allianceofbaptiststatementonjewish-christianrelations march41995/.

133. See Neil Malhotra and Yotam Margalit, "State of the Nation: Anti-Semitism and the Economic Crisis," *Boston Review*, May 1, 2009. "We directly asked respondents 'How much to blame were the Jews for the financial crisis?' with responses falling under five categories: a great deal, a lot, a moderate amount, a little, not at all. Among non-Jewish respondents, a strikingly high 24.6 percent of Americans blamed 'the Jews' a moderate amount or more, and 38.4 percent attributed at least some level of blame to the group." Ibid.

After the Madoff scandal, the ADL reported an increase in anti-Semitic postings on internet websites. "Anti-Semitism and the Madoff Scandal," Anti-Defamation League, December 19, 2008, www.adl.org/news/article/anti-semitism-and-the-madoff -scandal#overview.

134. Eric Cortellessa, "Almost 6 Percent of Congress Now Jewish—28 Democrats and 2 Republicans," *Times of Israel*, January 3, 2017, www.timesofisrael.com /almost-6-of-congress-now-jewish-28-democrats-and-2-republicans.

135. Russell Berman, "Bernie Sanders Bid for Jewish History," *The Atlantic*, January 27, 2016, www.theatlantic.com/politics/archive/2016/01/bernie-sanders -bids-for-jewish-history/429252. Rabbi Jonah Pesner, director of the Religious Action Center of Reform Judaism, said, "You have a guy who is from New York with a Brooklyn accent named Bernie who is a viable presidential candidate and nobody is discussing it, which to me is just a remarkable statement of the success of the American Jewish community to be fully integrated and distinct at the same time." Ibid.

136. "Americans Express Increasingly Warm Feelings Toward Religious Groups." "Americans express warm feelings toward Jews, with half of U.S. adults rating them at 67 degrees or higher on the 0-to-100 scale. Four-in-ten Americans rate Jews in the middle of the thermometer, between 34 and 66, and only about one-in-ten

express feelings that fall at 33 degrees or cooler. These warm ratings are not significantly affected by the ratings of Jews themselves, because Jews make up just 2 percent of the U.S. adult population." Ibid. In an earlier 2014 study Jews received an overall rating of 63. Even more striking: both Protestants and Catholics rated Jews more positively than any other religious group except their own. "How Americans Feel About Religious Groups," Pew Research Center, July 16, 2014, www.pewforum .org/2014/07/16/how-americans-feel-about-religious-groups.

137. Seymour Martin Lipset, "A Unique People in an Exceptional Country," in *American Pluralism and the Jewish Community*, ed. Seymour Martin Lipset (New Brunswick, NJ: Transaction Books, 1990), 22. Lipset was referring to a 1985 poll among contributors to the San Francisco Jewish Community Federation. That year, he noted, in addition to the three members of Congress, the city's two state senators, the mayor, and a "considerable part" of the city council were also Jewish.

138. "AJC Survey of American Jewish Opinion 2017," AJC, September 13, 2017, 20, https://www.ajc.org/survey2017.

139. Market Facts, "1997 Annual Survey of American Jewish Opinion," American Jewish Committee, February 3–11, 1997, www.jewishdatabank.org/Studies /downloadFile.cfm?FileID=3669. Of the 95 percent of respondents who characterized anti-Semitism as a problem in 1997, 40 percent thought it was a "very serious problem" and 55 percent thought it was "somewhat of a problem"; 5 percent said it was "not a problem at all," and 1 percent were "not sure."

140. In 1990 Congress passed the Hate Crime Statistics Act, 28 USC, sec. 534. The act has been subsequently amended to add crime motivated by disabilities, gender bias, and gender identity. See FBI, "2016 Hate Crime Statistics Released," November 13, 2017, www.fbi.gov/news/stories/2016-hate-crime-statistics.

141. One must acknowledge the limitations of the FBI data. The FBI collects and aggregates its data from hundreds of state and local law enforcement agencies. These law enforcement agencies are probably not consistent in terms of their reporting practices or their diligence. For example, Miami reported no hate crimes in 2015, which seems unlikely for such a large and diverse city. See "Crimes Against Whites Equals Small Percentage of Hate Crimes, FBI Statistics Show," *Chicago Tribune*, January 6, 2017, www .chicagotribune.com/news/nationworld/ct-whites-hate-crimes-20170106-story.html.

142. In 2016 the FBI reported a total of 7,321 hate crime "offenses," of which 2,122 were anti-black, 876 were anti-white, 834 were anti-Jewish, and 765 were anti-gay (male). See "2016 Hate Crime Statistics," FBI, Table 4, Offenses, Offense Type by Bias Motivation, 2016, https://ucr.fbi.gov/hate-crime/2016/tables/table-4. It's important to note that the FBI counts hate crimes in two ways: as "offenses" and as "incidents." A single criminal incident can include more than one criminal offense. In 2016, for example, the FBI counted 684 anti-Jewish incidents and 834 offenses. See "2016 Hate Crime Statistics," FBI, Table 1, Incidents, Offenses, Victims, and Known Offenders by Bias Motivations, 2016, https://ucr.fbi.gov/hate-crime/2016/tables/table-1.

143. There are, of course, exceptions. One such crime occurred in April 2014 in Overland Park, Kansas, when a seventy-three-year-old man with a long history of anti-Semitism killed two people outside a Jewish community center and a third on the grounds of a nearby Jewish assisted-living facility. When he was arrested, he shouted, "Heil, Hitler!" As it turned out, none of his victims were Jewish. See Laura Bauer, Dave Helling, and Brian Burnes, "Man with History of Anti-Semitism Jailed in Fatal Shooting of Three at Johnson County Jewish Centers," *Kansas City Star*, April 13, 2014, www.kansascity.com/news/local/article344979/Man-with-history-of-anti-Semitism-jailed-in-fatal-shooting-of-three-at-Johnson-County-Jewish-centers.html#storylink=cpy.

The article further reported,

"Other Jewish-related facilities have been the targets of violence in recent years.

In 2009, a white supremacist shot and fatally wounded a security guard at the crowded U.S. Holocaust Memorial Museum in Washington, D.C., in an attack that sent tourists running for cover. The shooter, eighty-eight-year-old James W. von Brunn, was wounded in the head during the assault and died the following year. Prosecutors said he had been planning the assault—which they described as a suicide mission—for months and wanted "to send a message to the Jewish community" that the Holocaust was a hoax.

In 1999, avowed white supremacist Buford Furrow Jr., who had been recently released from prison, rushed into a day care at a Jewish community center on the northern edge of Los Angeles. He shot and wounded five people, including three children. Later in the day, Furrow shot and killed a postman. Authorities said Furrow described his attacks as a wake-up call to kill Jews and non-whites."

144. In 2016 the FBI reported sixty-one "simple assaults" and twelve "aggravated assaults" motivated by anti-Jewish bias. Both figures were lower than those in 2015. However, these numbers may undercount the total numbers because many school-related fights may go unreported. See "2016 Hate Crime Statistics," FBI, Table 4, Offenses, Offense Type by Bias Motivation, 2016, https://ucr.fbi.gov/hate-crime/2016/tables/table-4.

145. Of the 834 anti-Jewish offenses reported by the FBI in 2016, 489 (59 percent) involved vandalism or the damage or destruction of property. Ibid.

146. In 1996 the FBI reported a total of 1,109 anti-Semitic criminal incidents. By 2016 the number had dropped to 684. "Anti-Semitism in the United States: Statistics on Religious Hate Crimes," Jewish Virtual Library, www.jewishvirtuallibrary.org/statistics-on-religious-hate-crimes.

147. Since 1979, the ADL has reported "anti-Semitic incidents" in an annual report. See, e.g., "ADL Audit: U.S. Anti-Semitic Incidents Surged in 2016–17," https://www.adl.org/sites/default/files/documents/Anti-Semitic%20Audit%20Print_vf2.pdf.

148. Jason Slotkin, "Anti-Semitic Incidents Up 86 Percent Compared with Same Time Last Year," April 24, 2017, NPR, www.npr.org/sections/thetwo-way /2017/04/24/525398277/anti-semitic-incidents-up-86-percent-compared -to-same-time-last-year.

149. Spencer Blakeslee, *The Death of American Antisemitism* (Westport, CT: Praeger, 2000), 52–53. Blakeslee notes that it is difficult to draw conclusions from the data because the reporting has been inconsistent. But by 1997 the reported total had dropped to 1,571. Ibid.

150. Ibid., 53.

151. See "2017 Audit of Anti-Semitic Incidents, Major Findings," ADL, www .adl.org/resources/reports/2017-audit-of-anti-semitic-incidents#major-findings.

152. See "2017 Audit of Anti-Semitic Incidents, Themes and Trends," ADL, www.adl.org/resources/reports/2017-audit-of-anti-semitic-incidents#themes-and -trends.

153. The ADL reported 1,266 anti-Semitic incidents in 2016, a 34 percent spike. Approximately 30 percent (369) of these incidents occurred in November and December. Slotkin, "Anti-Semitic Incidents Up 86 Percent."

154. See "2017 Audit of Anti-Semitic Incidents," ADL, www.npr.org/sections /thetwo-way/2018/02/27/589119452/anti-semitic-incidents-see-largest-single-year -increase-on-record-audit-finds. The ADL press release is "Anti-Semitic Incidents Surged Nearly 60% in 2017, According to New ADL Report," ADL, www.npr .org/sections/thetwo-way/2018/02/27/589119452/anti-semitic-incidents-see-largest -single-year-increase-on-record-audit-finds.

155. Isabel Kershner, Adam Goldman, Alan Blinder, and Richard Pérez-Peña, "Jewish Center Bomb Threat Suspect Is Arrested in Israel," *New York Times*, March 23, 2017, www.nytimes.com/2017/03/23/us/jcc-bomb-threats.html.

156. Adam Vaccaro, Aimee Ortiz, and Reena Karasin, "Boston's Holocaust Memorial Damaged for Second Time This Summer," *Boston Globe*, August 14, 2017, www.bostonglobe.com/metro/2017/08/14/holocaust-memorial-boston-damaged -for-second-time-this-summer/ujYan70j3kXzFWS3TGcZ0J/story.html.

157. Heidi Beirich and Susy Buchanan, "2017: The Year in Hate and Extremism," *Intelligence Report, 2018*, Spring Issue, February 11, 2018.

158. See, for example, Cheryl Gay Stolberg and Brian M. Rosenthal, "Man Charged After White Nationalist Rally in Charlottesville Ends in Deadly Violence," *New York Times*, August 12, 2017, www.nytimes.com/2017/08/12/us /charlottesville-protest-white-nationalist.html?_r=0.

159. See David Gelles, Karl Russell, and Ashwin Seshagiri, "The Business Leaders Who Were on Trump's Advisory Councils," *New York Times*, August 16, 2017, www.nytimes.com/interactive/2017/08/15/business/trump-councils.html.

160. Kershner et al., "Jewish Center Bomb Threat Suspect Is Arrested in Israel."

161. Counting the bomb threats, the number of harassment incidents increased by 41 percent in 2017. The ADL report acknowledged that if the bomb

threats were not counted, the increase would be 18 percent. "2017 Audit of Anti-Semitic Incidents," ADL, www.adl.org/resources/reports/2017-audit-of-anti-semitic-incidents#major-findings.

162. "Israeli-U.S. Teen Indicted for Bomb Threats, Hate Crimes: U.S. Justice Department," *Reuters*, February 28, 2018, www.reuters.com/article/us-usa-security-jewish/israeli-u-s-teen-indicted-for-bomb-threats-hate-crimes-u-s-justice-department-idUSKCN1GD3MN.

163. Dinnerstein, *Antisemitism in America*, 151.

164. Novick, *The Holocaust in American Life*, 113.

165. The ADL indicates that "over the years there have been slight changes in the wording of the 11 Index statements to keep them relevant and contemporary, but the basic structure of the Index has remained consistent since 1992." "A Survey About Attitudes Towards Jews in America," Anti-Defamation League, www.adl.org/sites/default/files/documents/ADL_MS_Survey_Pres_1_25_17.pdf.

166. Ibid.

167. See Blakeslee, *Death of American Antisemitism*, 225. "The index possesses no ability to differentiate between people who don't like Jews and people who don't like anyone else who is different from themselves, regardless of what their attributes, behavior, or racial/ethnic/religious composition may be."

168. "A Survey About Attitudes Towards Jews in America." This figure has held fairly steady since 2007, ranging from 25 to 30 percent.

169. Claude Steele, *Whistling Vivaldi: How Stereotypes Affect Us and What We Can Do* (New York: W. W. Norton & Company, 2010), 5.

170. "What Is BDS?" BDS, https://bdsmovement.net/what-is-bds.

171. Ibid.

172. "BDS: The Global Campaign to Delegitimize Israel," Anti-Defamation League, www.adl.org/education/resources/backgrounders/bds-the-global-campaign-to-delegitimize-israel. The ADL also suggests that "many of the strategies employed in BDS campaigns are anti-Semitic" because they include "overt anti-Semitic expression and acts" and "anti-Semitic rhetoric and narratives." To the extent this is true, such tactics should be condemned.

173. See Lawrence Summers, "Academic Freedom and Anti-Semitism," remarks made on January 29, 2015, before the Columbia Center for Law and Liberty.

174. "The Monitor," August 2014, Special Edition, https://2009-2017.state.gov/documents/organization/231166.pdf.

175. See Karen W. Arenson, "Harvard President Sees Rise in Anti-Semitism on Campus," *New York Times*, September 21, 2002, www.nytimes.com/2002/09/21/us/harvard-president-sees-rise-in-anti-semitism-on-campus.html. Summers later elaborated on his ideas in "Academic Freedom and Anti-Semitism."

176. See generally Douglas Stone, Bruce Patton, and Sheila Heen, *Difficult Conversations: How to Discuss What Matters Most* (New York: Penguin Books, 2000).

177. Summers, "Academic Freedom and Anti-Semitism."

178. Judith Butler, "No, It's Not Anti-Semitic," *London Review of Books*, August 21, 2003, www.lrb.co.uk/v25/n16/judith-butler/no-its-not-anti-semitic.

179. Summers, "Academic Freedom and Anti-Semitism."

180. Sarna, "Anti-Semitism and American History," 47.

181. See *Engel v. Vitale*, 370 U.S. 421 (1962); see also *Abington School Dist. v. Schempp*, 374 U.S. 203 (1963).

182. Sarna, "Anti-Semitism and American History," 46.

183. Ibid.

CHAPTER 9: THE CHALLENGE OF ISRAEL

1. See "A Portrait of Jewish Americans," 82–83. Of the Pew respondents, 30 percent reported being "very attached" to Israel, and 39 percent reported being "somewhat" attached. "Caring" about Israel was an "essential part of being Jewish" for 43 percent of Jewish respondents, and "important but not essential" for an additional 44 percent. A majority of the respondents sixty-five years or older (53 percent) reported that caring about Israel was an "essential" part of what it means to be Jewish, and most of the remainder (39 percent) indicated it was an "important but not essential" element. For younger respondents the percentages are lower. For those eighteen to forty-nine, 35 percent reported it was an essential part, and an additional 48 percent said it was important. Ibid.

2. Dov Waxman, *Trouble in the Tribe: The American Jewish Conflict Over Israel* 3 (2016).

3. See Robert Mnookin and Ehud Eiran, "Discord 'Behind the Table': The Internal Conflict Among Israeli Jews Concerning the Future of Settlements in the West Bank and Gaza," *Journal of Dispute Resolution* 1 (2005): 11–44; Robert Mnookin, Ehud Eiran, and Sreemati Mitter, "Barriers to Progress at the Negotiation Table: Internal Conflicts Among Israelis and Among Palestinians," *Nevada Law Journal* 6 (2005), 299; Robert Mnookin, "The Israeli-Palestinian Conflict: Is There a Zone of Possible Agreement ('ZOPA')," in *Negotiating in Times of Conflict*, ed. Gilead Sher and Anat Kurz (Tel Aviv: Institute for National Security Studies, 2015), 213–215.

4. "Camp David Accords and the Arab-Israeli Peace Process," State Department, Office of the Historian, https://history.state.gov/milestones/1977-1980/camp-david; "Camp David Accords," Israel Ministry of Foreign Affairs, September 17, 1978, www.mfa.gov.il/mfa/foreignpolicy/peace/guide/pages/camp%20david%20accords .aspx; Oslo Accords, 1993, http://cis.uchicago.edu/oldsite/sites/cis.uchicago.edu/files /resources/CIS-090213-israelpalestine_38-1993DeclarationofPrinciples_Oslo Accords.pdf. For the Clinton Parameters, see Foundation for Middle East Peace, "Clinton Parameters, December 23, 2000," https://fmep.org/resource/clinton-parameters/.

5. When the British mandate ended, Jordan took control and occupied the West Bank. But Jordan never asserted national sovereignty over the West Bank by incorporating it into its national state. See James L. Gelvin, *The Israel-Palestine*

Conflict: One Hundred Years of War (New York: Cambridge University Press, 2014), 134; see also "In Jordan, Longstanding Split," *New York Times*, March 26, 1983, www.nytimes.com/1983/03/26/world/in-jordan-longstanding-split.html.

6. This number does not include the 176,000 Jewish inhabitants of those portions of Jerusalem in the West Bank that were annexed to Israel in 1968. Yehezkel Lein, *Land Grab: Israel's Settlement Policy in the West Bank*, B'TSELEM, May 2002, 17, www.btselem.org/download/200205_land_grab_eng.pdf. See also Dror Etkes, director of Peace Now's Settlements Watch Project, "Testimony Before the Near Eastern & South Asian Affairs Subcommittee of the Senate Foreign Relations Committee," October 15, 2003, transcript available at www.foreign.senate.gov/imo/media/doc/EtkesTestimony031015.pdf.

7. For a transcript of the president's announcement, see "Full Video and Transcript: Trump's Speech Recognizing Jerusalem as the Capital of Israel," *New York Times*, December 6, 2017, www.nytimes.com/2017/12/06/world/middleeast/trump-israel-speech-transcript.html.

8. See Mnookin, "The Israeli-Palestinian Conflict," 213–225.

9. See Mnookin and Eiran, "Discord 'Behind the Table,'" 15–19. See generally Mnookin, Eiran, and Mitter, "Barriers to Progress at the Negotiation Table."

10. See Mnookin, Eiran, and Mitter, "Barriers to Progress at the Negotiation Table," 301.

11. In its annual survey of American Jewish opinion, the AJC asks whether "in the current situation" the respondent favors or opposes the establishment of a Palestinian state. Opinion is rather evenly divided, with 55 percent favoring it and 40 percent opposing it. "AJC Survey of American Jewish Opinion 2017," AJC, www.ajc.org/survey2017. See also Waxman, *Trouble in the Tribe*, Figure 4.1, 128.

12. Waxman, *Trouble in the Tribe*, 127 (emphasis added). Only a small fraction favors dismantling all settlements. The 2013 Pew survey reported that 44 percent of the respondents said that settlement construction hurt Israeli security, while 46 percent thought it made no difference or actually helped Israeli security. "A Portrait of Jewish Americans," 91. A November 6, 2016, J Street survey had 28 percent wanting Israel to stop all settlement construction in the future; 50 percent wanted to limit it to the existing settlement blocks; and 22 percent wanted Israel to continue settlements anywhere on the West Bank. "From GBA Strategies to J Street, 2016 Post-Election Jewish Surveys Summary Findings: National and Florida Surveys of Jewish Voters," J Street, November 9, 2016, 3, http://jstreet.org/wp-content/uploads/2016/11/J-Street-Election-Night-Survey-Analysis-110916.pdf.

13. These differences can be overstated, however. A 2014 survey of young American Jews taken before and after the 2014 war found that a vast majority thought that Israel's actions in the war were mostly or completely justified. See Theodore Sasson, Leonard Saxe, and Michelle Shain, "How Do Young American Jews Feel About Israel?" *Tablet*, February 24, 2015, www.tabletmag.com/scroll/189210/how-do-young-american-jews-feel-about-israel.

14. Mnookin, Eiran, and Mitter, "Barriers to Progress at the Negotiation Table," 313–317. That it might be too late, see, for example, Luke Baker, "Israel's Settlement Drive Is Becoming Irreversible, Diplomats Fear," Reuters, May 31, 2016, www.reuters.com/article/us-israel-palestinians-settlements/israels-settlement -drive-is-becoming-irreversible-diplomats-fear-idUSKCN0YM1MY.

15. On December 23, 2016, the UN Security Council passed Resolution 2334 condemning Israeli settlement activity as a "flagrant violation" of international law. The United States abstained. This was the first time the United States did not veto a UN resolution condemning Israel. Among other things, the resolution stressed "that the status quo is not sustainable and that significant steps...are urgently needed in order to (i) stabilize the situation and to reverse negative trends on the ground, which are steadily eroding the two-State solution and entrenching a one-State reality."

16. Waxman, *Trouble in the Tribe*, 94–108. Waxman's Table 3.1 encapsulates the differences among these four positions. Ibid., 94.

17. According to its president, the ZOA opposed "like crazy" the 2005 decision of the Israeli government to withdraw from Gaza and has criticized three different Israeli prime ministers when they "made their offers" in negotiations with the Palestinians that it considered too generous. See Ron Kampas, "Will US Jewish Groups Pivot Left if Herzog Wins?" *Times of Israel*, December 17, 2014, quoted in Waxman, *Trouble in the Tribe*, 173n102.

18. See the JVP's position paper, "Jewish Voice for Peace on One State or Two," Jewish Voice for Peace, March 21, 2007, https://jewishvoiceforpeace.org/jewish -voice-for-peace-on-one-state-or-two. JVP states it would support "any solution that is consistent with the national rights of both Palestinians and Israeli Jews, whether one binational state, two states, or some other solution," so long as it achieves "a lasting peace for Palestinians and Jewish Israelis based on equality, human rights, and freedom." Ibid. "About Us," Jewish Voice for Peace, www.jvpnyc.org/who-we-are.

19. Many Israeli Arabs and Palestinian intellectuals dream of some sort of single, secular binational state—not based simply on one man, one vote but instead a consociational democracy, perhaps along the lines of Belgium. Belgium has Flemish and Walloon regions, with language and educational rights for each people. Belgium has a national government as well, and therein lies the rub for the Israeli-Palestinian conflict. To prevent either group from enacting legislation that would be discriminatory to the other, Belgium has all sorts of special requirements giving each ethnic group a veto. This results in endless conflicts and frequent deadlocks at the national level. Belgium survives—barely—because the Flemish and the Walloons have never had a history of violent conflict; moreover, its national government is relatively unimportant because the country is embedded in the European Union. Given the history of violent conflict between the Israelis and the Palestinians, however, a binational consociational democracy would be a disaster. See generally Robert Mnookin, "Ethnic Conflicts: Flemings & Walloons, Palestinians & Israelis," *Daedalus* 136, no. 1 (2007): 103–119.

20. The $70 million annual revenue figure was reported for 2013. The organization's clout stems from several factors. Although AIPAC itself does not raise money for political candidates, it has informal ties with many pro-Israel PACs, and its members include many formidable fundraisers. It has a substantial staff of experienced lobbyists in Washington who maintain relationships with congressional and executive branch staff. It tracks every congressperson's voting record and disseminates that information. And because of its national network, AIPAC has an army of local volunteers in congressional districts throughout the country. Waxman, *Trouble in the Tribe*, 166; Armin Rosen, "No One Is Afraid of AIPAC," *Tablet*, January 3. 2017, www.tabletmag.com/jewish-news-and-politics/220665/no-one-is-afraid-of-aipac; Connie Bruck, "Friends of Israel," *New Yorker*, September 1, 2014, www.newyorker .com/magazine/2014/09/01/friends-israel.

21. J Street's website describes itself as "the political home for pro-Israel, propeace Americans who want Israel to be secure, democratic and the national home of the Jewish people." It sees itself as "advocat[ing] for policies that advance shared US and Israeli interests as well as Jewish and democratic values, leading to a two-state solution to the Israeli-Palestinian conflict." "About Us," https://jstreet.org/about-us.

22. Theodore Sasson, *The New American Zionism* (New York: New York University Press, 2014), 43.

23. Morton A. Klein and Daniel Mandel, "ZOA Report: J Street—Siding with Israel's Enemies," Zionist Organization of America, April 8, 2013, https://zoa .org/2013/04/10196411-zoa-report-j-street-siding-with-israels-enemies.

24. As of 2013 J Street had forty-five local chapters, 20,000 donors, roughly 180,000 registered supporters, and a Rabbinic cabinet of hundreds of rabbis. J Street U had over fifty campus chapters and 7,500 members. Waxman, *Trouble in the Tribe*, 80; see also J Street, "Our Future, Our Choice," 2014 Financial Statements, https:// s3.amazonaws.com/s3.jstreet.org/images/2014_Financial_Statements_-_Final.pdf.

25. For the list of members, see Member Organizations, Conference of Presidents of Major American Jewish Organizations, www.conferenceofpresidents.org /about/members.

26. Michael Kaplan, "Rick Jacobs Threatens to Pull URJ Out of Presidents Conference After J Street Fiasco," May 1, 2014, https://forward.com/news/breaking -news/197474/rick-jacobs-threatens-to-pull-urj-out-of-president. To his credit, ADL national director Abraham Foxman said his organization had supported the admission of J Street "not because we agree with them, not because we support their views, but in order to ensure the integrity and credibility of American Jewish advocacy and of the Conference of Presidents." Maya Shwayder, "Conference of Presidents Votes Against J Street Inclusion," *Jerusalem Post*, May 1, 2014, www.jpost.com /Jewish-World/Jewish-Features/Conference-Of-Presidents-votes-against-J-Street -inclusion-350972. Leon Wieseltier in *The New Republic* condemned J Street's rejection as a "scandal." Rather than AIPAC or ZOA, he blamed the Orthodox, whom he characterized as J Street's "most energetic opponents." They and the

various organizations they controlled were not at all representative of the American Jewish community as a whole, he claimed; they were "blind to their irrelevance to the fate of Jews who are not like themselves, which is to say, to the fate of the overwhelming majority of American Jewry." Leon Wieseltier, "J Street's Rejection Is a Scandal," *New Republic*, May 7, 2014, https://newrepublic.com /article/117680/presidents-conference-j-street-rejection-disgrace.

27. Wendy Sherman, email to Robert Mnookin, December 5, 2017.

28. Karoun Demirjian and Carol Morello, "How AIPAC Lost the Iran Deal Fight," *Washington Post*, September 3, 2015, www.washingtonpost.com/news /powerpost/wp/2015/09/03/how-aipac-lost-the-iran-deal-fight/?utm_term= .e478dc7c5bfc.

29. See Scott Clement, "Jewish Americans Support the Iran Nuclear Deal," *Washington Post*, July 27, 2015, www.washingtonpost.com/news/the-fix/wp/2015/07/27 /jewish-americans-support-the-iran-nuclear-deal/?utm_term=.7ddfb21b6b7f. Indeed, the proportion of American Jews supporting Obama on this issue was higher than the proportion of Americans generally. Ibid. See also JTA, "Jews Back Iran Deal by Narrow Margin, Poll Says," *The Forward*, September 11, 2015, https://forward .com/news/breaking-news/320816/jews-back-iran-deal-by-narrow-margin-poll-says (reporting on the 2015 AJC poll of American Jewish Opinion).

30. There are two primary sources of polling data: (1) the 2013 Pew Research Center Survey, "A Portrait of Jewish Americans," and (2) the American Jewish Committee's annual "Survey of American Jewish Opinion." The advantage of the AJC's survey is that it is done on a regular basis with a consistent methodology, which permits comparison over time. Waxman notes, however, that the AJC surveys "include only people who identify themselves as Jewish by religion and exclude 'Jews of no religion.'" The Pew survey suggests that "Jews of no religion" account for 22 percent of the American Jewish population; on average they tend to be less attached to Israel and may be more liberal. As a result, "the AJC surveys do not provide a completely accurate representation of American Jewish opinion." Waxman, *Trouble in the Tribe*, 256n2.

31. Ibid., 124. The Pew survey supports these contentions. For example, 61 percent of American Jews think that Israel could peacefully coexist with a future Palestinian state. "A Portrait of Jewish Americans," 87. Nonetheless, most American Jews are "distrustful of Palestinians" and do not think that Palestinian Authority president Mahmoud Abbas has been making "a sincere effort to reach a peace agreement with Israel." Waxman, *Trouble in the Tribe*, 124. Nor do American Jews believe that Prime Minister Netanyahu is making sincere efforts to bring about a two-state resolution of the conflict. Bruce Stokes, "Are American Jews Turning Away from Israel?" *Foreign Policy*, March 10, 2016, http://foreignpolicy.com/2016/03/10/are-american -jews-turning-away-from-israel; "A Portrait of Jewish Americans," 13.

Most American Jews strongly favored the Oslo peace process and blame the Palestinians for its failure. But even during the Second Intifada most favored dismantling some Jewish settlements in the West Bank, at least in the context of a peace agreement with the Palestinians. Waxman, *Trouble in the Tribe*, 126.

32. The annual American Jewish Year Book summarizes BDS activities. See, for example, Arnold Dashefsky and Ira Sheskin, eds., *American Jewish Year Book 2014: The Annual Record of the North American Jewish Communities* (Cham, Switzerland: Springer, 2015), 149–151.

33. To date no American university has ever agreed to divest from investments connected with Israel or implemented a policy to boycott Israeli academic institutions. Some small scholarly groups have endorsed boycotts of Israeli academic institutions, but leading academic administrators and major academic associations have condemned such boycotts. Aiden Pink, "U. of Michigan Regents Won't Divest Despite Students' Anti-Israel Campaign," *The Forward*, December 14, 2017, https://forward.com/fast-forward/390134/u-of-michigan-regents-wont-divest-despite-students-anti-israel-campaign; Richard Pérez-Peña and Jodi Rudoren, "Boycott by Academic Group Is a Symbolic Sting to Israel," *New York Times*, December 16, 2013, www.nytimes.com/2013/12/17/education/scholars-group-endorses-an-academic-boycott-of-israel.html.

34. Judy Maltz, "From the BDS Front Lines: How the On-campus Brawl Is Turning Young Jews Off Israel," *Haaretz*, May 9, 2016, www.haaretz.com/jewish/features/1.717781. This tendency to disengage has even affected the Birthright program, which was once so popular on campus that it had to turn away applicants for its free trips to Israel. See Amanda Pazornik, "Waitlists Hinder Birthright Goal of Giving Free Israel Trips," *Jewish News of Northern California*, September 10, 2010, www.jweekly.com/2010/09/10/waitlists-hinder-birthright-goal-of-giving-free-israel-trips. In recent years Birthright has experienced a drop in popularity and has raised the age limit from twenty-six to thirty to fill the slots available. Judy Maltz, "As Numbers Drop, Birthright Targets Candidates with Little or No Jewish Connection," *Haaretz*, April 23, 2014, www.haaretz.com/jewish/.premium-1.586857.

35. See "Hillels Around the World," Hillel International, www.hillel.org/about/hillels-around-the-world.

36. Hillel was founded in the 1920s. Before the establishment of the State of Israel, Hillel viewed itself as "non-Zionist"—that is, neither for nor against the creation of a Jewish homeland. Like the Methodist Wesley Foundation and the Newman Catholic Foundation, campus Hillel chapters did not have a partisan political orientation but instead held religious services and educational and social events. See John B. Judis, "Hillel's Crackdown on Open Debate Is Bad News for American Jews," *New Republic*, January 6, 2014, https://newrepublic.com/article/116100/hillel-college-campuses-fractures-students-debate-israel. Indeed, in 1944 the Harvard Hillel chapter explicitly announced that it would be "neither Zionist nor anti-Zionist...neither Orthodox nor Reform." See Batya Ungar-Sargon, "How the Israel Lobby Captured Hillel," *Foreign Policy*, November 23, 2015, http://

foreignpolicy.com/2015/11/23/how-the-israel-lobby-captured-hillel-international -college-campus. After the state was established, the national organization was supportive of Israel but adopted no official position regarding it. It saw itself as being more involved in Israel education rather than advocacy, open to Jewish students of "any political bent." Local chapters were free to decide what speakers and programs to provide. See Judis, "Hillel's Crackdown on Open Debate."

37. Ungar-Sargon, "How the Israel Lobby Captured Hillel."

38. The Standards of Partnership provide that "Hillel will not partner with, house, or host organizations, groups, or speakers that as a matter of policy or practice: Deny the right of Israel to exist as a Jewish and democratic state with secure and recognized borders; Delegitimize, demonize, or apply a double standard to Israel; Support boycott of, divestment from, or sanctions against the State of Israel; Exhibit a pattern of disruptive behavior towards campus events or guest speakers or foster an atmosphere of incivility." "Hillel Israel Guidelines," Hillel International, www .hillel.org/jewish/hillel-israel/hillel-israel-guidelines.

39. See "FAQ," Open Hillel, www.openhillel.org/faq.

40. For example, in October of 2013 the Jewish Student Union at the University of California at Berkeley denied membership to J Street U. Connor Grubaugh, "Jewish Student Union Votes to Deny Membership to J Street U," *Daily Californian*, October 8, 2013, www.dailycal.org/2013/10/08/jewish-student-union-votes-deny -membership-j-street-u. Early the next year 129 alumni of Berkeley sent a letter to Berkeley Hillel arguing that the Jewish Student Union should be open to various views on Israel and become an "open Hillel" that rejected the Hillel International guidelines. Daniel Tutt, "UC Berkeley Alumni Urge Berkeley Hillel to Welcome More Views on Israel Policy," *Daily Californian*, February 25, 2014, www.dailycal .org/2014/02/25/uc-berkeley-alumni-urge-berkeley-hillel-welcome-views-israel -policy. Boston University Hillel rejected J Street U as an affiliate in the spring of 2014 but accepted it later that year. Mina Corpuz, "BU Hillel Student Board Approves J Street U as Student Group," *Daily Free Press*, December 9, 2014, http://dailyfreepress .com/2014/12/09/bu-hillel-student-board-approves-j-street-u-as-a-student-group. In 2016 the student board of Harvard Hillel voted to exclude J Street U. I learned this as a member of Harvard Hillel's governing board, a majority of whom expressed the view that this action was inappropriate.

41. Corpuz, "BU Hillel Student Board Approves J Street U."

42. Reader comments in response to Corpuz, "BU Hillel Student Board Approves J Street U."

43. In 2015 I heard this view in interviews with members of the Harvard Hillel Student Board.

44. Bradley Burston, "At Berkeley, Love of Israel Means No Fear—Except Fear of J Street," *Haaretz*, October 14, 2013, www.haaretz.com/blogs/a-special-place-in -hell/.premium-1.552374.

45. Debra Nussbaum Cohen, "Hillel Faces Backlash After CEO Fingerhut Withdraws from J Street Conference," *Haaretz*, March 19, 2015, www.haaretz.com /jewish/features/.premium-1.647710.

46. Michelle Boorstein, "Tensions Among U.S. Jews over Israel on Display as Hillel Leader Pulls Out of Speech," *Washington Post*, March 23, 2015, www .washingtonpost.com/news/acts-of-faith/wp/2015/03/23/tensions-among-u-s-jews -over-israel-on-display-as-hillel-leader-pulls-out-of-speech/?utm_term=.ec4f77594b64.

47. JTA, "Hillel Chief Eric Fingerhut to Meet with J Street Students," *The Forward*, March 25, 2015, http://forward.com/news/breaking-news/217426/hillel -chief-eric-fingerhut-to-meet-with-j-street..

48. In 2017 the Hillel at Ohio State University created a stir when it expelled an LGBTQ Jewish student organization, B'nai Keshet, which had agreed to host an event to help queer refugees. The sole reason for the expulsion was that the coalition of organizations supporting the event included an organization that supported BDS, in violation of the Hillel International guidelines. To protest the expulsion, the J Street U National Student Board issued a powerful statement arguing that the action sent "exactly the wrong message to campus activists—including pro-Israel advocates—committed to building broad coalitions to advance social change." They said the action set "a worrying precedent about the limits Hillel seeks to impose on Jewish students who want to take part in critical social justice projects on campus." The statement argued that "partnering with a broad array of other individuals and groups—even those with whom we, sometimes strongly, disagree"—should not be flatly prohibited. There is "no contradiction between vocally opposing BDS and selectively partnering on other issues with groups who may support it." J Street U National Student Board, "Hillel Must Allow Space for Vital Student Activism," March 23, 2017, http://jstreet.org/hillel-must-allow -space-vital-student-activism/#.WkA0rLaZM6U.

Also in 2017, at Washington University in St. Louis, the campus Hillel told J Street U that it would not back a three-day event commemorating the Six Day War as the start of the "occupation." The J Street event was to feature former IDF soldiers who oppose the continued occupation. They are members of an Israeli NGO called Breaking the Silence (BtS). Although admittedly on the left wing of Israeli politics, BtS states on its website that it "has never supported the movement to boycott Israel, nor have we ever been funded by the movement." Despite this disclaimer by BtS, a J Street U member wrote in the campus newspaper, "We were told that the event would be too radical and divisive.... Respectfully, that's unacceptable." Jewish students at Washington University were divided about whether J Street U should lose its Hillel-affiliated status because it planned to host BtS. See Rachel Frommer, "Washington U Hillel Hailed for Refusing to Fund J Street–Hosted Breaking the Silence Event," *Algemeiner*, April 25, 2017, www.algemeiner.com/2017/04/25 /washington-u-hillel-hailed-for-refusing-to-fund-j-street-hosted-breaking-the -silence-event.

49. Isabel Kershner, "Israeli Minister Says Reform Jews Are Not Really Jewish," *New York Times*, July 7, 2015, www.nytimes.com/2015/07/08/world/middleeast /israeli-minister-says-reform-jews-are-not-really-jewish.html.

50. These examples are all referred to in Jonathan A. Greenblatt, "ADL Head: Ultra-Orthodox Using Hate Speech Against Reform Jews," *Haaretz*, March 28, 2016, www.haaretz.com/opinion/.premium-1.710885.

51. See, for example, Asher Schechter, "Israel Tells Reform Jews: You're Not Really Jewish, but Your Money Is Just Jewish Enough," *Haaretz*, July 10, 2015, www.haaretz.com/jewishjewish/features/.premium-1.665301. See also Kershner, "Israeli Minister Says Reform Jews Are Not Really Jewish."

52. Greenblatt, "ADL Head: Ultra-Orthodox Using Hate Speech Against Reform Jews."

53. Netanyahu said he reminded Azoulay that "Israel is a home for all Jews and that as Minister of Religious Affairs, he serves all of Israel's citizens." Kershner, "Israeli Minister Says Reform Jews Are Not Really Jewish."

54. Jay Ruderman, an American Jewish philanthropist, called on Prime Minister Netanyahu to make clear that Azoulay's "statements do not represent the position of his government" and suggested that he expel Azoulay from his cabinet if he makes any more comments along these lines. Rick Cohen, "Not Quite Jewish Enough for Israel: Netanyahu Cabinet Minister Slams Reform Jews," *Nonprofit Quarterly*, July 10, 2015, https://nonprofitquarterly.org/2015/07/10/not-quite-jewish-enough-for-israel-netanyahu -cabinet-minister-slams-reform-jews.

55. An egalitarian space already exists for Reform and Conservative Jews, but it is hidden behind a wall, and worshippers must reach it through a side entrance. The new space would have included elements that Reform and Conservative Jews consider extremely important for both practical and symbolic reasons. For example, worshippers would have reached the new space through the same entrance used by the Orthodox, the area would no longer have been hidden by a wall topped with barbed wire, and it would have been administered by a new board that included representatives from the Reform and Conservative communities. See, for example, Judy Maltz, "Fact-Checking Netanyahu's False Claims to U.S. Jews About the Western Wall," *Haaretz*, November 15, 2017, www.haaretz.com/israel-news/.premium-1.822964.

56. Stuart Winer and *TOI* Staff, "Key US Donor Suspends Activities over Western Wall, Conversion Spat," *Times of Israel*, July 2, 2017, www.timesofisrael.com/key -israel-fundraiser-in-us-suspends-activities-over-western-wall-conversion-spat.

57. Debra Kamin, "Are American Jews Giving Up on Israel?" *Foreign Policy*, July 28, 2017, http://foreignpolicy.com/2017/07/28/are-american-jews-giving-up- on-israel/, quoting Rabbi Rick Jacobs.

58. Judy Maltz, "Kotel Crisis: Jewish Agency Instructs Emissaries to Tell Israel About Diaspora Anger," *Haaretz*, July 27, 2017, www.haaretz.com/israel -news/1.798148. Natan Sharansky, a Russian Jewish dissident who emigrated to Israel and is now the chairman of the Jewish Agency for Israel, played a critical role in the plan

to create egalitarian prayer space at the Western Wall. In January of 2016 Netanyahu's government had initially approved the deal, which was then suspended in June of 2017.

59. Debra Kamin, "There's a Rift Growing Between Israel and American Jews," *Foreign Policy*, July 29, 2017, www.businessinsider.com/theres-a-rift-growing-between -israel-and-american-jews-2017-7.

60. Ibid.

61. In a Pew poll conducted in Israel in 2015 fewer than 3 percent of Israeli Jews identified with the Reform movement, and only 2 percent with the Conservative movement. See Pew Research Center, "Comparisons Between Jews in Israel and the U.S.," March 8, 2016, www.pewforum.org/2016/03/08/comparisons-between -jews-in-israel-and-the-u-s.

62. In 1996 the children of haredi Jews in Israel represented 10 percent of all first graders; now they represent 30 percent. "Bennett: 32% of Grade 1 Students Are Haredim, Israel Will Not Survive Without Their Integration," *Jerusalem Post*, October 14, 2013, www.jpost.com/Diplomacy-and-Politics/Bennett-32-percent-of-grade-1 -students-are-haredim-Israel-will-not-survive-without-their-integration-328663.

CHAPTER 10: THE CHALLENGE OF INTERMARRIAGE

1. In this chapter I am *not* counting as an "intermarried couple" one in which the non-Jewish partner converts to Judaism before the marriage.

An estimated 1 to 2 percent of American Jews are converts. According to a comprehensive 2011 study of downstate New York Jewry conducted by UJA-Federation of New York, comprising 5,993 interviews, only 2 percent of those identified as Jewish were "Jewish by conversion." Steven M. Cohen, Jacob B. Ukeles, and Ron Miller, "Jewish Community Study of New York: 2011, Comprehensive Report," UJA-Federation of New York, June 2012, 36, http://jewishdatabank.org/studies/details.cfm?StudyID=597. This accords with the findings in the 1990 National Jewish Population Survey. According to the 1990 NJPS (2,500 households), of the 6,840,000 American Jews counted at the time, an estimated 185,000 were "Jews by Choice," of which 70 percent— 129,500—had undergone a formal conversion. This comes to roughly 1.89 percent and is less than the estimated 210,000 individuals who were born or raised Jewish but have converted out and now identify with another faith. Barry A. Kosmin, Sidney Goldstein, Joseph Waksberg et al., "Highlights of the CJF 1990 National Jewish Population Survey," Council of Jewish Federations, 1991, www.bjpa.org/search-results /publication/13841. It is also in line with the findings of the 2013 Pew Study, which reported a 2 percent conversion rate to Judaism.

2. "A Portrait of Jewish Americans," 35.

3. Although I have found no systematic national surveys for the early years, this seems to be the scholarly consensus. See David Desser and Lester D. Friedman, *American Jewish Filmmakers: Traditions and Trends* (Urbana: University of Illinois Press, 2004), 26; see also Julius Drachsler, *Intermarriage in New York City: A Statistical Study of the Amalgamation of European People* (New York, 1921), 49–50, quoted in Lila Corwin Berman,

"Sociology, Jews and Intermarriage in Twentieth-Century America," *Jewish Social Studies* 14, no. 2 (Winter 2008): 37–38. According to a 1908–1912 survey of 170,000 Bronx and Manhattan marriage licenses, the intermarriage rate for Jews was 1.17 percent. I note, however, that this data may have understated the national intermarriage rate because it was based on New York City, which had a large Jewish population.

4. See pp. 32–35 in chapter 2.

5. "Reform Judaism and Mixed Marriage," *CCAR Responsa: American Reform Responsa* XC (1980), 86–102 (explaining "that mixed marriages are contrary to the tradition of the Jewish religion and should, therefore, be discouraged").

6. Keren R. McGinity, *Still Jewish: A History of Women and Intermarriage in America* (New York: New York University Press, 2009), 77. "Religious advocates warned against intermarriage because, as the strict definitional borders between the three major religions in the United States blurred, increasing intermarriage rates diminished religious and denominational distinctiveness."

7. See "Rabbi Officiating at a Mixed Marriage," *CCAR Responsa* XCII (1982), 213–215 (describing that it is "the task of the rabbi to strengthen Judaism" and that mixed marriage tends to weaken it).

8. See sources cited in note 3 of this chapter.

9. Desser and Friedman, *American Jewish Filmmakers*, 26.

10. Gregory A. Smith and Alan Cooperman, "What Happens When Jews Intermarry," Pew Research Center, November 12, 2013, www.pewresearch.org/fact-tank/2013/11/12/what-happens-when-jews-intermarry.

11. "A Portrait of Jewish Americans," 55 (indicating that only 19 percent of American Jews viewed "observing Jewish law" as essential to being Jewish).

12. Shmuel Rosner, "Study Finds More Than Half of Young Jews Have 'No Religion,'" *Jewish Journal*, September 6, 2017, http://jewishjournal.com/rosnersdomain/224032/study-finds-half-young-jews-no-religion/ (discussing the Pew study, which found that 22 percent of Jews say they have no religion and 53 percent of those under thirty say they have no religion).

13. "A Portrait of Jewish Americans," 37. The term "Jews of no denomination" includes both "Jews by religion" and "Jews not by religion." Ibid., 177. Although not shown in this table, Pew found that those who were "Jewish not by religion"—those who claimed to have no religion but thought of themselves as Jewish for cultural reasons—had the greatest tendency to intermarry (79 percent). Ibid., 36.

14. The authors of the Pew study cautioned, "It is not clear whether being intermarried tends to make U.S. Jews less religious, or being less religious tends to make U.S. Jews more inclined to intermarry, or some of both. Whatever the causal connection, the survey finds a strong association between secular Jews and religious intermarriage." Ibid., 2.

15. According to a 2015 Pew survey, 44 percent of Jews have an annual household income of $100,000 or more, compared to an 18 percent national average. This was the highest of any religious group. "America's Changing Religious Landscape: Christians Decline Sharply as Share of Population; Unaffiliated and Other Faiths Continue to

Grow," Pew Research Center, May 12, 2015, 57–58, www.pewforum.org/2015/05/12/chapter-3-demographic-profiles-of-religious-groups. In education 59 percent of Jews hold at least a bachelor's degree and 31 percent have earned a postgraduate degree, compared to 17 percent and 11 percent national averages, respectively. Ibid., 56.

16. Alberto Bisin, Giorgio Topa, and Thierry Verdier, "Religious Intermarriage and Socialization in the United States," *Journal of Political Economy* 112, no. 3 (2004): 616 (explaining that sociological literature has documented very low religious intermarriage rates in the past).

17. Ruby Jo Reeves Kennedy, "Single or Triple Melting-Pot? Intermarriage Trends in New Haven, 1870–1940," *American Journal of Sociology* 49, no. 4 (January 1944), quoted in Will Herberg, *Protestant-Catholic-Jew: An Essay in American Religious Sociology* (Chicago: University of Chicago Press, 1955), 32–34.

18. Robert Putnam and David E. Campbell, *American Grace: How Religion Divides and Unites Us* (New York: Simon & Schuster, 2012), 153.

19. Ibid., 148–149.

20. Sylvia Barack Fishman, *Double or Nothing?: Jewish Families and Mixed Marriage* (Waltham, MA: Brandeis University Press, 2004) 4.

21. Deborah D. Moore, *American Jewish Identity Politics* (Ann Arbor: University of Michigan Press, 2009), 304. "Recent research shows that fewer than half of American Jews today actively oppose mixed marriage."

22. Market Facts, *2000 Annual Survey of American Jewish Opinion* (New York: American Jewish Committee, 2000), 97.

23. Calvin Goldscheider, *Studying the Jewish Future* (Seattle: University of Washington Press, 2004), 21 (explaining that in the Jewish community during most of the twentieth century "people who intermarried repudiated their religion, their families, and their communities. And their religion, families, and communities abandoned them").

24. Barry A. Kosmin and the Council of Jewish Federations, "Highlights of the CJF 1990 National Jewish Population Survey" (New York: Council of Jewish Federations, 1990), 16. According to the 1990 National Jewish Population Survey (NJPS), only 28 percent of intermarried couples said they were raising their children Jewish by religion, compared to about half of in-married couples.

25. A United Jewish Communities Report, *The National Jewish Population Survey 2000–01: Strength, Challenge and Diversity in the American Jewish Population* (New York: United Jewish Communities, 2003), 17. This study, conducted in 2000, had found that among married Jews raised in mixed-married families, 74 percent had intermarried, compared to 22 percent of those raised with two Jewish parents.

26. "A Portrait of Jewish Americans," 67–68. In the 2013 Pew survey, for each child in the household, respondents were asked, "In what religion, if any, is this child being raised? Is he or she being raised Jewish, in another religion, in no religion, or partly Jewish and partly something else?" Apparently, 96 percent of in-married Jewish respondents answered "Jewish." Among those who had married out, only 20 percent said they were raising their children Jewish by religion, and 25 percent

reported raising their children partly Jewish by religion. Another 16 percent were raising their children Jewish without religion or mixed, and about a third (37 percent) were not raising their children as Jewish at all.

27. Ibid., 37. Among married Jews "who are themselves the children of intermarriage," 83 percent had intermarried. By contrast, among married Jews with two Jewish parents, only 37 percent had intermarried.

28. Theodore Sasson, "New Analysis of Pew Data: Children of Intermarriage Increasingly Identify as Jews," *Tablet*, November 11, 2013, www.tabletmag .com/jewish-news-and-politics/151506/young-jews-opt-in. Among those aged fifty to sixty-four (baby boomers), 37 percent identified as Jewish, and among those aged thirty to forty-nine (Generation X), 39 percent identified as Jews.

29. Ibid. Among children of intermarriage in the Silent Generation, only 7 percent identified as Jews by religion. Among millennials, 29 percent identified as Jews by religion.

30. Leonard Saxe, "The Sky Is Falling! The Sky Is Falling!" *Tablet*, December 3, 2014, www.tabletmag.com/jewish-news-and-politics/187165/pew-american-jewry -revisited.

31. Social scientists don't yet agree on the date range for this generation. In 2016 Pew defined millennials as those who were born between 1981 and 1997 or those aged eighteen to thirty-four in 2015. Richard Fry, "Millenials Approach Baby Boomers as America's Largest Generation in the Electorate," Pew Research Center, April 3, 2016, www.pewresearch.org/fact-tank/2018/04/03/millennials-approach -baby-boomers-as-largest-generation-in-u-s-electorate.

32. Saxe, "The Sky Is Falling! The Sky Is Falling!" A later study seemed to support this causal connection between increased Jewish education and the rising rate of Jewish identification among millennials. The study's authors noted that other factors may also have contributed to the generational shift, including the decline of anti-Semitism and the increasingly positive view of Judaism in the general culture. Theodore Sasson, Janet Krasner Aronson, Fern Chertok, Charles Kadushin, and Leonard Saxe, "Children of Intermarriage: Religious Upbringing, Identification, and Behavior Among Children of Jewish and Non-Jewish Parents," *Contemporary Jewry* 37, no. 1 (2017): 118.

33. Saxe, "The Sky Is Falling! The Sky Is Falling!" "The 1990 NJPS finding about intermarriage sparked not only Birthright Israel, but a host of initiatives that reshaped Jewish education writ large."

34. Sasson, "New Analysis of Pew Data: Children of Intermarriage Increasingly Identify as Jews." Sasson is also a senior research scientist at the Cohen Center for Modern Jewish Studies at Brandeis University.

35. As Saxe explained in an article that preceded the study's publication, "Our goal in part was to assess the claim that intermarriage was the greatest threat to American Jewish life....We tried to understand what would lead adults, as well as children, from both in-married and intermarried families to be engaged in Jewish life, raise Jewish children and feel connected to Israel." Leonard Saxe,

"Intermarriage in Perspective," Jewish Telegraphic Agency, March 17, 2008, www
.jta.org/2008/03/17/news-opinion/opinion/intermarriage-in-perspective.

36. Fern Chertok, Benjamin Phillips, and Leonard Saxe, "It's Not Just Who
Stands Under the Chuppah: Intermarriage and Engagement," Brandeis University
Steinhardt Social Research Institute, May 2008, 24.

37. Ibid., 1–2. The study focused on Reform Jews, both in-married and intermarried. Although intermarried parents were indeed less likely than in-married
parents to raise Jewish children, the authors argued that this was not the result of
intermarriage itself but of the fact that Jews who intermarry tend to have had "less
intense Jewish upbringings than those who marry other Jews" and tend to pass on
those weaker moorings to their children. Ibid., 7–9, 24.

38. The small Reconstructionist movement recognized patrilineal descent
before the Reform movement and, like Reform, has made substantial efforts to reach
out to intermarried couples.

39. Outside the United States, Reform Judaism does not necessarily accept patrilineal descent. Sue Fishkoff, "Why Is Patrilineal Descent Not Catching On in Reform
Worldwide?" Jewish Telegraphic Agency, February 15, 2011, www.jta.org/2011/02/15
/life-religion/why-is-patrilineal-descent-not-catching-on-in-reform-worldwide.

40. Penny Schwartz, "More Reform Rabbis Agreeing to Officiate at Intermarriages," Jewish Telegraphic Agency, July 3, 2012, www.jta.org/2012/07/03/news
-opinion/united-states/more-reform-rabbis-agreeing-to-officiate-at-intermarriages.

41. In 1973 the CCAR affirmed its opposition by urging members to "desist"
from officiating at interfaith weddings but left the decision up to the individual
rabbi. Jack Wertheimer, *A People Divided: Judaism in Contemporary America*
(Hanover, NH: Brandeis University Press, 1993), 101, quoted in Sylvia Barack Fishman, *Double or Nothing?*, 126. The Reconstructionist movement, like the Reform
movement, is officially opposed but appears to give each rabbi some discretion.
Reconstructionist Rabbinical Association Resolution Committee on Intermarriage,
1980, https://therra.org/resolutions/intermarriage-committee-80.pdf. Rabbis affiliated with Humanistic Judaism have no objection.

42. Schwartz, "More Reform Rabbis Agreeing to Officiate at Intermarriages."

43. Ibid.

44. Pew reports that 73 percent of Conservative Jews have married other Jews.
"A Portrait of Jewish Americans," 37.

45. Yair Ettinger, "In Unprecedented Move, U.S. Conservative Movement Allows Non-Jewish Members," *Haaretz*, March 7, 2017, www.haaretz.com
/us-news/.premium-1.775538 ("Conservative congregations will be able to accept as
rank-and-file members worshippers and family members who are not Jews according to halakha").

46. Adina Lewittes, "Intermarriage, I Do!" *Tablet*, February 4, 2015, www
.tabletmag.com/jewish-life-and-religion/188465/intermarriage-i-do. Other Conservative rabbis share this concern. "The laity are voting by their unhappiness when we

refuse to marry their children," says Rabbi Seymour Rosenbloom, "and their children are voting by not coming back to our synagogues after we've rejected them." Emma Green, "We're Headed Toward One of the Greatest Divisions in the History of the Jewish People," *The Atlantic*, July 16, 2017, www.theatlantic.com/politics /archive/2017/07/intermarriage-conservative-judaism/533637.

47. Bradley Shavit Artson, Arnold M. Eisen, Julie Schonfeld, and Steven C. Wernick, "The Conservative Movement Can, and Should, Welcome the Intermarried," *Times of Israel*, October 18, 2017, www.timesofisrael.com/the-conservative -movement-can-and-should-welcome-the-intermarried. Conservative rabbi Charles Simon, the former head of the Federation of Jewish Men's Clubs, was an early voice urging Conservative synagogues to open dialogues on the topic of intermarriage and become more welcoming of intermarried couples. See, for example, Ben Sales, "Conservative Movement Reaffirms Intermarriage Ban and Rabbis Ask Why," Jewish Telegraphic Agency, October 20, 2017, www.jta.org/2017/10/20/news-opinion/united -states/conservative-movement-doubles-down-on-intermarriage-and-its-rabbis-ask-why.

48. JTA, "40% of Conservative Rabbis Would Perform Intermarriages," *Forward*, October 23, 2015, https://forward.com/news/breaking-news/323204/40-of -conservative-rabbis-would-perform-intermarriages. The article cites a survey of 249 rabbis that was conducted by Big Tent Judaism, a now-defunct organization that promoted outreach to interfaith families. The article also notes, however, that a spokesperson for the Rabbinical Assembly dismissed the study as "unscientific" and "unrepresentative" because it was an opt-in survey conducted by email.

49. Green, "We're Headed Toward One of the Greatest Divisions in the History of the Jewish People." See also Seymour Rosenbloom, "It's Time to Allow Conservative Rabbis to Officiate at Interfaith Weddings," Jewish Telegraphic Agency, April 4, 2016, www.jta.org/2016/04/04/news-opinion/united-states/op-ed-its-time -to-allow-conservative-rabbis-to-officiate-at-interfaith-weddings.

50. Green, "We're Headed Toward One of the Greatest Divisions in the History of the Jewish People."

51. Lewittes, "Intermarriage, I Do!"; See also Rabbi Amichai Lau-Lavie, *Joy: A Proposal*, June 2017, http://amichai.me/wp-content/uploads/2017/06/Welcome _Book_2017.pdf.

CHAPTER 11: RAISING A JEWISH CHILD

1. "A Portrait of Jewish Americans," 6. According to a recent study, however, Christmas observance among Jewish couples may be growing. Among millennial children with two Jewish parents, about 18 percent reported doing "something to celebrate Christmas while growing up." See Theodore Sasson, Leonard Saxe, Fern Chertok, Michelle Shain, Shahar Hecht, and Graham Wright, "Millennial Children of Intermarriage: Touchpoints and Trajectories of Jewish Engagement," Maurice and Marilyn Cohen Center for Modern Jewish Studies (Brandeis University, 2015), 19, www.brandeis.edu/cmjs/pdfs/intermarriage/MillennialChildren Intermarriage1.pdf.

2. "A Portrait of Jewish Americans," 6. Overall, about a third of Jews (32 percent) said they had a Christmas tree in their home, most of whom were intermarried.

3. "Most mixed-married families report some connection to both Christmas and Hanukkah, Passover and Easter." Sylvia Barack Fishman, *Double or Nothing?: Jewish Families and Mixed Marriage* (Waltham, MA: Brandeis University Press, 2004), 61.

4. Sasson et al., "Millennial Children of Intermarriage," 18–19.

5. Fishman, *Double or Nothing?*, 62.

6. Raising children in two religions is a different matter. This approach gives children a full religious foundation in both traditions. Susan Katz Miller, whose book *Being Both: Embracing Two Religions in One Interfaith Family* (Boston: Beacon Press, 2013), ch. 3, supports the practice, suggests that many dual-faith children feel their lives have been enriched by being educated in both faiths. I believe that if you raise children as both, it increases the risk that the children won't identify as Jews, given that we live in a predominantly Christian culture. Raising children as "nones" runs similar risks. Even if the Jewish parent emphasizes the child's ethnic heritage, it's hard to transmit the cultural dimensions of Jewishness in the complete absence of the religious tradition.

7. Paul Cowan with Rachel Cowan, *Mixed Blessings: Overcoming the Stumbling Blocks in an Interfaith Marriage* (New York: Penguin, 1987), 131.

8. See Douglas Stone, Bruce Patton, and Sheila Heen, *Difficult Conversations: How to Discuss What Matters Most* (New York: Penguin Books, 2000).

9. InterfaithFamily is a Jewish organization with programs in eight major US cities that helps interfaith families connect to Jewish life. See "InterfaithFamily: Supporting Interfaith Families Exploring Jewish Life," InterfaithFamily, 2018, www.interfaithfamily.com.

10. Open Hearts & Open Door is a program at Chicago Sinai Congregation that encourages interfaith couples "to discuss important topics in a safe, nurturing and respectful environment." "Interfaith Marriage and Families in Chicago," Chicago Sinai Congregation, www.chicagosinai.org/jewish-interfaith-relationships-chicago/interfaith -marriage-interfaith-couples-chicago. The Rabbinic Center for Research and Counseling provides research on intermarriage, including a variety of programs, and lists rabbis who officiate at interfaith weddings. In addition, the Center provides intermarried couples and families with premarital and marital counseling. Rabbinic Center for Research and Counseling, http://rcrconline.org. Various articles and books provide support and advice for interfaith couples and families. See Edmund Case, "Supporting Interfaith Families Exploring Jewish Life," EJP, July 16, 2013, http://ejewishphilanthropy.com /supporting-interfaith-families-exploring-jewish-life; see also Ronnie Friedland and Edmund Case, eds., *The Guide to Jewish Interfaith Family Life: An InterfaithFamily.com Handbook* (Woodstock, VT: Jewish Lights Publishing, 2002); Anita Diamant, *New Jewish Wedding* (New York: Simon & Schuster, 2001).

11. Fishman, *Double or Nothing?*, 159; Fern Chertok, Benjamin Phillips, and Leonard Saxe, "It's Not Just Who Stands Under the Chuppah: Intermarriage and Engagement," Brandeis University Steinhardt Social Research Institute, May 2008, 11–16, http://bir .brandeis.edu/bitstream/handle/10192/23017/Intermarriage.052908.pdf?sequence=1.

12. ReformJudaism.org is a particularly complete resource, offering detailed information about holidays, recipes, life-cycle rituals, blessings, synagogue etiquette, and other topics. "ReformJudaism.org: Jewish Life in Your Life," Union for Reform Judaism, https://reformjudaism.org.

13. Marion Usher, "Raising Jewish Children," *Love and Religion: An Interfaith Workshop for Jews and Their Partners*, February 8, 2017, www.jewishinterfaithcouples .com/2017/02/raising-jewish-children.

14. See, for example, "Jewish Life at Home," Central Synagogue, www.central synagogue.org/engage/youth-family-engagement/jewish-life-at-home.

15. The 1885 Pittsburgh Platform in many ways had provided the foundation for Classical Reform. See "Our Mission," Society for Classical Reform Judaism, http://renewreform.org/about/our-mission.

16. My paternal grandparents must have been members of two Kansas City congregations—the traditional synagogue that they attended as well as the Reform temple. I recently discovered that my father's younger sister, who died when she was only sixteen, had been "confirmed" in Kansas City's Reform congregation.

17. Rabbi Kerry M. Olitzky and Paul Golin, *How to Raise Jewish Children… Even When You're Not Jewish Yourself* (Los Angeles: Torah Aura Productions, 2010), 35. Traditionally the youngest person at the Seder asks the Four Questions relating to "Why is this night different from all other nights?" The text for the Passover Seder service is called a Haggadah, and there are now many hundreds to choose from. Indeed, many families create their own Haggadah to add a personal family touch to the Passover Seder. There is a web-based platform to facilitate the creation of a custom Haggadah. See www.haggadot.com.

18. The dreidel is a four-sided top with a Hebrew letter on each side. For game pieces players can use pennies, chocolate chips, peanuts, buttons, Cheerios—whatever is around the house. Each player puts one game piece in the pot. Players take turns spinning the dreidel and taking the action indicated on the side facing up: Nun: the player takes nothing; Gimel: the player takes all; Hey: The player takes half; Shin: The player puts one piece in. The winner is the person who collects all the game pieces. Noam Zion, "How to Play Dreidel," My Jewish Learning, www .myjewishlearning.com/article/how-to-play-dreidel/.

19. "About PJ Library," PJ Library, https://pjlibrary.org/about-pj-library.

20. The PJ Library website offers instructions about how children can make their own tzedakah boxes at home.

21. "Featured Books," Jewish Book Council, www.jewishbookcouncil.org/books/.

22. See "Alternative Bar and Bat Mitzvah Ceremonies: How to Have a Meaningful Ceremony Even if You Don't Belong to a Synagogue," My Jewish Learning, www.myjewishlearning.com/article/alternative-bar-and-bat-mitzvah-ceremonies.

23. See Marvin Schick, *A Census of Jewish Day Schools in the United States 2008–2009* (The AVI CHAI Foundation, 2009), 10, http://avichai.org/knowledge _base/a-census-of-jewish-day-schools-in-the-united-states-2008-09-2009.

24. "Mission," BBYO, http://bbyo.org/about/mission.

25. See Emma Green, "Convincing Millennials to 'Marry a Nice Jewish Boy,'" *The Atlantic*, November 7, 2013, www.theatlantic.com/national/archive/2013/11/convincing -millennials-to-marry-a-nice-jewish-boy/281229.

26. See Michael M. Lorge and Gary P. Zola, eds., *A Place of Our Own: The Rise of Reform Jewish Camping* (Tuscaloosa: University of Alabama Press, 2006), 111, 161. See also Harold S. Himmelfarb, "The Study of American Jewish Identification: How It Is Defined, Measured, Obtained, Sustained and Lost," *Journal for the Scientific Study of Religion* 19, no. 1 (March 1980), 58; Fishman, *Double or Nothing?*, 30–31; Paul Lewis, "The Value of Jewish Summer Camp," eJewish Philanthropy, August 21, 2012, http://ejewishphilanthropy.com/the-value-of-jewish-summer-camp; "Reform Judaism: History & Overview," Jewish Virtual Library, www.jewishvirtuallibrary .org/history-and-overview-of-reform-judaism; Rabbi Scott Nagel, "What Can Camp Teach Us About Judaism at Home?" ReformJudaism.org, June 15, 2017, https:// reformjudaism.org/blog/2017/06/15/what-can-camp-teach-us-about-judaism-home; Jeri Zeder, "How Summer Camp Became a Jewish Thing," My Jewish Learning, www.myjewishlearning.com/article/summer-camps; Foundation for Jewish Camp, Summer Camp Community and Resources, https://jewishcamp.org.

27. Some social programs have the added agenda, implicit or explicit, of build- ing friendships that may lead to marriage. According to the executive director of BBYO, Matt Grossman, "if they're in an environment where their closest friends are Jewish, the likelihood that they're going to end up dating people from those social circles, and ultimately marry someone from those social circles, increases dramati- cally." Green, "Convincing Millennials to 'Marry a Nice Jewish Boy.'" According to a recent BBYO poll of its alumni, 84 percent were married to or living with Jewish partners. Ibid.

28. "For Jewish students, friendship and dating patterns are linked to partici- pation in formal Jewish life on campus." Amy L. Sales and Leonard Saxe, *Particu- larism in the University: Realities and Opportunities for Jewish Life on Campus* (New York: Avi Chai Foundation, 2006), 7.

29. "The Jewish fraternity is a very positive institution on campus that allows Jews to hang out with one another," said Steven Bayme, the director of Contemporary Jewish Life at the American Jewish Committee. "At the same time, I fully have no problem with the idea of non-Jews inside Jewish fraternities. I think it's a statement of our maturity in America that [Jews are] so well integrated into American societies." The Forward and Britta Lokting, "Are Jewish Fraternities in America Only for Jews?," *Haaretz*, September 15, 2016, www.haaretz.com/world-news/americas/are-jewish-fraternities-in-america -only-for-jews-1.5436179; see also "Jewish Fraternities and Sororities," Wikipedia, https://en.wikipedia.org/wiki/List_of_Jewish_fraternities_and_sororities.

30. Sasson et al., "Millennial Children of Intermarriage," 31–47. The study focused on how best to strengthen the Jewish identities of children of intermarriage during the college years.

31. Ibid., 47. These interventions do not, however, seem to increase the students' desire to marry a Jew. Millennial children of intermarriage "see themselves as proof that inmarriage is not a necessary ingredient for having a Jewish home or raising children as Jews." Ibid., 43.

32. "About Birthright Israel," Taglit Birthright Israel, http://taglit-birthright israel.com/TaglitBirthrightIsraelStory/Pages/About-Birthright-Israel.aspx.

33. Caroline Burt, "How Traveling to Your Roots Changes Your Life," Hillel International, March 2, 2015, www.hillel.org/hillel-stories/hillel-stories-item/hillel -stories/2015/03/02/how-traveling-to-your-roots-changes-your-life.

34. Ibid. See also Leonard Saxe, Ted Sasson, and Shahar Hecht, "Taglit-Birthright Israel: Impact on Jewish Identity, Peoplehood, and Connection to Israel," Brandeis University, June 2006, 2, www.brandeis.edu/cmjs/pdfs/bri2006.evaluationimpact .pdf (noting that the Birthright experience is not only about fun, but is "Jewishly meaningful," and that participants seriously engage in their Jewishness).

35. One of the recent Brandeis studies explored the impact of this relationship. "For children of intermarriage, being 'very close' to Jewish grandparents while growing up had a positive impact on many Jewish attitudes and behaviors in young adulthood," it found. Sasson et al., "Millennial Children of Intermarriage," 36. Those attitudes and behaviors included identifying as Jewish by religion, celebrating Jewish holidays, feeling a connection to Israel and the Jewish people, and wanting to marry someone Jewish. Ibid., 48.

36. Jimmy and Wendy's oldest son, Seth, and his wife, Sara, have two children. They live in Brookline, Massachusetts, and belong to a Reform temple, where their children attend Sunday school. Daughter, Abby, and her wife, Laura, live with their two children in Brattleboro, Vermont, where there are fewer opportunities for organized religion. They tend to celebrate Jewish holidays with other young Jewish couples, many of whom are also intermarried. Younger son, Jacob, and his wife, Isabel, are a proud uncle and aunt.

CONCLUSION

1. Rabbi Lord Jonathan Sacks, "The Genesis of Jewish Genius," What Is Genius?, www.slate.com/bigideas/what-is-genius/essays-and-opinions/rabbi-lord-jonathan -sacks-opinion.

2. As used in the Mishnah, the term referred to the rabbinic practice of amending the law both to protect the disadvantaged and to benefit society at large. See, for example, Jill Jacobs, "The History of 'Tikkun Olam,'" Zeek, June 2007, www.zeek .net/706tohu. See also "Tikkun Olam: Repairing the World," My Jewish Learning, www.myjewishlearning.com/article/tikkun-olam-repairing-the-world.

3. "Why Facing History and Ourselves," Facing History and Ourselves, www .facinghistory.org/why-facing-history.

4. Jonathan Sacks, *Not in God's Name: Confronting Religious Violence* (New York: Schocken Books, 2015), 13.

INDEX

ROBERT H. MNOOKIN is the Samuel Williston Professor of Law at Harvard Law School, the chair of the Program on Negotiation at Harvard Law School, and the director of the Harvard Negotiation Research Project. A leading scholar in the field of conflict resolution, Professor Mnookin has served as a consultant to governments, international agencies, major corporations, and law firms; has resolved numerous complex commercial disputes as a neutral arbitrator or mediator; and has facilitated many "track-two" meetings between high-ranking Israelis and Palestinians. He has written or edited numerous scholarly articles and nine books, including *Bargaining with the Devil: When to Negotiate, When to Fight* and most recently *Kissinger the Negotiator: Lessons from Dealmaking at the Highest Level* (with James K. Sebenius and R. Nicholas Burns).

Before joining the Harvard faculty, Professor Mnookin was the Adelbert H. Sweet Professor of Law at Stanford Law School and the director of the Stanford Center on Conflict and Negotiation. At Stanford he chaired the Jewish Community Federation and served as president of the Stanford Hillel Foundation. Between 1994 and 2003 he served on the International Board of the New Israel Fund as its treasurer. He is presently the vice president of the Harvard Hillel Foundation and on the International Advisory Board of the Israel Democracy Institute.

Professor Mnookin received his AB in economics from Harvard College in 1964 and his law degree from Harvard Law School in 1968. After serving as a law clerk to Supreme Court Justice John M. Harlan, he practiced law in San Francisco before becoming a law professor, first at Berkeley (1972–1980) and then at Stanford (1981–1993). Professor Mnookin has been a visiting fellow at Wolfson College, Oxford University; a visiting professor of Law at Columbia Law School; and a fellow at the Center for Advanced Study in the Behavioral Sciences at Stanford University.

PublicAffairs is a publishing house founded in 1997. It is a tribute to the standards, values, and flair of three persons who have served as mentors to countless reporters, writers, editors, and book people of all kinds, including me.

I. F. STONE, proprietor of *I. F. Stone's Weekly*, combined a commitment to the First Amendment with entrepreneurial zeal and reporting skill and became one of the great independent journalists in American history. At the age of eighty, Izzy published *The Trial of Socrates*, which was a national bestseller. He wrote the book after he taught himself ancient Greek.

BENJAMIN C. BRADLEE was for nearly thirty years the charismatic editorial leader of *The Washington Post*. It was Ben who gave the *Post* the range and courage to pursue such historic issues as Watergate. He supported his reporters with a tenacity that made them fearless and it is no accident that so many became authors of influential, best-selling books.

ROBERT L. BERNSTEIN, the chief executive of Random House for more than a quarter century, guided one of the nation's premier publishing houses. Bob was personally responsible for many books of political dissent and argument that challenged tyranny around the globe. He is also the founder and longtime chair of Human Rights Watch, one of the most respected human rights organizations in the world.

· · ·

For fifty years, the banner of Public Affairs Press was carried by its owner Morris B. Schnapper, who published Gandhi, Nasser, Toynbee, Truman, and about 1,500 other authors. In 1983, Schnapper was described by *The Washington Post* as "a redoubtable gadfly." His legacy will endure in the books to come.

Peter Osnos, *Founder*